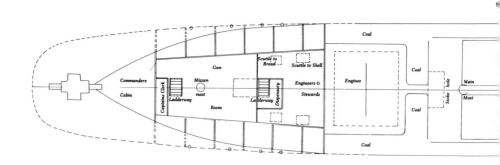

*s & Co.*

*Deck*

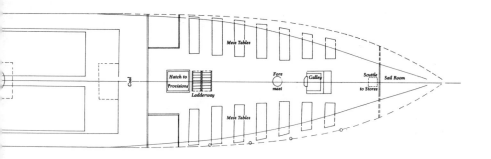

Coal

Mess Tables

Hatch to
Provisions

Ladderway

Fore
mast

Galley

Scuttle
to Stores

Sail Room

Mess Tables

*Works*

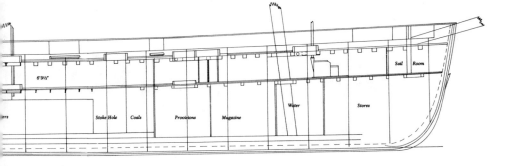

6'9½"

Stoke Hole  Coals  Provisions  Magazine  Water  Stores  Sail Room

# Gray Thunder

## Exploits of the Confederate States Navy

## by R. Thomas Campbell

BURD STREET PRESS

This Burd Street Press publication was printed by
Beidel Printing House, Inc.
63 West Burd Street
Shippensburg, PA 17257 USA

In respect for the scholarship contained herein, the acid-free paper used in this book meets the guidelines for permanence and durability of the Committee on Production Guidelines for Book Longevity of the Council on Library Resources.

For a complete list of available publications please write:
Burd Street Press
*Division of White Mane Publishing Company, Inc.*
P.O. Box 152
Shippensburg, PA 17257 USA

Library of Congress Cataloging-in-Publication Data

Campbell, R. Thomas, 1937-
　　　Gray thunder : exploits of the Confederate States Navy / by R. Thomas Campbell.
　　　　　p.　　cm.
　　　Includes bibliographical references and index.
　　　ISBN 0-942597-99-0 (alk. paper). -- ISBN 1-57249-277-5 (pbk.)
　　　　　1. Confederate States of America. Navy--History. 2. United States--History--Civil War, 1861-1865--Naval operations, Confederate. 3. Confederate States of America--History, Naval. I. Title.
E596.C36　1996
973.7'57--dc20

95-47854
CIP

PRINTED IN THE UNITED STATES OF AMERICA

DEDICATED TO

THOSE WHO WORE THE NAVY GRAY

AND THE LOVED ONES THEY LEFT BEHIND

AND TO MY FATHER,

ROY L. CAMPBELL

JUNE 21, 1907–MARCH 25, 1995

# Table Of Contents

# Preface

The Confederate States Navy was established by an act of the Confederate Congress on February 21, 1861. It existed for almost four years and nine months until finally, its last flag was lowered by the CSS *Shenandoah* at Liverpool, England on November 6, 1865. During this period the Confederate government proceeded to build from scratch, a courageous and innovative naval force. The fact that they achieved all that they did, in spite of the South's limited resources, is what makes the study of the C.S. Navy so intriguing. Their history, however, is not just the story of cruisers, ironclads, and gunboats. While the vessels themselves are important, and some are fascinating in their construction detail and operation, the real heart and soul of the Confederate navy during the War Between the States was her cadre of professional officers and dedicated men.

The courage and determination displayed time and time again by her sailors and marines allowed the Confederate navy to achieve much more than its limited numbers and equipment would lead one to believe was possible. Outnumbered ten to one, outgunned usually 100 to one, they continued to challenge the Federal forces until the very last, regardless of the obvious outcome. With bravery, boldness, and the element of surprise, they often achieved brilliant successes. Many times, however, they suffered humiliation and ultimate defeat. In spite of this, they persisted. Much like the often maligned Army of Tennessee, they never seemed to realize when they were beaten.

A complete and accurate history of the Confederate navy has yet to be written. This book, the first of three, is not intended to be that work. Instead, selected exploits have been chosen from the four arduous years of the war that best illustrate the Confederate navy's activities as a whole. Activities that, in reality, form a microcosm of the entire story. As much as possible, I have elected to quote from the writings of the participants themselves. They were there during those momentous events, and it was they who faced the storm of shot and shell.

Within the following pages, the reader will be introduced to Southern Americans who were fiercely devoted to God, their cause, their flag, and their country. Southern independence and defense of the Southern homeland were the primary thoughts of these officers and men who knew beforehand the great odds that they were about to encounter, and yet, there was no flinching, no turning back. Even in defeat, they conducted themselves with courage and dignity.

With their courageous deeds revealed before me, I would be remiss if I did not respectfully dedicate the narration of these few exploits to the officers and men of the Confederate States Navy. To all those who wore the navy gray, this is their story.

# Acknowledgments

I wish to acknowledge the help and assistance of my wife, Carole. Without her encouragement, her patience, and especially her editing expertise, this book would not have been possible.

All photos, unless otherwise noted, are courtesy of the Naval Historical Foundation, Washington, D.C.

# Chapter One

## The Iron Turtle of New Orleans

The infant Confederate States Navy had been in existence for only seven months when on a late September day in 1861, the steamer CSS *McRae* reversed her engines and glided to a stop in the harbor of New Orleans. Alongside the rakish hull of the *McRae* was a very strange looking vessel. A lead-colored convex iron shell covered its entire frame, causing her to look like a giant floating turtle with two smokestacks poking up through the middle of its shell. Given the name *Manassas*, in honor of the recent great victory in Virginia, she had been launched only lately and taken on her first trial run down the Mississippi River. First Lieutenant Thomas B. Huger, commander of the *McRae*, ordered a boat lowered, and Lieutenant Alexander F. Warley, revolver in hand, ordered the boat's crew to pull toward the *Manassas*. Lieutenant Huger had been ordered by Commodore George C. Hollins, commander of the Confederate fleet at New Orleans, to seize the *Manassas* in the name of the Confederate States Navy.[1]

The *Manassas*, which Warley was grimly approaching, was originally known as the *Enoch Train*. Built for service as an icebreaker in Bedford, Massachusetts in 1855 by James O. Curtis, she was purchased and brought to New Orleans in 1859 and used there as a heavy tugboat. At that time she was a single-decked, two-masted steamer, 128 feet in length, 28 feet abeam, drawing twelve and one-half feet of water. Her twin en-

*1*

*Battles and Leaders of the Civil War*

**First Lieutenant Alexander F. Warley, commander of the
Confederate ram CSS *Manassas.***

gines each drove a single screw, and she was one of the most powerful
tugs in the harbor.[2]

In May of 1861, John A. Stevenson, Secretary of the New Orleans
Pilots' Benevolent Association, traveled to Montgomery, Alabama and
laid before the newly-formed Confederate government his proposal to
*alter and adapt some of our heavy and powerful tow-boats on the Mississippi
so as to make them comparatively safe against the heaviest guns afloat, and by
preparing their bow in a peculiar manner...render them capable of sinking by
collision the heaviest vessels ever built.*[3] Stevenson's motives were not all
patriotic, however, as he envisioned not a war vessel for the government, but his own privateer. As a privateer, Stevenson would be
awarded twenty percent of the value of any enemy merchant vessel he

might capture and bring into a Confederate port.[4] Being assured he would receive a letter of "Marquee and Reprisal," Stevenson hurried to return to New Orleans. With subscription books in hand, Stevenson and his business colleagues arrived at the New Orleans Merchant Exchange where they quickly raised $100,000, $50,000 of which was subscribed for on the first day. This was enough to purchase the *Enoch Train* and begin her conversion into a ram.[5]

Taken across the river from New Orleans, her conversion from a tugboat to a privateering ironclad ram was begun by the shipyard of John Hughes & Co. of Algiers, La. All of the upper works of the tug were cut away and upon the remaining frame a convex deck of oak was built. This convex frame was twelve inches thick, and bolted to it was one and one-half inches of iron plate which was obtained from railroad iron. (Some reports give the thickness of the frame as no more than five to six inches.) Two smokestacks, with their supporting wires and braces, were mounted amidships.

To enable her to ram enemy vessels, the *Enoch Train's* bow was solidly filled with timbers for a length of twenty feet, and a cast iron ram was affixed to the bow below the water line. In order to give her ram an extra punch, a gun port was cut in the forward end of the shield. Here a 9-inch Dahlgren 32-pounder smoothbore gun, obtained from the navy, was mounted which was impossible to train or elevate and almost impossible to load. Because of these restrictions, it was intended to be fired only moments before ramming. An ingeniously designed shutter covered the port which was opened by the muzzle of the gun as it was run out to be fired, while the recoil of the gun inboard allowed the shutter to close.

Two hatchways, one forward of the smokestacks and one aft, were the only means of access to the interior. A novel system was devised whereby high-pressure steam and scalding water could be pumped over the convex shield to repel boarders. When the work was completed, the *Manassas* was now 143 feet in length, 33 feet abeam, and drew 16 and one-half feet of water while weighing 387 tons.[6]

Completed in August of 1861, the *Manassas* began trial runs on the Mississippi, where she was viewed by hundreds of inquisitive spectators. Stevenson enlisted a crew of 36 men from among the tough dock workers around Algiers and New Orleans and a letter of marquee and reprisal was applied for.[7] While awaiting this certificate to begin privateering, the *Manassas* was moored on the Algiers side of the river, opposite Jackson Square and St. Louis Cathedral.[8]

In September of 1861, a Union fleet of four vessels, the *Richmond*, 22 guns; the *Preble*, 10 guns; the *Water Witch*, 4 guns; and the *Vicennes*, 20 guns, arrived at the Head of the Passes, a section of the river about 70

The CSS *Manassas*, a wash drawing incorrectly depicting only one smokestack, but otherwise an accurate representation.

miles below New Orleans and 15 miles from where the river empties into the Gulf of Mexico. At this point the Mississippi separates into three channels leading to the open sea: Pass A Loutre, South Pass, and Southwest Pass. By blockading the head of these passes, the Federal navy was effectively able to close New Orleans to any and all blockade runners trying to enter port.

Commodore George N. Hollins, a native of Maryland, who had been placed in command of all Confederate naval forces at New Orleans on July 31, 1861, was determined to drive the Federals out of the river. Naval vessels at his disposal included the *McRae*, a small bark-rigged steamer mounting eight guns and commanded by First Lieutenant Thomas B. Huger; the *Ivy*, a small tug sporting a brand new English Whitworth rifle and commanded by First Lieutenant Joseph Fry; the *Tuscarora*, a sidewheel steamer with two guns and com-

Scharf's *History of the Confederate State Navy*

**Captain George N. Hollins, commander of the Confederate fleet during the engagement at the "Head of the Passes."**

manded by Lieutenant Beverly Kennon; the *Calhoun,* another sidewheel steamer and Hollins' flagship in the forthcoming encounter at the Head of the Passes. The *Calhoun* mounted five guns and was under the command of Lieutenant Jonathan H. Carter. Also available to Hollins was the *Watson,* Lieutenant Samuel W. Averett commanding, and the *Jackson* with First Lieutenant Washington Gwathmey in charge. Both were small sidewheel steamers carrying two small guns apiece.[9]

It was in late September, 1861, that Hollins determined to add the services of the *Manassas* to his squadron. A polite request that she par-

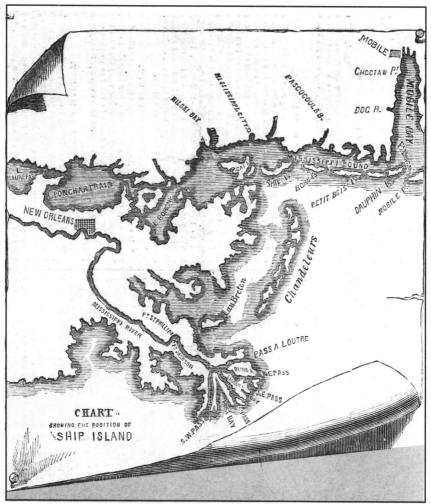

Chart showing the lower Mississippi River below New Orleans including the "Head of the Passes."

ticipate with the navy ships in expelling the Federals from the Head of the Passes was rebuffed by Stevenson. Considering the *Manassas* as the most formidable vessel available, Hollins informed Stevenson that he intended to take her by force if necessary.

James Morris Morgan, a midshipman on the *McRae*, has left us a graphic account of the seizing of the *Manassas*: He (Hollins) had the *McRae, with her crew at quarters, ranged up alongside the Manassas whose crew, composed of some 30 odd men, were standing on the turtleback hurling defiance at the navy men whom they pretended to hold in the greatest contempt. The McRae lowered a boat manned by an armed crew of eight men under the command of Lieutenant A. F. Warley. The only other officer in the boat was the writer of this account, who was at the time a midshipman in his 16th year, and very small for his age.*

*As the boat approached the ram her crew ceased their defiant billingsgate and stood on the turtleback in speechless, as well as helpless, amazement. There was a makeshift Jacob's ladder over the armor, reaching from its apex to the water-line, and under orders, the small midshipman steered for it. Arriving alongside, Mr. Warley ordered the small midshipman to keep the boat's crew in their seats until he called for them, and then, revolver in hand, he lightly tripped up the ladder. The crew of braggarts, who had a few moments before hurled defiance at him, took to their heels and disappeared down a small hole forward which served the purpose of a hatchway. Mr. Warley followed them below and soon they scampered up on deck again through a similar hole aft, some of them being so badly scared that they jumped overboard and swam to shore which, fortunately, was not far away. It was in this way that the first ironclad built in America became a part of the Confederate Navy.*[10] Captain Stevenson and his investors were later paid $100,000 by the Confederate government to compensate them for the seizure of the *Manassas*.

Most of the crew of longshoremen, not wanting to serve in the regular navy and having heard that Warley was a stern disciplinarian, packed their bags and left for New Orleans. Serving on the *Manassas* would also mean no prize money. Volunteers were requested from among the ships of the squadron and soon Warley had enough crew members to properly man the *Manassas*.

Lieutenant Warley, a native of South Carolina, was not impressed with his new command. He claimed she was a *bug-bear ... no power, no speed, no strength of resistance and no armament.* In addition to these misgivings, he and his crew would have little time to become acquainted with their charge, for Hollins was ready to attack the enemy at the Head of the Passes.[11]

The little *Ivy*, proudly sporting her new Whitworth gun, had been conducting daily reconnaissances in the vicinity of the Federal blockaders. On October 9, 1861, she steamed within long range and brazenly opened fire on the Federals. With the annoying *Ivy* dropping her shells in their midst, Captain "Honest John" Pope, commander of the Union fleet, began to panic: *It is evident that we are entirely at the mercy of the enemy. We are liable to be driven from here at any moment, and, situated as we are, our position is untenable. I may be captured at any time by a pitiful little steamer mounting only one gun. The distance at which she was firing I should estimate at 4 miles, with heavy rifled cannon, throwing her shot and shell far beyond us. This may be an experiment to ascertain the range of our guns, which they now have, and of course will quickly avail themselves of the knowledge.*

The next day, Hollins sailed from New Orleans with the *Calhoun*, *Jackson*, and *Tuscarora*. The *Manassas* had sprung a leak in a condenser or valve and was undergoing emergency repairs, but on the following morning of 10 October, she was ready. By noon, throngs of people were crowding the levee to see the *Manassas* off. The sailing of Hollins' "Mosquito Fleet," as it was being called, was a great morale booster for the citizens of New Orleans, for at here last, something aggressive was being done about the "Yankee" blockade. As the *Manassas* cast off her lines and headed south, the crowd cheered wildly as "she steamed down the river with fine speed."[12]

Hollins had his squadron anchor under the guns of Fort Jackson which was only 20 miles above the Head of the Passes. Calling his officers to the *Calhoun*, he explained his plan in detail. The attack on the Federal blockaders would take place before daylight on October 13. The *Manassas* would lead the attack followed at a distance by the *McRae*, the *Ivy*, and the *Tuscarora*. When the enemy was sighted, she was to ram the first suitable target and immediately send up a rocket as a signal for the rest of the squadron. Upon seeing this, three fire rafts were to be ignited and turned loose to float downstream toward the Federal ships, while the rest of the squadron attacked.

The night of October 12, 1861 was moonless and overcast with a gray mist hanging over the water. The Southern vessel's hulls were hidden within the damp veil of fog with only their masts and spars discernible. Silently, one by one, the ships of the "Mosquito Fleet" cast off their lines and moved into position. Turning their heads downstream, the *Manassas* took the lead followed by two tugs pulling three fire rafts. Behind the tugs steamed the *McRae*, the *Ivy*, and the *Tuscarora*. The *Calhoun*, because of her exposed machinery, and the *Jackson* with her noisy high-pressure engines brought up the rear. With no lights showing, the little fleet moved out and proceeded cautiously down the river. The low-lying mist began to thicken, and only the muffled throb of the engines, the steady splashing of paddle wheels, and the churning of propellers marked the passage of the Confederate ships.[13]

Downstream, at the Head of the Passes, the unsuspecting Federal warships lay quietly at anchor. The *Richmond*, *Preble*, and *Water Witch* were near the eastern bank of the river and the *Vicennes* was anchored near the head of Southwest Pass. In spite of the alarm caused by the *Ivy*, no guard boats or pickets had been posted. A coaling schooner, the *Joseph H. Toone*, was tied along the port side of the *Richmond* and by the light of lanterns, coal was being loaded on board. The prize schooner *Frolic* was anchored near the *Richmond*.

Master's Mate Charles Austin was piloting the *Manassas* and knew this stretch of the river well; however, he could see little through the four-inch opening in the forward hatch. At approximately 3:30 a.m. the *Manassas* carefully approached the Head of the Passes. Barely perceptible in the darkness was the dim light from the lanterns being used in the coaling operation at the *Richmond*. Lieutenant Warley ordered Austin to turn to port and head for the lights. At 3:40 a.m. the master of the *Frolic* spotted the *Manassas* and shouted a warning to the *Richmond*, which went unheard because of the noise of the coaling. As the *Manassas* passed the *Preble*, one of that ship's officers also spotted her, but by now it was too late to sound an alarm.

Suddenly, the *Richmond* loomed up out of the mist in front of the charging *Manassas*. Austin shouted to Engineer William E. Hardy, *Let her out, Hardy, let her out now!* The engineer began throwing tar, tallow and sulfur into the furnace to get a hotter fire. Steam pressure surged in the boilers. Crashing through the lines securing the coal schooner, which was not seen by Warley or Austin, the *Manassas* smashed into the *Richmond* at over ten knots. The *Richmond* shuddered from the blow and a large hole was torn in her side. While the Union ship was damaged, the impact of the ramming was hard on the *Manassas* as well. Every man on board was thrown from his feet and a hawser from the coal schooner sliced off both smokestacks even with the deck. As the badly vibrating ironclad reversed her engines and began to back away, pandemonium broke loose among the Federal ships. Bells clanged and foghorns blared. The *Richmond*'s broadside guns spurted flame as they opened fire into the darkness sending their shells screaming over the low lying *Manassas*. The *Preble* joined in, her gunners shooting blindly into the night. Captain Pope hoisted a red danger light to the masthead as each Federal ship, struggling to get underway, slipped their cables and began steaming for the Southwest Pass.

Warley ordered Austin to head for the *Preble* and Austin called to the engine room again: *Now let her out, Hardy, and give it to her!* But Hardy quickly reported back that only one engine was running. The shock of the collision had broken a condenser and one engine was disabled. As the *Manassas* drifted away, all four Federal ships began firing wildly into the darkness. Solid shot and explosive shells screamed in all directions, lighting up the waters of the Mississippi, while the *Manassas* struggled to regain some semblance of control.

In the midst of all this confusion, a midshipman clambered out on the shield and lit the fuse of the promised rocket. Unfortunately, he held it incorrectly, and it burned his hands causing him to drop it. Like a Hollywood cartoon, it happened to be pointed at the open hatch and down it whizzed into the interior of the *Manassas* hissing and sputtering like some angry demon. Thinking it was an enemy shell about to explode, Confederate sailors bowled over each other trying to get out of the way and attempted to hide behind any protective bulkhead they could find. Sheepishly, the midshipman got it right on the second try and the signal rocket arched into the blackened sky.

In the meantime, the *Manassas* was quickly filling with deadly sulfuric fumes. Engineer Hardy seized an ax and headed for the open hatch. As he suspected, one of the damaged smokestacks had fallen over a ventilator and the interior was rapidly becoming a death trap. Brushing Warley aside, who tried to stop him, Hardy scrambled up the ladder. Austin, realizing that he would certainly be swept overboard trying to stand on the wet and slippery iron shield, was close behind. With enemy shells shrieking overhead, and Austin holding on to him from the ladder, Hardy began to hack away at the tangled wires holding the wreckage of the stack. At last, his efforts proved successful as the mangled stack tumbled overboard freeing the ventilator.

Upon sighting the signal rocket, the two tugs ignited the fire rafts and cast them loose. The wind, however, blew them ashore on the east bank where they burned themselves out, doing no damage to the Federals who were now hurriedly retreating down the Southwest Pass.[14]

Lieutenant Fry with the *Ivy* now arrived on the scene, and with the first streaks of light beginning to appear in the eastern sky, searched apprehensively for the Confederate ironclad. *My anxiety for the Manassas was intense,* he wrote. *I believed her calculated to run down a single vessel, not to sustain a cross-fire at short distance directed at her sides. My delight was unbounded to see her slowly emerge from the smoke, an immense volume of it conveying the impression she herself was on fire. Her progress was so slow I was convinced she was crippled; but her commander declined my offer of assistance until she got aground.*

The *Manassas*, hard to control on only one engine, had run aground and Fry passed Warley a line which unfortunately snapped. A second line also broke and Fry steamed back up the river looking for help. Finding the *Tuscarora* also aground, it occurred to Fry that with daylight breaking, the Federals might discover the stranded Confederate vessels and return to attack them. With Hollins and the rest of the squadron just arriving, Fry turned the *Ivy* around and headed down the Southwest Pass firing his Whitworth gun at the fleeing Federals. Once the *Tuscarora* was freed from the sandbar, she and the *McRae* followed the *Ivy* and joined in lobbing shells at the Union vessels.[15]

The Federals were having additional problems. Captain Pope had ordered all his ships to cross the bar into the Gulf, and the *Preble* and the *Water Witch*, with the *Frolic* in tow, had cleared the barrier. The *Richmond* and the *Vicennes*, however, both ran hard aground; the former broadside to the river and the latter with her stern pointing upstream. With the two Federal vessels aground, the *McRae*, *Tuscarora*, and *Ivy* continued to shell them at a respectable distance. At approximately 10:00 a.m., with Lieutenant Warley now having the *Manassas* afloat, Commodore Hollins signaled his ships to cease firing and ordered them to steam back to New Orleans. Lieutenant Fry, disgusted with Hollins for calling off the attack because his Whitworth was playing havoc with the Federals, had kept a count of the number of shots fired by each Union and Confederate vessel. The *Richmond* fired 107, the *Water Witch* 18, and the *Vicennes* 16. On the Confederate side, the *Ivy* fired 26, the *McRae* 23, and the *Tuscarora* 6 shots.[16]

When Hollins reached Fort Jackson around 2:30 p.m., he went ashore and sent a telegram to New Orleans: *Last night I attacked the blockaders with my little fleet, and succeeded, after a very short struggle, to drive them all aground on the Southwest bar, except the sloop-of-war Preble, which I sunk. I have captured a prize from them, and after I got them fast on the sand I peppered them well. No casualties on our side. A complete success.* The city went wild. Even though a later evaluation would show Hollins' report to be a bit over optimistic (the *Preble* had not sunk and only two of the Federals were aground), the people of the city felt an enormous sense of relief that the Federals had been driven from the river. Known derisively in the North as "Pope's Run," New Orleans was proud of their Confederate heroes and the victory they had achieved. When Hollins and the men of the "Mosquito Fleet" returned to the city they were greeted by military bands each vying for an opportunity to serenade and entertain them. It was indeed a happy moment, not only for the citizens of New Orleans, but for the entire Confederacy.[17] As Lieutenant Warley surveyed the battered *Manassas*, however, he was keenly aware that the Federals were gone mostly because of the courage and determination of men like Austin, Hardy, and the rest of the crew of his ironclad.

Once moored back at New Orleans, the *Manassas* underwent repairs to her boilers and engines, while the smokestacks and her iron ram were replaced. Based on Lieutenant Warley's report of the engagement at the Head of the Passes, Acting Engineer Hardy was given the official rank of third engineer, and Austin was promoted to master.

With the threat to New Orleans eased somewhat near the end of November, 1861, and in compliance with orders from the War Department, Hollins led his "Mosquito Fleet" north up the Mississippi to support Confederate forces at Columbus, Kentucky. While details are sketchy, some reports have Warley and the *Manassas* accompanying the fleet and present at the engagements in the upper Mississippi. Hollins, however, who is the better authority since it was his command, stated before an investigating committee of the Confederate Congress that, *she came part of the way up, but she was sent back again, having run aground and injured herself.*[18]

During the winter months, with the *Manassas* being the only formidable vessel left at New Orleans, the Confederates worked feverishly on two new ironclads at Jefferson City just north of the city. Neither the mammoth named *Mississippi* nor the smaller *Louisiana* would be completed, however, before the Union invasion in the spring. The *Mississippi* would be burned and the *Louisiana*, her propellers not yet connected, could act only as a floating battery. Lieutenant Warley with the *Manassas*, therefore, would be the only Confederate ironclad able to maneuver and challenge Farragut's fleet if and when they attempted to fight their way past the forts.

On Good Friday, April 18, 1862, Union Commander David Porter's 20 mortar schooners opened fire on Fort Jackson from a hidden tree line around a bend in the river. Because each boat was instructed to fire its huge 13-inch mortar every ten minutes, Fort Jackson was subjected to a 216 pound shell exploding in its midst every 30 seconds. It was not long, therefore, before many of its guns were disabled and the fort was in flames. The Confederate gunners continued to return the Federal's fire, damaging several mortar schooners and sinking one of them. Fort St. Philip joined in, although situated across the river and about 700 yards upstream, their fire was at extreme range and less effective. Brigadier General Johnson K. Duncan, commander of the forts and a native of Pennsylvania, knew that it was only a matter of hours until Farragut's warships would attempt to pass the chain obstructions in the river, sail by the forts, and steam up the river to New Orleans.

To contest the passage of the Federal invading force, Commander John K. Mitchell, who had replaced Hollins as Confederate naval commander at New Orleans, had at his disposal only the *McRae, Manassas, Jackson*, the immovable *Louisiana* and two steam launches. To augment his little "fleet," the army had seized and converted as rams, six steamboats; the *Warrior, Stonewall Jackson, Defiance, General Lovell, R. J. Breckinridge*, and *Resolute*, all of which were crewed by Mississippi riverboat men and all under the command of that ward of the navy, John A. Stevenson. Needless to say, Captain Stevenson was in no mood to cooperate with the Confederate navy. In addition to the "River Defense Fleet," the state of Louisiana had commissioned and put into service two gunboats, the *Governor Moore* and the *General Quitman*.[19]

On Wednesday, 23 April, Lieutenant Warley and the *Manassas*, along with her tender, the *Phoenix*, were moved down and anchored on the east side of the river just above Fort St. Philip. The *Manassas* was tied with her head pointing upstream with the *Phoenix* alongside in order to quickly turn her down the river. By the end of the day, Warley knew that a desperate struggle was at hand. *On the evening before the attack,* he wrote, *I went on board of the Confederate steamer McRae, carrying some letters to put in the hands of my friend Captain Huger, and found him just starting to call on me, on the same errand. Both of us — judging from the character of the officers in the enemy's fleet, most of whom we knew — believed the attack was at hand, and neither of us expected support from the vessels that had been sent down to help oppose the fleet.* The poignant meeting on the *McRae* to exchange personal letters would be the last time Lieutenant Warley would see his good friend Thomas B. Huger alive.[20]

Scharf's *History of the Confederate States Navy*

**Commander John K. Mitchell, who commanded Confederate naval forces during the Battle of New Orleans.**

The dark night of April 23–24, 1862 was starlit and chilly. The moon had still to rise, when at 3:30 a.m. a sergeant in a water battery at Fort Jackson discerned the ghostly shape of a ship approaching the chain barrier. Notifying Captain William B. Robertson, they watched as *several black, shapeless masses, barely distinguishable from the surrounding darkness, moved silently, but steadily up the river.* Almost immediately the darkness was shattered by thundering salvos of screaming shells as the guns of Forts Jackson and St. Philip opened fire. Blue-coated tars jerked their lanyards and the Federal guns thundered in response. The night was illuminated from tongues of flame, exploding shells, and sputtering fuses. Captain Robertson wrote of this moment: *The flashes of the guns, from both sides, lit up the river with a lurid light that revealed the outlines of the Federal steamers more distinctly.*

*I do not believe there ever was a grander spectacle witnessed before in the world,* Robertson continued, *than that displayed during the great artillery duel which then followed. The mortar-shells shot upward from the mortar-*

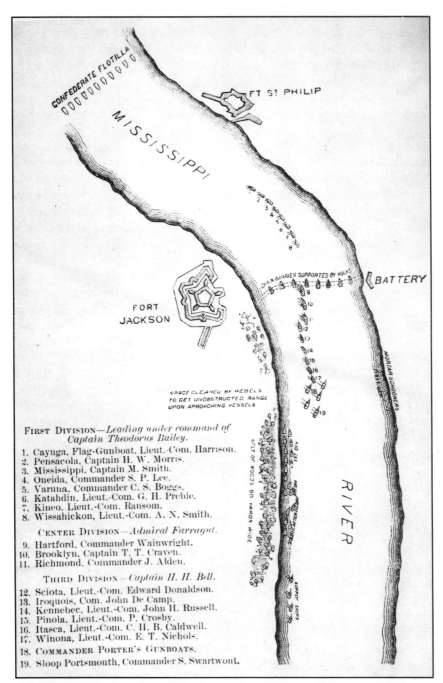

CONFEDERATE FLOTILLA

FT ST PHILIP

MISSISSIPPI

CHAIN BARRIER SUPPORTED BY HULKS

BATTERY

FORT JACKSON

MORTAR SCHOONERS FLEET NO 2

SPACE CLEARED BY REBELS TO GET UNOBSTRUCTED RANGE UPON APROACHING VESSELS

RIVER

FIRST DIVISION—*Leading under command of Captain Theodorus Bailey.*

1. Cayuga, Flag-Gunboat, Lieut.-Com. Harrison.
2. Pensacola, Captain H. W. Morris.
3. Mississippi, Captain M. Smith.
4. Oneida, Commander S. P. Lee.
5. Varuna, Commander C. S. Boggs.
6. Katahdin, Lieut.-Com. G. H. Preble.
7. Kineo, Lieut.-Com. Ransom.
8. Wissahickon, Lieut.-Com. A. N. Smith.

CENTER DIVISION—*Admiral Farragut.*

9. Hartford, Commander Wainwright.
10. Brooklyn, Captain T. T. Craven.
11. Richmond, Commander J. Alden.

THIRD DIVISION—*Captain H. H. Bell.*

12. Sciota, Lieut.-Com. Edward Donaldson.
13. Iroquois, Com. John De Camp.
14. Kennebec, Lieut.-Com. John H. Russell.
15. Pinola, Lieut.-Com. P. Crosby.
16. Itasca, Lieut.-Com. C. H. B. Caldwell.
17. Winona, Lieut.-Com. E. T. Nichols.
18. COMMANDER PORTER'S GUNBOATS.
19. Sloop Portsmouth, Commander S. Swartwout.

The Federal order of attack for the passage of Forts Jackson and St. Philip, April 24, 1862.

*boats, rushed to the apexes of their flight, flashing the lights of their fuses as they revolved, paused an instant, and then descended upon our works like hundreds of meteors, or burst in mid-air, hurling their jagged fragments in every direction. The guns on both sides kept up a continual roar for nearly and hour, without a moment's intermission and produced a shimmering illumination, which though beautiful and grand, was illusive in its effect upon the eye, and made it impossible to judge accurately of the distance of the moving vessels from us.*[21]

As the first shots thundered out across the dark Mississippi, the crew of the *Manassas* rushed to their assigned stations. Coal heavers shoveled more coal into the furnace. Blowers were started. Steam pressure rose, and commands were shouted to the *Phoenix*, who, with tow lines, began swinging the ram's bow out into the river. Warley was impressed with his crew's efficiency in starting for battle: ... *the Manassas was cut away from the bank, turned downstream, cast off from the tug, and was steaming down to the fleet in quicker time than I had believed to be possible.*[22]

The first vessel that the *Manassas* encountered, rather than an enemy, was the *Resolute* from the River Defense Fleet which came charging out of the fire-streaked darkness fleeing up river from the oncoming Federals. Warley shouted to Chief Engineer Dearning (Hardy had been transferred to the *Tuscarora*) to reverse the engines, but it was too late. The *Manassas'* bow struck the *Resolute* abeam the wheel house, and as Warley tried to back away, a passing Federal discharged a broadside into the fleeing army ram. Free of the *Resolute*, Warley headed for the middle of the river. In the flickering light of flashing guns, Warley spotted a large side-wheeler cutting diagonally across the water that looked very familiar. It was the USS *Mississippi*, aboard which Warley had made a round-the-world cruise in the old navy. Warley ordered pilot William T. Levine to ram her. With the aid of the current and her engines at full throttle, the *Manassas* rushed the Union ship. The bow port shutters clanged open as the old smoothbore was run out and all hands braced themselves for the collision. The *Mississippi*, at the last moment, saw her coming and sheared to port trying to ram the *Manassas*. Levine spun the ironclad's wheel to starboard, spoiling the Federal's aim, and then quickly reversed it back hard-a-port. Within ten feet of the *Mississippi*, Warley's gunner pulled the lock-string and the Dahlgren roared to life. Within seconds the *Manassas* smashed into the Union ship just aft of the giant paddle wheel on her port quarter. Striking a glancing blow, the *Manassas* tore out a solid section of timber seven feet long and four inches deep, shearing off fifty copper bolts. The Dahlgren's shell smashed through timbers and bulkheads and came to rest in one of the *Mississippi's* cabins. As the *Manassas* backed off, the *Mississippi* unleashed a tremendous broadside that whistled close over the ironclad's arched shield. Steaming on and firing into Fort St. Philip on her starboard side, the *Mississippi* was soon lost in the smoke and darkness.[23]

First officer Frank Harris turned the *Manassas'* head downstream as he and Warley searched desperately for the next Federal ship passing the forts. Harris spotted the *Pensacola* and called to Engineer Dearning for a full head of steam, but the *Pensacola's* executive officer spotted the ram and the large Union ship sheared out of the way. As she passed she fired her after-pivot gun at point blank range cutting off the flag staff of the *Manassas*.[24]

The *Oneida, Cayga, Pinola, Richmond, Iroquois,* and *Wissahickon* all sent shot and shell screaming toward the *Manassas* as they passed. Finding that all of the Federals had passed the forts, Warley decided to steam south and attack Porter's mortar boats. With the river ablaze with fire rafts and burning hulks of the River Defense Fleet, however, the excited army gunners in the forts were firing at everything that moved on the water. St. Philip's guns were now firing furiously at the *Manassas* and Fort Jackson scored several hits before Warley could reverse his course and move back out of range.[25]

Determining that it was impossible to attack the mortar boats downstream because of the heavy fire from the forts, Warley decided to pursue the Federals upstream. Turning around, and with the first streaks of light beginning to show in the eastern sky, the *Manassas* pounded slowly up river fighting the strong Mississippi current. The Federals may have gotten by, but Lieutenant Warley was not finished with them

The CSS *Manassas,* attacking the USS *Mississippi* at the Battle of New Orleans, April 24, 1862.

yet! Soon the shape of a large Union vessel loomed out of the smoke which Warley thought was the *Hartford* but was, in fact, the *Brooklyn*. Harris shouted to the engine room again for full speed. The coal heavers threw resin into the furnace and the *Manassas* shook and trembled as she pounded toward the unsuspecting Federal. Once again the clanging of the iron shutter announced that the bow gun had been run out and was ready to fire. The *Brooklyn* had just finished fighting off on her port side one of the few River Defense rams to put up a fight, *when a column of black smoke*, wrote her commander, James R. Bartlett, *which came from the dreaded Manassas, was seen on the starboard side, and the cry was passed along by men who were looking out of the ports, "The ram, the ram!"*[26]

*The Manassas*, Warley wrote, *was driven at her with everything open, resin being piled onto the furnaces. The gun was discharged when close on board. We struck her fairly amidships; the gun recoiled and turned over and*

*Battles and Leaders of the Civil War*

**A bird's eye view of the passage of the forts below New Orleans, April 24, 1862.**

*remained there, the boiler started, slightly jamming the Chief Engineer Dearning, but settled back as the vessel backed off.* The Dahlgren's heavy iron ball tore through the heavy chain links protecting the *Brooklyn's* sides, penetrated the planking, continued on through some spare rigging stored inside, and buried itself in a wall of sandbags protecting the steam boiler. The *Manassas* struck the heavy Union ship where one of her full coal bunkers was located and thus little damage was apparent until later. When the bunker was emptied, it was found that the *Brooklyn* was so heavily damaged as to be completely unseaworthy.[27]

The *Manassas* was also badly shaken. Her boiler had been torn from its mounts, and the bow gun was now useless. *Just then,* Warley continued, *another steamer came up through the fire of the forts. I thought her the Iroquois, and tried to run into her, but she passed as if the Manassas had been at anchor.*[28]

*Steaming slowly up the river — very slow was our best — we discovered the Confederate States steamer McRae, head up-stream, receiving the fire of three men-of-war. As the Manassas forged by, the three men-of-war steamed up the river, and were followed, to allow the McRae to turn and get down to the forts, as she was very badly used up.*[29]

The *McRae* was indeed "badly used up," and it was fortunate that the *Manassas* came along when she did. As the Union vessels pulled away, upon sighting the approaching *Manassas*, one of their parting shots mortally wounded Warley's close friend, Lieutenant Huger. Command of the *McRae* was assumed by her first officer, Lieutenant Charles W. Read, who would continue to fight the Union ships until the *McRae* was shot through like a sieve.[30]

Lieutenant Warley and the *Manassas* were not quite beaten yet, and he ordered Levine to continue up the river. But the end of this agonizing night was near. *Day was getting broader,* Warley wrote, *and with the first rays of the sun we saw the fleet above us; and a splendid sight it was, or rather would have been under other circumstances. Signals were being rapidly exchanged, and two men-of-war steamed down, one on either side of the river. The Manassas was helpless. She had nothing to fight with, and no speed*

*Battles and Leaders of the Civil War*

**Flag-Officer Farragut's flagship, the USS *Hartford*.**

*to run with. I ordered her to be run into the bank on the Fort St. Philip side, her delivery-pipes to be cut, and the crew to be sent into the swamp through the elongated port forward, through which the gun had been used. The First Officer, gallant Frank Harris, reported all the men on shore. We examined the vessel, found all orders had been obeyed, and we also took to the swamp.*[31] Warley was convinced, in his official report that, *God was good to me in allowing me to save all the people under my command. Cut up as the vessel was, there were no causalities on board beyond a few slight scratches.*[32]

The *Mississippi* and the *Kineo* pulled up along side of the abandoned *Manassas* and several Federal sailors in a small boat rowed over and set fire to her. The two Federal ships backed away and began angrily firing broadsides at the burning hull turning her into a shambles of flaming wood and splintered iron. Occasionally, one of the Federals would fire a load of grape-shot into the swamp trying to kill their tormentors who were now hiding there. The concussion of the shells slamming into the *Manassas* knocked her loose from the river bank and she drifted out into the middle of the river.

Twisting and turning in the swirling eddies of the Mississippi, she slowly and aimlessly drifted downstream. Crackling flames were licking out of her hatches and from the many holes that had been punched in her thin iron plating. Finally, mercifully, for the Confederates watching from the banks of the river, at 7:30 a.m. the fire reached her magazine, and with a deep rumble her iron shield lifted into the crisp, early morning air. With a last gasp of smoke and steam, the mighty little *Manassas* sank in the river she had fought so valiantly to defend.[33]

# *Chapter Two*

## "A Matter of First Necessity"

The secretary of the new Confederate States Navy was bone tired as his train pulled into the Richmond station on June 3, 1861. It had been a long journey from Montgomery, Alabama. Waiting for him at Mechanics Hall, an ungainly building on 9th Street which housed the various newly arrived offices of the War and Navy departments, was a telegram dated May 30 from Captain French Forrest at Norfolk. One sentence stood out: *We have the Merrimac up and just pulling her into dry dock.*[1] Little did Secretary Mallory realize, as he wearily skimmed the captain's dispatch, that this one sentence would signal a revolutionary change in all naval warfare.

**Secretary of the Confederate States Navy, Stephen R. Mallory from Florida.**

The vessel to which the Confederate navy captain was referring to was the burned and charred remains of the U.S. Auxiliary Steam Frigate *Merrimac,* formerly of the United States Navy. Burned and scuttled by Federal troops

*19*

when they evacuated Norfolk on April 20, her hull, engines, and machinery, though rusted and covered with mud, were undamaged. Also undamaged in the conflagration that engulfed parts of the Gosport Navy Yard at Portsmouth, which was across the Elizabeth River from Norfolk, was the priceless granite dry dock.

Mallory had been pondering for some time the benefits of an iron-plated vessel for the Confederacy. The previous month, while the government was still in Montgomery, he had written to the chairman of the House Committee on Naval Affairs: *I regard the possession of an iron-armored ship as a matter of the first necessity. Such a vessel at this time could traverse the entire coast of the United States, prevent all blockades, and encounter, with a fair prospect of success, their entire navy. If we cope with them upon the sea we follow their example and build wooden ships, we shall have to construct several at one time; for one or two ships would fall an easy prey to her comparatively numerous steam frigates. But inequality of numbers may be compensated by invulnerability; and thus not only does economy but naval success dictate the wisdom and expediency of fighting with iron against wood, without regard to first cost.*

*Naval engagements between wooden frigates,* he continued, *as they are now built and armed, will prove to be the forlorn hopes of the sea, simply contests in which the question, not of victory, but of who shall go to the bottom first, is to be solved.* Since the Confederacy did not, as yet, have the facilities for building ironclads capable of challenging and defeating the Federal navy, Mallory recommended that they be built in Europe. Congress agreed, and on May 10 appropriated $2,000,000 for this purpose.[2]

Now, with the information contained in the telegram from Captain Forrest, there had arisen the intriguing possibility of building an ironclad in home waters. Late that same night, the exhausted Mallory conferred with Lieutenant John M. Brooke about the feasibility of building an ironclad within the Confederacy. Brooke, who would become renowned later for his double and triple banded "Brooke Rifles," probably the finest naval gun on either side, was one of the most capable Confederate naval officers at the

Lieutenant (later Commander) John M. Brooke, co-designer of the CSS *Virginia*. Brooke also became famous for his design of the superb "Brooke Rifle."

beginning of the war. Recognizing his talents, Mallory sought his advice. Before the meeting adjourned, the secretary had asked Brooke to submit his calculations and ideas on building an ironclad warship.[3]

Naval constructor John L. Porter, co-designer of the CSS *Virginia*, and designer of numerous other Confederate ironclads.

Early in June, Brooke submitted to the secretary, *outline drawings,— sheer, body and deck plans, with explanations,—and he approved and adopted this novel form.* On Brooke's recommendation, Mallory contacted naval constructor John L. Porter and Chief Engineer William P. Williamson, both at Norfolk, and ordered them to Richmond for consultation on Brooke's design. On the June 23, Brooke, Porter, and Williamson met with the secretary in his office. Brooke now had pencil drawings of his design and Porter had brought along a wooden model of his own proposal. Both men suggested an armored shield with inclined sides and ends carried on a flat-bottomed hull. Porter's design had the hull terminating at the ends of the shield much like a barge, while Brooke's drawings showed the hull extended fore and aft. Concerned about the weight of the shield and the build-up of water ahead of it while under way, Brooke explained why he had extended the hull:

*It was apparent that to support such a shield the ends of the vessel would be so full as to prevent the attainment of speed; and that moving "end on" even a small sea would prevent working the bow or stern gun. It then occurred to me that fineness of line, protection of hull, and buoyancy with light draught, could be obtained by extending the ends of the vessel under water beyond the shield, provided the shield were of sufficient length to give the requisite stability.* Brooke's design was accepted by Mallory and the department, though Porter, who made the final line drawings, would later claim the design to be his. The two men, unfortunately, would wage a bitter quarrel for years to come as to who was actually responsible for the design of the *Virginia*.[4]

The next day, Brooke and Williamson went to the Tredegar Iron Works in Richmond searching for suitable engines for their ironclad. Tredegar, who was already swamped with orders from the army, informed them that there was no way they could build the engines they needed. Disappointed, the two men journeyed to Norfolk, while Porter stayed behind to work on the final drawings. After an exhaustive search, nothing was found at the navy yard that could be adapted to power their design. In desperation, Williamson suggested that they use the burned-out hulk of the *Merrimac*. Returning to Richmond, they discussed Williamson's proposal with Porter who agreed that it was feasible. Brooke and Porter, however, felt that the draft of the *Merrimac* was too great, but agreed that there was really no other choice.[5] Based on this meeting, the three men submitted their recommendations to Secretary Mallory, part of which stated:

*In obedience to your orders, we have carefully examined and considered the various plans and propositions for constructing a shot-proof steam battery, and respectfully report that, in our opinion, the steam-frigate* Merrimac, *which is in such condition from the effects of fire as to be useless for any other purpose, without incurring very heavy expense in rebuilding, etc., can be made an efficient vessel of the character, mounting 10 heavy guns, 2 pivot and 8 broadside guns of her original battery, and from further consideration that we cannot procure suitable engines and boilers for any other vessel without building them, which would occupy too much time. It would appear that this is our only chance to get a suitable vessel in a short time.*[6]

Mallory agreed with their findings and Porter returned to Norfolk where he could make accurate measurements of the *Merrimac*. Working with his assistants at the navy yard, Porter completed the detailed construction drawings that he needed and returned to Richmond. A final review meeting was held at the Navy Department on July 11, after which Secretary Mallory issued the following to Captain Forrest at the Gosport Navy Yard:

*Sir: You will proceed with all practicable dispatch to make the changes in the form of the* Merrimac, *and to build, equip, and fit her in all respects according to the design and plans of the constructor and engineers, Messrs. Porter and Williamson. S. R. Mallory, Secretary of the C. S. Navy.*

Forrest, however, had only administrative control on the project. It was Porter who would oversee the actual construction of the ironclad's upper structure including the shield, while Williamson was given responsibility for cleaning and refurbishing the engines, boilers, and all other machinery. Brooke would maintain his office in Richmond and work with Tredegar to produce the 1,000 tons of iron plates needed to sheath the vessel's casemate. His responsibilities also included testing different angles of inclination on armored targets to determine the best angle to use on the ironclad's shield. In addition, Brooke was to design a new and more powerful rifled gun which would provide the converted *Merrimac* with the most formidable ten gun battery of anything afloat.[7]

Porter got to work immediately. All the charred and splintered timber of the *Merrimac's* upper structure was cleared away. She was then cut down to her berth deck which, when the vessel was without the shield, was three and one-half feet from the water line. Both ends were covered over for a distance of twenty-nine and one-half feet forward of the shield and fifty-five feet aft. Soon thereafter, work began on the shield itself. Porter's plans called for a wooden frame 170 feet long and seven feet high to be erected amidships. The walls of this frame were of solid oak and pine beams, making a total thickness of twenty-four inches. These were inclined, based on Brooke's testing, at an angle of 36 degrees which was the best compromise between deflecting shot and still having enough room to work the guns. The ends of the shield or casemate were rounded, and the upper deck, which was fourteen feet wide, was an iron grating two inches thick and cut for four hatchways. A conical pilot house was at the forward end, while fourteen elliptical gunports were cut in the shield, four on each side and three to an end.[8]

Meanwhile, Brooke had been busy testing iron plates. Setting up targets on Jamestown Island, he fired shots at them from 300 yards using the heaviest ordnance then in service with the Federal navy. After experimenting with different angles of inclination and thicknesses of iron, he determined that four inches of iron, backed by twenty-four inches of wood, and inclined at between thirty-five and forty-five degrees would deflect any shot from any range. Unfortunately, no rolling mill in the entire Confederacy could roll four-inch iron plates. It was obvious that two layers of two-inch plates would have to suffice, and Brooke requested Tredegar, who was currently rolling one-inch plates, to modify their machinery accordingly. Tredegar agreed, but the ensuing down time for retooling caused considerable delay in production.

With the plates, which were seven inches wide and eight feet long, now being produced by the rolling mill, the task of finding available rail transportation became another problem. With Virginia's inadequate rail systems already overburdened carrying troops and supplies for the Confederate armies, it was next to impossible to get shipments through to Norfolk. By re-routing to different rail lines, however, enough shipments of iron plates were able to get through in time to keep the workers busy.[9]

Once the plates began reaching the navy yard, the first layer of 2-inch iron was bolted horizontally to the casemate while the second layer was attached vertically. One-inch iron plates were bolted to the hull and extending two to three feet below the water line, while one-inch iron plates also covered the decks fore and aft. A cast iron 1500-pound prow for ramming was imperfectly attached to the bow and projected two to four feet (sources disagree) from the stem below the water line. The rudder and the single two-blade seventeen foot propeller were unprotected.[10]

In November, Mallory assigned Lieutenant Catesby ap R. Jones to the *Virginia* as her executive officer with orders to expedite construction, acquire and mount her guns, assemble a crew, and prepare the ship for sea. Jones, who had served on the *Merrimac* before the war, was an extremely competent naval officer. (Federal Admiral David Porter once stated that he regretted the loss of only two officers to the South: John M. Brooke and Catesby Jones.)[11] During the winter, Jones set up a battery for test firing near the naval hospital. These included six 9-inch Dahlgren smoothbores, two newly designed 6.4-inch Brooke rifles, and two new 7-inch Brooke rifles which would be used in the forward and aft pivot positions, the other guns being used in broadside.[12]

With construction now falling behind schedule, workers at the yard began working seven days a week to hasten the *Virginia's* completion. On January 11, blacksmiths, machinists, and bolt-drivers volunteered to work until eight o'clock every night without extra pay. Finally, by January 27, 1862, her armor was finished, but much work remained to be done. Porter was constantly plagued by detractors who believed the big ironclad would sink like a stone once she was launched. Some predicted she would capsize as soon as she hit the water, and even Captain Sidney Smith Lee, brother of General Robert E. Lee and executive officer of the yard, asked the day before the launch, *Mr. Porter, do you really think she will float?*

Considering the importance of the event, the launching of the *Virginia* on Monday, February 17, 1862, was very anticlimactic. No brass bands played, and there was no crowd of Portsmouth citizens or dignitaries on hand as the water began to flow into the dry dock. Only two of her officers were present, and they, preferring the safety of dry land, stood on the granite walls of the dry dock. As she slowly began to rise off the stocks and slide toward the river, only five Confederate marines stood nervously on board.[13] She did not sink, however, and later in the day she was officially commissioned the CSS *Virginia*. Her size, dictated by the hull of the *Merrimac*, made her one of the largest ironclads the Confederacy would ever put in commission. She was now 262 feet, nine inches long, 38 feet wide and weighed 3,200 tons with a draft of 22 feet when fully loaded. Her maximum speed would prove to be about nine knots, an improvement of three knots over the old *Merrimac* on steam alone.[14]

There was still more work to be done, however, to bring the *Virginia* up to fighting condition. On February 20, Jones was writing

The CSS *Virginia* in the granite dry-dock at the Gosport Navy Yard after her conversion from the *Merrimac*.

Mallory that, *we are living aboard, and are as uncomfortable as possible — there has not been a dry spot aboard her, leaks everywhere — mechanics are at work at a thousand things which should have been done months ago.* Like any new experimental ship, the *Virginia* had certain weaknesses, the most serious being her engines.[15] These had been condemned as unserviceable by the Federals while the *Merrimac* was berthed at Norfolk, and Williamson had to work hard to put them in serviceable order. In addition, the *Merrimac*'s engines were never intended for more than "auxiliary" power, and with the added weight now of the *Virginia*'s armor, they were woefully under powered. Her single propeller made it difficult to maneuver and it would take 30 to 40 minutes to make a 180-degree turn in the shallow waters of Hampton Roads. In spite of her shortcomings, however, the *Virginia* was still a fearsome warship.[16]

By February, most of the ship's officers had been assigned, but obtaining a crew of 320 men would be a problem. While many southern officers had resigned their commissions and offered their services to the new Confederacy, most of the enlisted seamen were from the North and remained in Federal service. Lieutenant John Taylor Wood, nephew to President Davis, had been assigned to the *Virginia* in January with the responsibility of collecting and training the ironclad's crew. Wood found some experienced seamen who had escaped to Norfolk after the destruction of their gunboats in the sounds of North Carolina when the Federals invaded the eastern part of that state. For the remainder, however, he was forced to visit several army commands including General Magruder's army at Yorktown. Finally, with a crew of mostly army volunteers, training began amid the sounds of carpenters and machinists who were busily trying to finish last minute tasks.[17]

On February 24, Captain Franklin Buchanan, a Maryland native and the first superintendent of the U.S. Naval Academy at Annapolis,

A wash drawing by Clary Ray of the CSS *Virginia*, sketched in 1898.

was appointed by Mallory to command the defenses of the James River. His squadron would consist of the *Virginia*, and the gunboats *Patrick Henry, Jamestown, Teaser, Raleigh*, and the *Beaufort*. Naturally, he would fly his flag from the *Virginia*, thus by default, becoming her commander. Buchanan, who was almost 61, had spent 46 years in the Federal service and was commander of the Washington Navy Yard at the beginning of the war. He sadly resigned his commission on April 22, 1861, when, after the riots in Baltimore, it looked as though Maryland would secede. Maryland, which was occupied by Federal troops, was prevented from leaving the Union and Buchanan, who applied for reinstatement, was told he had been stricken from the rolls. Dejected and saddened by the end of his career and by the events surrounding him, he retired to his Maryland farm determined to take no part in the war. By September, seeing the North continuing to gather its forces for invasion and subjugation of the South, he could sit still no longer and offered his services to Secretary Mallory. Commissioned a captain in the Confederate navy, he was assigned command of the Office of Orders and Detail where he served until ordered to the *Virginia*.[18]

By the beginning of March, everything was on board except one important commodity ... gunpowder! While needing 18,000 pounds to service her ten guns, there was only one thousand pounds in the magazines. Captain Forrest urgently requested the gunboats of the James River Squadron to send to the *Virginia* all the powder they could spare. Ultimately, the army came to the rescue and by March 5, a full compliment of powder finally filled the magazines.

On March 2, Buchanan wrote to Commander John R. Tucker of the *Patrick Henry*: *It is my intention, if no accident occurs to this ship to prevent it, to appear before the enemy off Newport News at daylight on Friday Morning next (March 7). You will, with the Jamestown and Teaser, be prepared to join us. My object is first to destroy the frigates Congress and Cumberland if possible and turn my attention to the destruction of the battery on shore, and the gun-boats. You will, in the absence of signals, use you best exertions to injure or destroy the enemy. Much is expected of this ship and those who cooperate with her by her Countrymen, and I expect and hope that our acts will prove our desire to do our duty, to reflect credit upon the Country and the Navy ... No. 1 signal hoisted under my pennant indicates "Sink before you surrender."*[19] Bad weather on the 7th forced Buchanan to postpone his attack until the following day. In order to launch his attack at daylight, Buchanan planned on leaving the night before and anchoring in the Roads. Now he had another problem. Even though the obstructions in the Elizabeth River, down which the *Virginia* would have to steam, had been marked with lights, the pilots reported that they could not operate the huge ironclad safely in the darkness. With her deep draft of 22 feet, they were fearful they would run aground, and Buchanan had no alternative but to postpone their departure until morning.

It had been a long, dreary winter in Virginia, and the last couple of days had brought cold wind and rain. On this Saturday morning, March 8, it was refreshing to the men of the *Virginia* to arise to a brilliant blue sky, and feel the warmth of the morning sun. Fleecy white clouds drifted across the sky, hurried along by a gentle northwest breeze, while only light swells disturbed the waters of the river and the bay. At the dock in front of the navy yard, workmen were busy smearing tallow or "ship's grease" over the big ironclad's casemate, hoping it would help deflect enemy shells. Steam pressure was building in her boilers and wisps of black smoke were visible drifting up lazily from her stack.

Officers, looking smart in their new steel gray uniforms, could be seen rushing about performing last minute duties. The word was out that a "trial run" would be made this day, and the docks were becoming crowded as the curious began to gather. At 11:00 a.m., a signal gun boomed across the harbor; crewmen began casting off lines, bells rang, and thick black smoke began to pour from the *Virginia's* funnel. With the Stars and Bars already fluttering from her aft flag staff, the red pennant of a flag officer was run up on the forward staff as she began to move. Workmen, who had been attending to last minute tasks on board, rushed to leave, some having to jump to the dock as she pulled away. While onlookers cheered, the *Virginia* slowly turned her head down river, and accompanied by the *Raleigh* and *Beaufort*, headed north toward Hampton Roads and her rendezvous with history.[20]

Not everyone in the crowd of onlookers was convinced that the *Virginia* would be a success. Midshipman H. B. Littlepage remembered: *As we passed along we found the wharves crowded with people, men and women, the women cheering us on our way, and many of the men with serious countenances. One man, I remember, called out to us, "Go on with your old metallic coffin! She will never amount to anything else!*

While only Buchanan and Jones knew beforehand that they would head straight for the *Cumberland* and *Congress*, many of her crew and most of the officers suspected that this was not going to be a mere "trial run." With the untried engines running slowly, the *Virginia* was

making about five knots as it steamed past Norfolk. Knowing that it would take some time to steam the ten miles to the end of the river, Buchanan had the crew sent to lunch and called Chief Engineer H. A. Ramsey to the pilot house. Buchanan wanted to know what would happen to the engines and boilers in the event of a collision. *They are braced tight,* said Ramsey. *Though the boilers stand 14 feet, they are so securely fastened that no collision could budge them.* Buchanan was concerned, however, about some new rifled guns that the *Cumberland* reportedly carried (as part of her 24 gun battery, she carried one 70-pounder rifle), and declared to Ramsey, *The moment we are in the*

Captain Franklin Buchanan, commander of the James River Squadron and the CSS *Virginia*. Shown here just prior to the war in the uniform of a captain in the United States Navy.

Wartime chart of Hampton Roads, showing the Elizabeth and James Rivers and the entrance from the Chesapeake Bay.

*Roads I'm going to make right for her and ram her. How about your engines: should they be tested by a trial trip?*

*She will have to travel yet some 10 miles down the river before we get to the Roads,* Ramsey replied, *I think that will be a sufficient trial trip.*[21]

Ramsey was now called to the wardroom as it would be his last chance to get something to eat because the galley fires had to be extinguished before the magazines were opened. On passing along the gun deck, Ramsey remembered, *I saw the pale and determined countenances of the guns' crews, as they stood motionless at their posts, with set lips unsmiling. ... This was the real thing.* Arriving at the wardroom, Ramsey noticed several officers eating, but his attention was drawn to the end of the table, where Assistant Surgeon Algernon S. Garnet sat cleaning and polishing his instruments. *The sight took away my appetite,* remembered Ramsey.[22]

First Lieutenant William H. Parker, captain of the *Beaufort*, solemnly remembered this cruise down the Elizabeth: *As we steamed down the harbor we were saluted by the waving of caps and handkerchiefs; but no voice broke the silence of the scene; all hearts were too full for utterance; an attempt at cheering would have ended in tears, for all realized the fact that here was to be tried the great experiment of the ram and ironclad in naval warfare.*[23]

Following in the three-ship flotilla's wake was a hodgepodge of small vessels crammed to the rails with spectators. Among these was Captain Forrest and all the officers of the navy yard who were following in the ordnance transport *Harmony*. At about twelve-thirty, the *Beaufort* passed a towline to the *Virginia* and one of the ironclad's pilots came on board the gunboat. The *Virginia's* rudder was virtually dragging the river bottom, and she was becoming difficult to manage. In fact Lieutenant Wood commented that, *She was as unmanageable as a water-logged vessel.* Nearing Craney Island, a boat was lowered and the few remaining mechanics who were still on board were sent ashore. On the *Virginia's* gun deck, the gun crews stood grimly silent at their stations, lanyards in the hands of gun captains; all was quiet save the continuous throbbing of the propeller as the big ironclad steadily approached the mouth of the river.[24]

Approaching the Confederate batteries at Sewell's Point, the officers on board could see Federal occupied Fort Monroe straight ahead off the bow, while off the port side was Newport News which was crowded with Federal land batteries. As the lumbering ironclad made a turn to port to enter the South Channel leading toward the mouth of the James River, the *Cumberland*, with twenty-four guns, and the *Congress*, with forty-four guns, were plainly visible anchored a few hundred yards off the Point at Newport News. In the distance off the starboard bow, between these two Federal warships and Fort Monroe,

Scharf's *History of the Confederate States Navy*

**First Lieutenant William H. Parker, commander of the CSS *Beaufort* during the engagements in Hampton Roads.**

Scharf's *History of the Confederate States Navy*

**Captain French Forrest, commandant of the Gosport Navy Yard at Norfolk during the battles in Hampton Roads.**

could also be seen the masts of the fifty-gun screw frigates *Minnesota* and *Roanoke* and the forty-four-gun sailing frigate *St. Lawrence*, along with a host of gunboats and auxiliary vessels.[25]

It was about one-thirty now, and with the ironclad in deeper water, the *Beaufort* took back her towline. Both the *Raleigh* and the *Beaufort*, as pre-arranged, now eased into position on the port side of the *Virginia* where they would be somewhat shielded by the ironclad. With the enemy now in sight, Buchanan, who had been directing the *Virginia* from atop the casemate, descended to the gun deck. Standing on the ladder leading to the forward hatch, he called the crew together. *Men, the eyes of your country are upon you. You are fighting for your rights, your liberties, your wives and children. You must not be content with only doing your duty, but do more than your duty! Those ships (pointing to the Union fleet) must be taken, and you shall not complain that I do not take you close enough. Go to your guns!*[26] The men returned quietly to their stations.

It was wash day in the Federal fleet, and as the *Virginia* steadily closed the distance, her crew could see navy blues and whites fluttering from the *Cumberland's* rigging. Blue-coated tars lounged about the decks soaking up the warm sunshine and paying little attention to the three vessels approaching from the southeast. No fire was in their furnaces and no steam in their boilers as they swung lazily at their anchors. Earlier, a few officers on board the gunboat *Zouave* had noticed the wisps of black smoke coming from the Elizabeth River, and they had signaled the *Congress* and *Cumberland*, but no one noticed their signal flags.

Eventually, the gunboat fired a round to get the larger ship's attention and the *Roanoke* finally took notice and fired a few of her own guns to warn the rest of the fleet. Signal flags were run up and the *Minnesota* and *Roanoke* began moving toward Newport News, the latter under tow with a broken propeller. As sailors on the *Cumberland* and *Congress* stared wide-eyed at the approaching shapes on the horizon, the long roll could be heard on shore as the army troops were called to assembly. Soon the "beat to quarters" was sounded on the Union ships, and Federal tars began casting loose and loading their guns.[27]

As the ironclad drew nearer, the Confederates could see Federal sailors dropping their small boats astern and the *Cumberland* was being swung on her anchor so that she would lay broadside across the James River channel. There were many other small craft in the bay and Chief Engineer Ramsey remembered: *As we rounded into view the white-winged sailing craft that sprinkled the bay and long lines of tugs and small boats scurried to the far shore like chickens on the approach of a hovering hawk.*[28]

In an attempt to give support to the *Virginia* and her consorts, Confederate land batteries on Sewell's Point opened fire on the frigates *Minnesota*, *Roanoke*, and *St. Lawrence*, but because they were firing at extreme range, their fire had little effect. Federal land batteries at Fort Wool and on the Rip Raps bellowed in reply. Federal guns at Newport News began dropping their shells near the *Virginia*, sending up giant waterspouts from near misses. Presently, the *Cumberland's* guns belched fire and smoke and now the *Congress* joined in. Their first shots were wide and high and the big shells splashed to the side and beyond the lumbering ironclad. The *Cumberland's* gunners worked feverishly to reload. They wouldn't miss next time.

On board the *Virginia*, the Confederate sailors saw the flash from the *Cumberland's* guns again, and this time her aim was true. The casemate shook and vibrated as shot and shell crashed into the forward end. Shattering against the shield, iron fragments went spinning wildly across the water, while concussions from the explosions rocked the ironclad. Lieutenant Charles C. Simms was in command of the forward pivot-rifle, which was loaded, run out, and sighted. Mustering all the patience he could command, Simms stood with the lanyard in his hand anxiously awaiting the signal from Buchanan to open fire. With the *Cumberland* now within easy range, Simms finally got his signal, and with a quick jerk of the lanyard, the 7-inch Brooke rifle roared to life. The *Virginia* shook as the gun recoiled; smoke and flame erupted from the muzzle, and the explosive shell streaked across the water toward the Federal ship. Simms' aim was deadly. The Confederate shell smashed through the starboard-rail sending splinters flying and wounding several marines, then exploded near the aft-pivot gun, killing and wounding most of the crew.[29]

Quickly, Simms' crew swabbed out the gun, and another powder bag was rammed down the barrel followed by a wad and a 7-inch explosive shell. As the rammer was withdrawn, the crew heaved on the tackle running the gun out. The gunner inserted a new primer into the vent as Simms sighted on the *Cumberland's* forward pivot. "All clear! Fire!" The Brooke rifle roared again, and another shell screamed toward the *Cumberland*. With a blinding flash, the deadly missile exploded, this time against the forward pivot. The deck around the *Cumberland's* forward gun looked like a slaughter house for every one of the sixteen-man gun crew had been killed except the powder boy and the gun captain who, unmercifully, had both arms blown away.[30]

The remainder of the *Cumberland's* gunners were now firing furiously at the oncoming ironclad, and raging at the sight of their projectiles bouncing harmlessly off her shield. The bodies of their dead comrades were thrown to the port side to get them out of the way, while the wounded were carried below. Every first and second captain of the forward guns had been either killed or wounded.

The *Virginia* was now about four hundred yards from the *Cumberland*, and while Simms' gun crew sent round after round into her as fast as they could load and fire, the lumbering ironclad pulled abreast of the *Congress* on her starboard side. The two were only three hundred yards apart when the *Congress* unleashed a horrendous broadside. Lieutenant John R. Eggleston, commander of two of the *Virginia's* starboard guns, was peering out one of the gun ports when he saw the flashes from the Federal's guns. Jumping back, he held his ears as the din and racket inside the casemate was unbearable. Shells and solid bolts pummeled the casemate, cracking and scorching the iron plates but, fortunately, not penetrating to the interior. Eggleston was thankful that none of the shells found an open gun port. Two of *Virginia's* starboard guns were already loaded; the other two Eggleston quickly loaded with glowing hot shot, having been heated in the furnace down below. Upon command the *Virginia* unleashed her own broadside. Four tongues of flame leaped from her side, and all four projectiles went tearing into the *Congress*. The effect was devastating.[31]

One of *Virginia's* shells entered a gun port at gun number seven and exploded, killing and wounding the entire crew and knocking the gun from its mount. One hot shot smashed into the crew's quarters which burst into flames, while the second hot shot started a fire near the magazine.

The *Virginia* was now only a couple hundred yards from the *Cumberland* and the Federal gunners were frantic in their efforts to stop her. Nothing seemed to have an effect on this ugly monster! The *Cumberland's* pilot, A. B. Smith recalled: *As she came ploughing through the water ... she looked like a huge half-submerged crocodile, ... At her prow I could see the iron ram projecting, straight forward, somewhat above the water's edge, and apparently a mass of iron.*[32]

Meanwhile, the *Raleigh* and the *Beaufort* were firing at the *Congress,* trying desperately to take her attention away from the *Virginia.* Excitement was mounting on board the ironclad. Upon a call from Buchanan, Chief Engineer Ramsey hurried up the ladder from the engine room and headed for the pilot house. The racket from the impact of numerous shells and solid shot was terrible as he passed through the gun deck, *They struck our sloping sides,* he recalled, *were deflected upward to burst harmlessly in the air, or rolled down and fell hissing into the water, dashing the spray up into our ports.* Buchanan shouted into Ramsey's ear that, in case of a problem, the engineer was not to wait for a command to reverse the engines when they struck the *Cumberland.* He was to throw the levers immediately! Ramsey nodded and rushed back through the din of the gun deck and down to the engine room.

Within seconds of reaching his station, the signal gong rang twice, the signal to "stop engines" ... then three gongs, "reverse engines!" Ramsey's hands flew over the levers and valves, and then as he remembered, *there was an awful pause.*

Suddenly, there was a heavy jolt as though the big ironclad had run aground. The crew hung on as the iron prow smashed through some heavy timbers surrounding the *Cumberland,* placed there to ward off torpedoes, and crashed into the Federal's side below the water line, snapping planks, timbers, and bulkheads as though they were match sticks. At the instant of impact, Simms fired another round from his bow pivot that went plunging deep into the bowels of the stricken ship where it exploded, killing ten men. Most did not know what had happened until Lieutenant Robert Minor, waving his cap, came running through the gun deck shouting, "We've sunk the *Cumberland!*"[33]

The Union sloop heeled violently over to port upon impact and then rolled back sending men flying about her decks. Slowly, she began to settle by the bow as tons of water poured through a hole that Lieutenant Wood thought was *wide enough to drive in a horse and cart.*[34]

The *Virginia's* engines were laboring in reverse, but the big ironclad, her prow entangled in the wreckage, refused to budge. As the Federal ship began to sink, her weight bore down on the *Virginia's* bow threatening to take her to the bottom with her. The Confederate ironclad had swung around to where she was lying almost parallel to the *Cumberland*, and the two continued to fire into one another at point blank range. The Federal gunners courageously continued to serve their guns even as water rose about their knees. While their shots still would not penetrate their tormentor, the *Virginia's* explosive shells tore through the stricken Union ship causing more causalities. For several minutes the two blasted away at each other as one by one the *Cumberland's* forward guns continued to sink beneath the swells.

During this time the *Virginia's* stern was pointed toward the *Congress* and Lieutenant Wood finally got his opportunity with the afterpivot. Loading as fast as they could, Wood's gun crew sent round after round crashing into the Federal, while the *Beaufort* and *Raleigh* continued to do the same. The *Congress* had small fires raging in a couple of places, and the decimated Federal crew was struggling frantically to extinguish them.

Finally, with a rasping lurch the cast iron ram broke off the *Virginia's* prow, and she backed away. From a distance of twenty feet, the two warships now continued to trade broadsides for nearly thirty minutes as the *Cumberland* continued to slip slowly beneath the waves. The flashes from the guns were all that could be seen as thick smoke enshrouded the two. A shot from the *Cumberland* struck the muzzle of one of *Virginia's* guns, which had just been loaded with hot shot. Two feet of the Confederate gun disappeared in a shower of sparks and flying fragments, causing the gun to fire, and sending its sizzling round crashing into the *Cumberland*.

On board the *Virginia*, Engineer Ramsey eloquently remembered these thirty minutes:

*On our gun-deck the men were fighting like demons. There was no thought or time for the wounded and dying as they tugged away at their guns, training and sighting their pieces while the orders rang out: "Sponge, load, fire."*

*"The muzzle of our gun has been shot away," cried one of the gunners.*

*"No matter, keep on loading and firing — do the best you can with it," replied Lieutenant Jones.*

*"Keep away from the side ports, don't lean against the shield, look out for sharpshooters," rang the warnings. Some of our men who failed to heed them and leaned back against the shield were stunned and carried below, bleeding at the ears. All were in high courage and worked with a will; they were so begrimed with powder that they looked like Negroes.*

*"Pass along the cartridges!"*

*"More powder!"*
*"A shell for number six!"*
*"A wet wad for the hot shot gun!"*
*"Put out that pipe and don't light again on the peril of your life!"*[35]

Two guns had been struck, which left them shattered with broken off muzzles, but the crews continued to load and fire even though each discharge set the wooden bulwark around the gunports afire.

The effects of the *Virginia's* point blank fire was devastating to the *Cumberland*. Her decks resembled a demonic massacre with blood and pieces of bodies scattered everywhere. As the Federal ship settled, Union sailors struggled aft through the carnage trying to reach a gun that still had not gone under water in order to fire one more round at the *Virginia*. Finally, with their ship going down around them, they began jumping overboard, struggling to reach some floating debris or swimming frantically for shore. With a roar and the grating of breaking timbers, the *Cumberland* went under, her flag still flying bravely from her peak. Lieutenant Wood, watching the *Cumberland* go down declared: *No ship was ever fought more gallantly.*[36]

The stern of the *Virginia* was still pointed toward the *Congress* and it was time to devote the ironclad's full attention to her. In his report, Buchanan explained the complications involved in turning the heavy Confederate ship around:

*We were some time in getting our proper position, in consequence of the shoaliness of the water and the great difficulty of managing the ship when in or near the mud. To succeed in my object I was obliged to run the ship a short distance above the batteries on the James River in order to wind her. During all the time her keel was in the mud; of course, she moved but slowly. Thus we were subjected twice to the heavy guns of all the batteries in passing up and down the river, but it could not be avoided. We silenced several of the batteries and did much injury on shore.*[37]

As the *Virginia* pulled away to go up the James, Lieutenant Wood quickly sent three well-aimed shots crashing into the *Congress*, dismounting two of the frigate's stern guns. The crew of the battered Federal ship, seeing the ironclad moving away, rushed to the rail and began to cheer, thinking they had driven her off. The cheers went silent as they watched the ironclad ominously begin a slow turn, and then slowly start back down the river. As the *Virginia* was making its turn in the James, Buchanan's eyes fell upon a welcome sight. The *Teaser*, *Jamestown*, and *Patrick Henry*, under Commander Tucker, were steaming down the river and firing furiously at the Federal land batteries. The two small gunboats took position with the *Virginia*, but the *Patrick Henry* took a round through one of her boilers and had to be towed out of range. She would soon catch up after making temporary repairs.

The commander of the *Congress*, Lieutenant Joseph Smith, hoping to prevent his ship from being rammed like the *Cumberland*, ordered his top sails set and called for the tug *Zouave* to tow his ship toward the beach. With much difficulty, for the frigate was still on fire in places and the *Beaufort* and *Raleigh* continued to fire at her, a line was secured, and with the help of a little wind in her top sails, the *Congress* began to move. She grounded within one hundred yards of the Federal batteries on Signal Point. Unfortunately for the battered *Congress*, this left only her few undamaged stern guns able to bear on the slowly approaching ironclad. At least she could not be sunk.[38]

Not able to approach the *Congress* because of the shallow water, Buchanan moved the *Virginia* to a position two hundred yards astern of the Union ship and his guns opened fire. Again the side of the *Virginia's* casemate was enveloped in smoke and flame, and within minutes the stern of the *Congress* was a shambles. The *Jamestown* and the repaired *Patrick Henry* now added their fire to that of the *Virginia*, *Beaufort* and *Raleigh*. The *Congress's* commander, Lieutenant Smith, was killed instantly when a shell fragment took off his head, and the command was now assumed by Lieutenant Austin Pendergrast. The Union ship had become a death trap. Some wounded jumped overboard and were immediately drowned. Ax-men chopped through bulkheads so fire hoses could be dragged to the raging flames. Everywhere, above and below decks, there was slaughter and destruction. The wounded were dragged below only to be wounded again or killed. In a tragedy amid tragedies, one of the Federal officers struggling to survive in this inferno on the *Congress* was Paymaster McKean Buchanan, brother of Captain Franklin Buchanan, commander of the *Virginia*.

After absorbing this devastating Confederate fire for nearly an hour, the *Congress* finally hauled down her colors and ran up a white flag.[39]

When Buchanan saw the *Congress'* white flag, he ordered Jones to have his gunners cease firing. Signaling the *Beaufort* to come within hailing distance, Buchanan shouted for Parker to take his gunboat and the *Raleigh* along side the *Congress*, take her officers as prisoners, remove the wounded, and allow the rest to escape to shore. Once that was accomplished, he was to make sure the Union ship was burning.

Parker moved in along the port side of the *Congress* and sent some of his own men on board the Union ship to help move the wounded to the *Beaufort*. As the Federal wounded were being lowered to the Confederate boat, Lieutenant Pendergrast came on board and presented the *Congress'* flag and a ship's cutlass as a token of surrender. Begging Parker not to fire the vessel until the wounded could be removed, he requested permission to return to his stricken ship and help in getting them off. Parker gave his consent, and just as Pendergrast turned to leave, a volley of musketry from the shore ripped into the *Beaufort* and *Raleigh*, killing and wounding several Confederate officers and men. Ignoring the white flag flying over the *Congress*, the Federal troops continued firing at the two Confederate gunboats, while three artillery pieces began firing loads of canister. Several wounded Federal sailors lying on the deck of the *Beaufort* were killed.[40]

With the deadly fire continuing from shore, Parker blew his steamwhistle to recall his men and they came tumbling aboard. Moving away with what Federal wounded he was able to save from the *Congress*, Parker opened fire on the troops on shore, but with only one gun, it had little effect. Steaming off toward Sewell's Point, he ran alongside the *Harmony* and delivered twenty-three wounded Federals to Captain Forrest. Returning to the scene of action, the *Beaufort* later opened fire on the *Minnesota*.

From his position Buchanan was unaware of the devastation the Union infantry fire was having on the *Beaufort* and *Raleigh*, and when he saw the two gunboats move off, he assumed Parker had fired the vessel. Although the *Congress* had small fires burning in different locations, the squadron commander wanted to make sure she was destroyed. Not seeing any new flames breaking out, an angry Buchanan concluded that Parker had failed in his duty, and ordered Lieutenant Minor to take the ironclad's only remaining boat with eight or ten men, and pull to the *Congress* and burn her. *The Teaser* (was ordered) *to protect me*, Minor wrote, ... *as I drew near the Congress the soldiers on shore opened on me ... and very soon two of my men and myself were knocked down.* The lieutenant and his men were taken on board the *Teaser* and returned to the *Virginia*.[41]

Buchanan was furious. *Destroy that ____ ship!* he shouted to Jones. The *Virginia* backed up as close astern of the *Congress* as she could and poured salvo after salvo into her, raking her unmercifully and setting her fully ablaze. Buchanan, still livid with rage, seized a rifle and foolishly climbed to the top deck and began firing at the troops on shore. Predictably, a Federal minie-ball struck him, tearing through his thigh, and causing him to fall heavily to the deck. Carried below, he was placed in his cabin along with the wounded Lieutenant Minor. The executive officer, Lieutenant Catesby Jones, assumed command in place of the fallen Buchanan. The *Virginia's* guns continued to roar sending sizzling hot shot deep into the already burning ship. *Dearly did they pay for their unparalleled treachery*, Lieutenant Eggleston remembered, *We raked her fore and aft with hot shot and shell.*[42]

With the *Congress* now ablaze from stem to stern, Jones turned the *Virginia's* attention to the *Minnesota*. It was now after 5:00 p.m. and the *Jamestown* and *Patrick Henry* had been engaging the *Minnesota* as she lay grounded about a mile and one-half from the burning *Congress*. Jones moved the *Virginia* in as close as he dared, but the ironclad's deep draft kept her more than a mile away. At long range in the fading light, the *Virginia* opened fire. Now it was the *Minnesota*'s turn to feel the effects of the ironclad's heavy battery.

As evening approached, the sky was illuminated by the flashes of the guns, while the burning *Congress* lent a macabre atmosphere to the engagement. A Federal colonel, observing from shore, wrote afterwards that the battered *Minnesota ... seemed like a huge monster at bay. The entire horizon was lighted by the continual flashes of the artillery; clouds of white smoke rose in spiral columns to the skies, illumined by the evening sunlight, while land and water seemed to tremble under the thunders of the cannonade.* With the day growing shorter, the *Virginia's* pilots reported to Jones that they felt it was not wise to remain in the Roads, for the tide was falling, and there was the danger of running the ironclad aground in the dark. Reluctantly, Jones signaled the rest of the Confederate squadron to break off the engagement and steam to the mouth of the Elizabeth River.

Even as the *Virginia* pulled away, her guns were still thundering at the *Minnesota*. Jones remembered that, *We fought until it was so dark that we could not see to point the guns with accuracy.* At 6:30 p.m., Lieutenant Wood fired the last shot from his aft-pivot rifle which streaked across the darkened waters toward the *Minnesota*. As the echo of the big Brooke died away, behind the *Virginia* lay a shattered and defeated Federal fleet. At 8:00 p.m., the big ironclad and her consorts dropped their anchors under the protection of the army batteries on Sewell's Point. It had been a long day. Lieutenant Minor, although wounded, would later write: *the IRON and the HEAVY GUNS did the work. It was a great victory.*

As soon as the *Virginia* anchored, Jones had the two dead and six wounded, accompanied by Surgeon Phillips, carried ashore. Two additional wounded, Buchanan and Minor, were made as comfortable as possible in the captain's cabin. The *Beaufort* and *Raleigh* sustained ten casualties between them and the *Patrick Henry* had seven. There were no reported casualties on the other gunboats, which meant that within the whole Confederate fleet, there were only twenty-seven men killed or wounded. The Confederate officers were thankful their losses had been so small. As Lieutenant Eggleston complimented his new commander on *...a pretty good day's work*, Jones thoughtfully replied, however, *...Yes, but it is not over.*

The story was starkly different on the other side of the bay as stunned Federal officers tallied their losses. On the sunken *Cumberland*, out of a compliment of 376 men known to have been on board, 121 were killed or went down with the ship, and 30 more were listed as wounded. The best that Lieutenant Pendergrast could determine was that from the 434 men on the *Congress*, 110 were dead and 26 wounded, 10 of whom would later die. The *Minnesota* had 2 or 3 killed and about 9 wounded. Total Federal losses, including gunboats, shore batteries and the Federals taken on board the *Beaufort*, amounted to around 325 killed and wounded.[43]

On the *Virginia*, after a late evening meal, many of the officers and men too excited to sleep, gathered on the top deck to watch the *Congress* burn. She was about four miles away and Chief Engineer Ramsey described the scene eloquently: *All the evening we stood on deck watching the brilliant display of the burning ship. Every part of her was on fire at the same time, the red-tongued flames running up shrouds, masts, and stays, and extending out to the yard arms. She stood in bold relief against the black background, lighting up the Roads and reflecting her lurid lights on the bosom of the now placid and hushed waters. Every now and then the flames would reach one of the loaded cannon and a shell would hiss at random through the darkness. About midnight came the grand finale. The magazines exploded, shooting up a huge column of firebrands hundreds of feet in the air, and then the burning hulk burst asunder and melted into the waters, while the calm night spread her sable mantle over Hampton Roads.*

Before the *Congress* exploded, one of the *Virginia's* pilots, exhausted by the day's events but unable to sleep, saw the silhouette of a low, strange-looking vessel glide silently through the glare of the burning Union ship.[44]

# Chapter Three

## "It is Quite a Waste of Ammunition"

The crew of the *Virginia* was awakened especially early on Sunday morning. It had been only a few hours since the *Congress* had exploded, and it seemed to most that they had just gotten to sleep. Lanterns were lit and one by one they fumbled to get dressed by the flickering light. It was evident that Catesby Jones wanted to get an early start on the morning high tide. The galley fires had been started earlier, and the men stumbled through the morning darkness to breakfast. Most were still bone tired from the fighting the day before. Surgeon Phillips was probably more exhausted then most, for he had spent the entire night on shore caring for the ironclad's wounded. Now, having finished his breakfast, he moved along one of the dark passageways to the captain's cabin to check on Buchanan and Lieutenant Minor. Both men were awake, had eaten, and were resting fairly comfortably. Buchanan was adamant that he still wanted to remain on board during this day's upcoming engagements, even though his wound would confine him to his cabin. Phillips pleaded with him to reconsider. Not only for his and Lieutenant Minor's sake, but the space might be needed for additional wounded once the fight began. Grudgingly, Buchanan gave in and he and Minor were carried ashore, where they were later transported by steamer to the naval hospital in Norfolk.[1]

Meanwhile, the crew, having finished their breakfast, began the many tasks necessary to get the big ironclad under way. At the same time, intense activity was also taking place on the *Patrick Henry*, *Jamestown*, and *Teaser*, which would accompany the *Virginia* into Hampton Roads. (The *Beaufort* would follow later and the *Raleigh* was sent to Norfolk for repairs.) In the engine room, fires which had been banked during the night were stoked and the ashes shaken down. Coal heavers began shoveling more coal into the furnaces. Pumps were started and steam pressure began to build in the boilers, while the engine room crew hurried about oiling the many levers, rods, and gears of the machinery. On the gun deck above, gun crews were busy swabbing out the big Dahlgrens, two of which had one to two feet missing from the end of their barrels. No matter, there was no time to replace them; their gun crews would have to do the best they could. Lieutenant Simms' and Lieutenant Wood's crews were also busy cleaning and lubricating their Brooke pivot-rifles which had caused the Federals so much damage the day before. The magazines were opened and additional crew members took their stations in the passageways where they could pass powder and shells up to the gun deck.

At 6:30 a.m. on this March 9, 1862, just as it was becoming light, other crew members began raising the anchor, and the Confederate flag was hoisted on a makeshift pole, the staffs having been shot away

in the fight with the *Cumberland*. The signal gong rang in the engine room, and Engineer Ramsey threw the levers and opened the steam valves to start the engines. Slowly the heavy ironclad began to move; the pilot swung her head toward the deep water in the South Channel of Hampton Roads, while the three Confederate gunboats took up their assigned stations on either side. From all points of the compass, not a cloud was visible; it appeared as though it would be another beautiful day. Through a low-lying mist, which was quickly being burned off by the rising sun, the outline of the *Minnesota* could be seen four miles away, still hard aground.[2]

Something else, though, had caught Jones' eye. Standing on the

**Lieutenant Catesby ap R. Jones, in the uniform of a Confederate commander. Executive and ordnance officer of the CSS *Virginia*, he succeeded Buchanan as captain of the ironclad in the battle with the USS *Monitor*.**

iron grating of the top deck and using his marine glass, he could discern a smaller vessel anchored beside the *Minnesota*. The outline of this strange craft looked like nothing he nor anyone on board the *Virginia* had ever seen before.

What Jones had spotted, of course, was the USS *Monitor*. She had arrived in Hampton Roads the night before, shortly before the explosion of the *Congress*, and had even been spotted by one of the *Virginia's* pilots. The Confederates had received reports of the Federal ironclad being built in Greenpoint, Long Island, New York, but it was not expected that she could have been completed so soon. In fact, it had taken only three months from the time John Ericsson's radical design's keel was laid until she was launched on January 30, 1862. Fitted with a revolving turret which was armored with eight inches of iron plate, and containing two eleven-inch guns, she would prove to be a formidable foe, indeed.[3]

As the *Virginia* continued on her course toward the *Minnesota*, many speculated on the nature of the strange vessel lying alongside her. Lieutenant Eggleston thought she was the strangest looking craft he had ever seen before. Some suggested that perhaps the *Minnesota* was taking on water from a water tank on a barge, while still others thought it looked like one of the Federal ship's boilers being removed for repair. The executive officer on the *Patrick Henry*, Lieutenant James H. Rochelle, spoke for most of the Confederates when he wrote that *such a craft as the eyes of a seamen never looked upon before ... an immense shingle floating in the water, with a gigantic cheese-box rising from its center; no sails, no wheels, no smokestack, no guns. What could it be?* Regardless of what it was, Jones was determined to ignore it and concentrate on destroying the *Minnesota*.

Drawing closer, the *Virginia's* officers could see men leaving the *Minnesota* in small boats and making for shore. Her captain, Commander G. J. Van Brunt, unconvinced that the little *Monitor* could protect his ship, was sending some of his crew to safety. He was determined to fight the *Virginia* as long as he could and then send the remaining men ashore and destroy his ship. When they were approximately a mile from the *Minnesota*, the *Virginia's* cautious pilots reported that they could go no farther because of the shallow water. Disappointed that they could draw no closer to the Federal ship, Jones ordered Simms to open fire with his bow pivot. With a thunderous roar, the Brooke rifle sent its first shell crashing into the Union frigate.

Shortly before Simms jerked the lanyard to fire his first shot, Lieutenant John L. Worden had gotten the *Monitor* under way and steamed directly for the *Virginia*. Now, as the Confederates watched in amazement, the "cheese-box" revolved and suddenly, from one of two gun

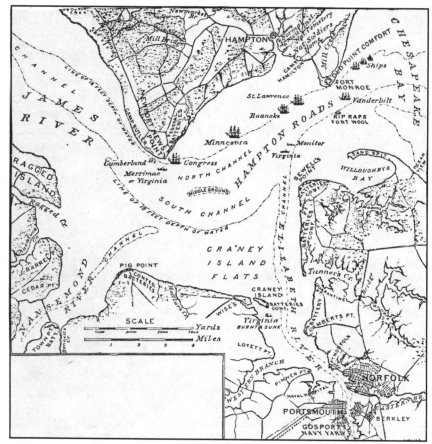

Hampton Roads, Virginia, showing the positions of the Federal vessels.

ports, it belched smoke and flame. A terrible crash resounded through the *Virginia's* gun deck. The *Monitor's* eleven inch solid bolt struck the casemate, cracking some of the iron plates, and then ricocheted hissing into the water far beyond the Confederate ship. With black smoke pouring from the *Virginia's* funnel, the two ironclads plowed toward one another. One of the most famous naval battles in history was about to be joined.[4]

It was now 8:45 a.m. and for the next two hours, the two ironclads were locked in a life and death struggle. They began to circle one another in spirals with ranges varying from over 100 yards to a few feet. The *Monitor* had a distinct advantage in these maneuvers. She was more responsive to the helm and drew only twelve feet of water, while the *Virginia*, with her great weight and draft, handled like "a water-logged vessel." The Confederate ship could bring, at times, up to five guns to bear on the *Monitor*, but all her shots, though leaving an indentation on the armored turret, bounced harmlessly away. Expecting to encounter only the wooden ships of the Federals, Jones had ordered the magazines stocked with exploding shells only; no solid shot had been brought on board. What the *Virginia* needed right now were large solid bolts for her heavy nine-inch Dahlgrens, but the bolts were sitting in the ordnance depot back at the navy yard.

The *Monitor's* guns were also firing under "a handicap." Because her guns were untested, and the fear that an exploding gun in her turret could sink her, regulations restricted her powder charges to fifteen pounds instead of the normal thirty. Historians have speculated for years on what might have happened if the *Virginia* had fired solid bolts and the *Monitor* had used thirty-pound powder charges.

The CSS *Virginia*, battles the USS *Monitor*, March 9, 1862.

Lieutenant Eggleston complained that *we never got sight of her guns except when they were about to fire into us*. Whenever the *Monitor* fired, her turret would revolve immediately, pointing the guns away from the Confederate ironclad where they could be reloaded in relative safety. The eleven inch solid shot continued to slam into the *Virginia's* casemate, each time causing the vessel to tremble and shake. Jones' gun crews were working like demons, loading and firing as fast as they could bring their guns to bear. Powder and shells continued to be passed along the darkened corridors and up to the gun deck, where powder boys ran them to the divisions, and where officers shouted commands which were barely audible above the roar of battle. Smoke drifted through the casemate, as blackened and sweating gunners continued to send their shells crashing against the *Monitor*. Adding to the inferno was the firing of the guns with damaged and shortened muzzles. Each time one discharged, the gun crew would have to beat out the flames in the wood backing around the gun port. Down below, the firemen were laboring in stifling temperatures as they strove to maintain the heat in the furnaces. Engineer Ramsey remembered that *the noise of the crackling, roaring fires, escaping steam, and the loud and labored pulsations of the engines, together with the roar of battle above and the thud and vibration of the huge masses of iron being hurled against us, altogether produced a scene and sound to be compared only with the poet's picture of the lower regions.*[5]

In the smoke and confusion of the circling battle, a potential disaster occurred. With a shudder felt throughout the ship, the *Virginia* ran hard aground! The *Monitor*, seeing the immovable Confederate, began circling her prey and pouring in shots from her two eleven-inch guns. Surgeon Phillips described the *Monitor* as circling the *Virginia ...like a fierce dog.* Eventually, the Federal ironclad took a position where the *Virginia* could not bring a gun to bear, and for nearly fifteen minutes she pummeled the stranded Confederate ship with heavy iron bolts. Some came close to entering an open gun port, while others cracked and bent the iron plates with such power that the wood backing was forced inward several inches. Several more shots like these and the *Virginia* would be destroyed. Seeing the *Virginia* in trouble, the *Patrick Henry* and *Jamestown* bravely started to her assistance, while with dry mouths and pounding hearts, the apprehensive gun crews continued to wait. Surgeon Phillips remembered: *Every one was watching and waiting, with an impatience which may well be imagined, to be relieved of the horrible night-mare of inactivity, from which we all suffered.*

The *Virginia* shook and vibrated as her thrashing propeller strained to pull her free. In the sweltering engine room, Ramsey was frantically doing everything he could to increase power. *We lashed down the safety valves, heaped quick-burning combustibles into the already raging fires, and brought the boilers to a pressure that would have been unsafe under ordinary circumstances. The propeller churned the mud and water furiously, but the ship did not stir. We piled on oiled cotton waste, splints of wood, anything that would burn faster than coal. It seemed impossible that the boilers could stand the pressure we were crowding upon them. Just as we were beginning to despair, there was a perceptible movement, and the Merrimack slowly dragged herself off the shoal by main strength.*[6]

A loud cheer rang through the gun deck as the *Virginia* backed out into deeper water. Again, her guns opened fire on the *Monitor*, but still not doing her any perceptible harm. It was now approaching 11:00 a.m. and Jones, descending from the spar deck, noticed a gun crew standing "at ease."

*Why are you not firing, Mr. Eggleston?* he shouted above the noise in the casemate.

*Why, it is quite a waste of ammunition to fire at her,* replied the lieutenant, *our powder is very precious, and after two hours incessant firing I find I can do her as much damage by snapping my finger at her every two minutes and a half.*

*Never mind,* Jones shouted, *we are getting ready to ram her.*[7]

Instructing Ramsey to reverse the engines the moment they struck the *Monitor*, Jones worked to bring the Confederate ironclad into a position where she could make a run at the Federal. Against the more agile *Monitor*, this was no easy task, but finally, after nearly an hour of maneuvering, the signal gong rang in the engine room for "all ahead full." Normally it would have taken the *Virginia* at least a mile to reach full speed, but she barely had half of that distance. At the last moment, the *Monitor* swung her helm hard away and the *Virginia* struck only a glancing blow. As the Federal slid along side, she fired both guns point blank into the *Virginia's* casemate right next to Wood's pivot gun. The concussion sent the men sprawling and started them bleeding from the ears and nose. The shield where the giant bolts struck was pushed in about three inches and a shaken Wood declared that, *Another shot at the same place would have penetrated.*[8] Many on board thought at first that they had done the *Monitor* much damage, but soon had to confess, as her iron bolts continued to slam into them, that she was barely harmed. On the contrary, the *Virginia's* carpenter reported that a serious leak had developed in the bow from the collision with the *Monitor*. Taking the initiative, Boatswain Charles H. Hasker crawled into the bow and shoved a bale of oakum against the stern apron, cutting the leak to a trickle. Jones sent Ramsey to check on the damage, and the engineer reported that while there was some water in the hold, with the bilge pumps running, she was in no immediate danger.[9]

The *Minnesota* had not been idle during this swirling battle of the ironclads. She continued to pour her heavy fire into the battered *Virginia*, some of her shells even striking the *Monitor*. Occasionally, when the two ironclads drew apart, the *Virginia* would reply, sending heavy explosive shells crashing through the Union ship. At one point, the *Monitor* withdrew for about thirty minutes so that the crew might replenish her ammunition from lockers below decks. Van Brunt recalled this moment: *The Merrimac, (the Federals always referred to the Virginia as the Merrimac) finding that she could make nothing of the Monitor, turned her attention once more to me. In the morning she had put one eleven-inch shot under my counter, near the water-line, and now, on her second approach, I opened upon her with all my broadside guns and ten-inch pivot — a broadside which would have blown out of the water any timber-built ship in the world. She returned my fire with her rifled bow-gun, with a shell which passed through the chief engineer's state-room, through the engineer's mess-room amidships, and burst in the boatswain's room, tearing four rooms all into one, in its passage exploding two charges of powder, which set the ship on fire, but it was promptly extinguished by a party headed by my first lieutenant.* One of *Virginia's* shells hit the tug *Dragon* which was alongside the Union frigate, and she exploded in a cloud of scalding steam.[10]

With the *Virginia's* explosives having no apparent effect on the *Monitor's* turret, the order was passed along the gun deck to concentrate on the armored pilot house. As the *Monitor* rounded the Confederate's stern, Lieutenant Wood sighted his pivot rifle on the two-foot-high pilot house and pulled the lanyard. With a blinding flash, the shell struck and exploded, sending fire and iron fragments blowing in through the viewing slits. Lieutenant Worden, who was looking through them, staggered backward clutching his face in excruciating pain, blinded by the burning powder. There was a moment of confusion on board the Union ironclad as their commander was helped down the ladder from the pilot house. When Worden was hit, the quartermaster on the *Monitor* immediately turned the ship's head away from the *Virginia*. Now, with her officers gathered around the injured lieutenant at the foot of the ladder, the *Monitor* was steaming farther and farther away from her enemy. Lieutenant Samuel D. Green assumed command, and after consultation with his officers, the decision was made to continue the battle. At least a half hour or more had been consumed in caring for the injured Worden.[11]

It was twelve noon, and with the *Monitor* now in shoal water where the *Virginia* could not follow, Jones ordered the pilots to steam toward the *Minnesota*. The pilots, however, warned Jones that they could not stay in the Roads any longer, for the tide was receding. If they remained, they would not be able to cross the bar at the mouth of the Elizabeth River. Jones descended to the gun deck and consulted with his lieutenants. *The Monitor has given up the fight and run into shoal water; the pilots cannot take us any nearer to the Minnesota; this ship is leaking from the loss of her prow; the men are exhausted by being so long at their guns; ... I propose to return to Norfolk for repairs. What is your opinion?* Jones' opinion was seconded by most of the officers and orders were issued to the pilots to head for the Elizabeth River. Ramsey was told that he could finally reduce the pressure in the boilers. *If there had been any sign of the Monitor's willingness to renew the contest,* Jones wrote later, *we would have remained to fight her.*[12]

Meanwhile Green, having turned the *Monitor* around, saw the *Virginia* over a mile away steaming slowly toward Norfolk, and assumed they had driven her off. After firing a long range shot, which Lieutenant Wood answered with his stern rifle, the *Monitor* turned and steamed back toward the *Minnesota*. Thus both sides, as they withdrew, thought they had been victorious over the other.

Accompanied by the *Patrick Henry, Jamestown, Teasor,* and *Beaufort,* the *Virginia* steamed cautiously up the Elizabeth, past Norfolk, and on toward the Gosport Navy Yard. Crowds of people lined the shores on both sides cheering, and waving flags and handkerchiefs. Jones mustered most of the crew on the top deck in order to acknowledge their applause, while small boats with brightly colored banners joined the procession. Captain Forrest, along with several other officers from the navy yard, came along side to offer his congratulations. Jones was gratified to be able to report to Forrest that there were no additional killed or wounded from the day's engagement. Docked at the navy yard, the *Virginia* was moved later that afternoon into dry-dock to undergo repairs and to complete her armor. Lieutenant Jones summarized her condition and the performance of his crew at the end of his official report:

*The stem is twisted and the ship leaks. We have lost the prow, starboard anchor and all the boats. The steam-pipe and smokestack are both riddled; the muzzles of two of the guns, shot away. It was not easy to keep a flag flying. The flag staffs were repeatedly shot away. The colors were hoisted to the smokestack and several times cut down from it.*

*The bearing of the men was all that could be desired; their enthusiasm could scarcely be restrained. During the action they cheered again and again. Their coolness and skill were the most remarkable for the great majority of them were under fire for the first time. They were strangers to each other and to the officers, and had but a few days' instruction in the management of the great guns. To the skill and example of the officers is this result in no small degree attributable.*[13]

Once the *Virginia* was in dry dock, the crew was released from duty and sent ashore. Constructor Porter made a careful inspection of the vessel and found 97 shot indentations in her iron armor. Six outer plates on her casemate had been broken but all underneath plates were intact. All her boats, railings, boat davits and flag staffs had been shot away, and as Jones reported, her smokestack and steam pipes were badly riddled.

The missing starboard anchor, the iron ram, and her two damaged guns would all have to be replaced.

Later in the day, Lieutenant Wood received a message to report to Captain Buchanan at the naval hospital. Writing a brief note for Secretary Mallory, Buchanan ordered Wood to proceed to Richmond with the dispatch, make a verbal report on the condition of the *Virginia*, and present the flag of the *Congress* to President Davis.[14]

Lieutenant Wood later described this interesting trip to Richmond and his report to the President:

*I took the first train for Petersburg and the capital. The news had preceded me, and at every station I was warmly received, and to listening crowds was forced to repeat the story of the fight. Arriving at Richmond, I drove to Mr. Mallory's office and went with him to President Davis', where we met Mr. Benjamin, who, a few days afterward, became Secretary of State, Mr. Seddon, afterward Secretary of War, General Cooper, Adjutant-General, and a number of others. I told at length what had occurred on the previous two days, and what changes and repairs were necessary to the Virginia. As to the future, I said that in the Monitor we had met our equal, and that the result of another engagement would be very doubtful. Mr. Davis made many inquiries as regarded the ship's draught, speed, and capabilities, and urged the completion of the repairs at as early a day as possible. The conversation lasted until midnight. During the evening the flag of the Congress, which was a very large one, was brought in, and to our surprise, in unfolding it, we found it in some places saturated with blood. On this discovery it was quickly rolled up and sent to the Navy Department, where it remained during the war; it doubtless burned with that building when Richmond was evacuated.*

The day after the *Virginia* was put into dry dock, the crew requested Reverend J. H. Wingfield, assistant rector of the Trinity Episcopal Church in Portsmouth, to come on board and conduct a thanksgiving service. As the entire crew knelt on the iron-grated top deck, Reverend Wingfield gave thanks to the Lord for their safe deliverance from battle, and assured them, *...The sunshine of a favoring Providence beams upon every countenance.*[15]

Scharf's *History of the Confederate States Navy*

**Commander Sidney Smith Lee,** **brother of Robert E. Lee, and executive** **officer of the Gosport Navy Yard.**

On March 23, the men of the James River Squadron were drawn up into a hollow square in the Gosport Navy Yard while officers in the middle read to them a resolution of thanks from the Confederate *Congress*. Because of his wound, the Navy Department relieved Buchanan of his command and replaced him with Captain Josiah Tattnall. Tattnall would fly his flag on the *Virginia* and Jones reverted to his position as executive officer. The next day Captain French Forrest was ordered to command the Bureau of Orders and Detail, and Captain Sidney Smith Lee was given command of the Gosport Navy Yard.[16]

Near the end of March, from his bed in the naval hospital in Norfolk, Buchanan, who had been informed that he would soon be promoted to admiral, completed his detailed report of the two engagements. Highly complimentary to the officers and men of the entire squadron, he prefaced his comments about each individual with, *...I feel it due to the gallant officers who so nobly sustained the honor of the flag and country on those days to express my appreciation of their conduct.* Singled out for commendation were Lieutenants Jones, Simms, Wood, and Eggleston, while Lieutenant Davidson was complimented for continuing to use one of the damaged guns. Captain Reuben T. Thom, commander of the company of marines on board, was commended for his coolness in action. One of the *Virginia's* broadside guns was served by Thom's Company C of Confederate "Leathernecks."[17]

Meanwhile repairs and alterations were proceeding slowly on the *Virginia*. The hull, four feet below the shield, was covered with two-inch iron plates, and wrought-iron shutters were installed at each gunport. The two damaged Dahlgrens were replaced; a new and heavier ram installed, this time more securely, and her rifled guns were supplied with special steel-pointed solid shot. With an additional 100 tons of ballast in her hull which would bring her lower in the water, the *Virginia* eased out of dry dock on April 4.

Tattnall called his squadron commanders together for a conference two days later. The grizzled sixty-seven year-old naval veteran was determined to destroy or capture the *Monitor*. One account reports him as stomping up and down the top deck of the *Virginia* muttering, *I will take her! I will take her if hell's on the other side of her!*[18]

Bluster or no, Tattnall had a plan. After outlining the weak points in the *Monitor's* defenses, he proposed that they attack a fleet of Federal army transports that were anchored at the mouth of Hampton Creek near Fort Monroe. Once the *Monitor* steamed to the defense of the transports, the *Virginia* would engage the Union ironclad while the other vessels in the squadron rushed along side and boarded her with hand-picked crews. Once on board, oil-soaked rags and gunpowder would be thrown down her stacks and ventilators. Wet sail cloths and tarpaulins would be thrown over her turret, smokestack openings, and the pilot house, while other men, with sledge hammers, would drive wedges between the deck and the turret so it could not revolve.[19]

It was a desperate plan, and the causalities would be heavy, but Tattnall, pressured by public out-cries to do something about the *Monitor*, was willing to gamble.

At 6:00 a.m. on April 11, the *Virginia, Patrick Henry, Raleigh, Beaufort,* and the *Jamestown* cast off their lines at the navy yard and steamed down the Elizabeth River toward Hamp-

Scharf's *History of the Confederate States Navy*

**Captain Josiah Tattnall, commander of the CSS *Virginia* at the time of her destruction.**

ton Roads. On the refurbished *Virginia*, Tattnall, at Lieutenant Wood's suggestion, mustered the crew on the top deck for a moment of prayer. Wood reported afterward that his *courage and spirits rose at once* as a result, and he hoped it would curb the cursing on board where he was *shocked hourly with oaths.*[20]

As the squadron approached the Confederate fortifications on Sewell's Point, Tattnall was disappointed to see that most of the Fed-eral transports were anchored near the north shore of the Roads and under the protection of the guns at Fort Monroe. Many of the Federal ships could be seen getting under way and heading for the open sea, while the rest of the Union fleet, including the *Monitor*, were quickly raising steam. Once again the day was a good one; the waters of the bay were calm as the *Virginia* plowed toward the Federal guns on the Rip Raps, a sandy spit of an island at the eastern end of the Roads. The *Monitor* could be seen clearly now. Smoke was rising from her funnel, and throughout the Confederate flotilla, nerves tightened as the crews prepared for a grave encounter. But to Tattnall's disgust, the *Monitor* did not move but remained near her moorings under the protection of the heavy guns at Fort Monroe. The *Virginia* began steaming in wide circles, some extending almost to Newport News, in an attempt to en-tice the *Monitor* to advance and give battle. Occasionally, Catesby Jones' gunners exchanged fire with the batteries on the Rip Raps and on the north shore, but still the Federal ironclad refused to come out.

Unknown to the Confederates, the Federal fleet was under orders not to risk the *Monitor* unnecessarily, and to continue to protect the entrance to the Chesapeake Bay and the York River. Lieutenant William N. Jeffers, now in command of the Federal ironclad, also hoped to be able to lure the *Virginia* nearer to Fort Monroe where the guns of the fort could help sink the Confederate vessel.

Spotting three transports along the north shore that had not taken refuge near the Federal fleet, Tattnall ordered signal flags hoisted and immediately the little *Jamestown* cut away from the squadron and headed for them. Securing the three Union vessels while under fire from the land batteries, First Lieutenant Joseph N. Barney, commander of the *Jamestown*, had the captured transports flags hoisted upside down and brazenly towed the Union ships away. Steaming triumphantly back to the Confederate squadron with her prizes in tow, the *Jamestown* passed near the British corvette *Rinaldo*, which was anchored in the Roads, her men hoping to see an engagement between the ironclads. As the Confederate gunboat passed near the Englishman's stern, the British warship dipped her flag in salute while her crew lined the rails and cheered the saucy little "Rebel."[21]

The Federal fleet, including the *Monitor*, made no attempt to challenge the seizures. All day the *Virginia* and the rest of the Confederate squadron remained in the Roads, challenging the *Monitor* to give battle, but to no avail. Finally near sunset, an angry Tattnall ordered a gun fired at the *Monitor*, hoisted the captured flags under his own, and steamed to Sewell's Point where the squadron anchored for the night. It had been a disappointing day, but the gruff Confederate commander was determined to try again.

A few days later, the *Virginia*, accompanied by the rest of the squadron, steamed into Hampton Roads again, and still the *Monitor* would not offer battle. After exchanging a few shots with the shore batteries, the *Virginia* developed engine problems that Engineer Ramsey could not overcome, and she had to return to the navy yard for repairs.

By now, General George B. McClellan's huge army was besieging Yorktown on the Peninsula and Secretary Mallory instructed Tattnall to keep the *Virginia* ready to make a dash past the Union forts and up the York River in order to aid the beleaguered Confederate army. Tattnall and Captain Lee both believed the *Virginia* was indispensable at Norfolk where she could protect the approaches to the city. In Richmond, however, Mallory, Davis, and Smith Lee's brother, General Robert E. Lee, were becoming more and more convinced that the *Virginia* was needed to help stop McClellan. Tattnall went to Richmond a few days after the last disappointing cruise in the Roads to confer with the government. No record of the meeting has survived, but when he returned he must have been convinced by Mallory's arguments, for he immediately ordered steam raised and preparations made for battle.

After dark, the *Virginia's* lines were cast off, her pilots evidently having more confidence now in their ability to avoid running aground, and soon she was under way. Steaming down the Elizabeth River, Tattnall ordered the pilots to steer for the channel leading to Fort Monroe, while on the dimly lit gun deck, men stood silently at their stations listening to the steady throb of the engines. Dense smoke poured from the *Virginia's* stack, quickly disappearing into the darkness, as Tattnall drove the big ironclad steadily toward Fort Monroe and the open sea. While passing the army batteries on Sewell's Point, Catesby Jones sighted a lantern signal being flashed from shore. *We have been ordered to return, Sir,* Jones reported.

The signal was from the Navy Department and had been sent through General Huger, army commander at Norfolk. Tattnall, watching Fort Monroe through his marine glass, ignored Jones' report.

*The order is peremptory, Sir!* Jones emphasized.

The crusty commander slowly lowered his marine glass but continued to gaze defiantly into the night. Finally, turning to Jones he grumbled, *Old Huger has outwitted me. Do what you please, I leave you in command. I'm going to bed.* Later that night, the *Virginia* was back at her moorings at the navy yard.[22]

On May 3, faced with McClellan's slow advance up the Peninsula and a variety of contributing reasons, Confederate authorities gave the order to begin the evacuation of Norfolk. Most of the machinery was to be sent to Richmond and Charlotte, while preparations were made to destroy the dry dock and all remaining facilities. Almost every day now, the *Virginia* steamed to the mouth of the Elizabeth River and into the Roads, but her appearance was nothing more than a screen to cover the evacuation of Norfolk.

At the navy yard on May 8, heavy firing was heard down the river in the direction of Sewell's Point. Raising steam, the *Virginia* hastened toward the sound of battle. Arriving at the Point around 2:45 p.m., Tattnall found the *Monitor* and a new Federal ironclad, the *Nagatuck,* along with numerous other Union vessels, bombarding the Confederate fortifications. Upon seeing the black smoke pouring from the *Virginia's* stack as she approached, the Federals hoisted signal flags, ceased firing, and steamed for Fort Monroe. Tattnall kept the *Virginia* in the Roads until after 4:00 p.m., when, with disgust he growled, *Mr. Jones, fire a gun to windward, and take the ship back to its buoy.*[23]

The next day, Tattnall went to Norfolk to confer with army and naval commanders on the best course of action for the *Virginia.* Most agreed that it was best for now that the Confederate ironclad remain at her buoy off Sewell's Point, where she could deny the Federals' access to Norfolk via the Elizabeth River. Once the evacuation of the navy yard and city were complete, Tattnall should try to follow the rest of his squadron up the James toward Richmond.

The morning after the conference, on May 10, Tattnall, who was back on board the *Virginia*, noticed that no flag was flying over the Confederate fortifications on Sewell's Point. Ordering a boat ashore to investigate, the crew hurriedly returned and announced that the works had been abandoned. Tattnall sent Lieutenant J. Pembroke Jones to Craney Island, where the flag was visible, to find out what was happening. Jones was told that the Federals were rapidly advancing on Norfolk, that Sewell's Point had been abandoned, and that the facilities on Craney Island would be next. Jones hastened to the city trying to find General Huger or Captain Lee, but was told they had left. The streets were mobbed with a confused mass of troops, artillery, and baggage wagons all moving out, while across the river, Jones could see the Gosport Navy Yard in flames. Union troops were only a half mile away from Norfolk as Jones hurried back down the river to the *Virginia*.

It was now 7:00 p.m. and whatever Tattnall was to do had to be done this night. The pilots had repeatedly said that if the *Virginia* was lightened to a draft of eighteen feet, they could take her up the James River and within forty miles of Richmond. Tattnall called the crew together and explained to them what had to be done to lighten the ship. With a cheer, the men went to work throwing everything overboard except powder and shot. Between one and two in the morning, Catesby Jones knocked at Tattnall's cabin door with bad news. After throwing all the iron ballast, baggage, and all unnecessary items overboard, they had reduced the *Virginia's* draft to twenty feet, and the men were still diligently searching for more items to unload. But now, there was another problem. As the weary commander sat on his bunk, Jones explained that the pilots now reported that it was useless to go on for they could not get the *Virginia* up the James.

Tattnall was furious. Calling Chief Pilot William Parrish to his cabin, he demanded an explanation. Parrish explained that with an easterly wind the James would be deep enough to allow a vessel with a draft of eighteen feet to pass over the bar at the river's mouth. For the last several days, however, the wind had been blowing from the west and northwest, and the river would be too shallow. The *Virginia* was now in serious trouble.[24]

Lieutenant Wood remembered this dilemma: *The ship had been so lifted as to be unfit for action; two feet of her hull below the shield was exposed. She could not be sunk again by letting in water without putting out the furnace fires and flooding the magazines. Never was a commander forced by circumstances over which he had no control into a more painful position than was Commodore Tattnall.*[25] With Federal troops in Norfolk, and unable to cross the bar at the mouth of the James, the *Virginia* had no place to go. The Confederates, long before this distressing night arrived, had resolved that no "Yankee" flag would ever fly over the *Virginia*. There was now only one way to be assured that this would not happen.

Tattnall called his officers together and presented his plan. With heavy hearts, they nodded their approval. Raising steam, Tattnall headed the ship toward Craney Island, where a few hundred yards out she grounded. Equipped with small arms and two days' provisions, the men began debarking to dry land using the ironclad's two small boats. As the crew was leaving, Midshipman Littlepage spotted the *Virginia's* flags lying on the gun deck. Taking his clothes out of his knapsack, he stuffed in the flags and hurried on to the waiting boats. It took nearly three hours to get all 300 men on shore, but once there, they moved out on a lonely trek to Suffolk, twenty-two miles away.

Lieutenants Wood and Catesby Jones were the last to leave. Shoving oil-soaked cotton and other inflammables into crevices in the bow and stern, Jones set the match and he and Wood dashed for the boat. Wood remembered this painful moment: *Setting her on fire fore and aft, she was soon in a blaze, and by the light of our burning ship we pulled for shore, landing at daybreak.*[26]

As the dejected crew trudged through the early morning darkness on the road to Suffolk, they could hear behind them the roar of the *Virginia's* guns, as the flames reached them, firing mournfully across the dark waters of Hampton Roads for the last time. Suddenly, about

**The destruction of the CSS *Virginia*, near Craney Island in the early morning hours of May 11, 1862.**

5:00 a.m., as the fire reached the magazines, the eastern sky flashed a bright orange-red and a tremendous rumble shook the forest and farm-houses for miles around. The *Virginia* was gone.

Five days later Catesby Jones and the men from the *Virginia* had succeeded in mounting five heavy guns at Drewry's Bluff on the James just south of Richmond. As the Union fleet approached, led by the *Monitor*, Midshipman Littlepage reached into his knapsack and once again unfurled the *Virginia's* tattered flags to the breeze.[27]

# Chapter *Four*

## Phantoms of the Night

At the beginning of the Southern people's struggle to defend themselves against invasion and gain their independence, it was painfully evident that the country would never be able to produce the materials necessary to maintain large armies in the field. While the Confederate government did work miracles in arming, clothing, and feeding its armies, it nevertheless depended heavily on those low, sleek, gray hulled vessels that slipped into Southern harbors almost every night to unload their precious cargoes of war material. Confederate records alone show that 60 percent of the arms carried by her troops in the field were imported. The blockade runners brought in 30 percent, or roughly three million pounds of lead for bullets, 75 percent of the army's saltpeter or 2,250,000 pounds, and nearly all of its cartridge paper. In addition, the runners also brought in other essential war materials such as food, cloth for uniforms, leather for shoes, accouterments, chemicals, paper, and medicines.[1]

Blockade runners were for the most part privately owned, though some were purchased entirely or in part by the Confederate government and operated by the Ordnance Bureau or the Navy Department. Men served as captains on these civilian ships for a variety of reasons, the predominate two being profits and patriotism. The government-owned runners were commanded by regular officers of the Confederate navy, and the crews, being mostly English, were usually shipped in from Nassau or Havana.

In spite of the ever-tightening Federal blockade, the probability of a runner getting through to a Confederate port was very good. It has been documented that over 300 steamers tested the Union blockade during the war, and of the 1300 attempts made, 1000 were successful. The Federals captured 136 vessels and destroyed an additional 85, yet approximately 400,000 bales of cotton were safely carried out by the blockade runners, thus enabling the Confederacy to purchase munitions and supplies abroad.[2]

Any study of the exploits of these blockade runners and their commanders, whether civilian or navy, illustrates the excitement, danger, and adventure of running the Federal blockade. The *Nassau* and the *Giraffe*, (later commissioned the *Robert E. Lee*), are just two examples of government-operated runners which were commanded by regular naval officers. The exploits of these vessels and their officers is representative of all blockade running and constitutes another chapter in the intriguing history of the Confederate States Navy.

Commander John Newland Maffitt, CSN, captain of the steam blockade runner *Nassau*.

The *Nassau*, built in New York in 1851, was a small, wooden side-wheeler with very powerful engines. She was a 518-ton steamer, 177 feet long and 27 feet in beam, and had been purchased by the Confederate government from the Fraser, Trenholm and Company of Charleston, South Carolina. In April of 1862, she was being loaded with her final consignment of cotton at Wilmington, North Carolina, when Lieutenant John Newland Maffitt arrived to take command.[3]

Maffitt was born in the middle of the Atlantic Ocean on February 22, 1819. On February 25, 1832, at the tender age of thirteen, he had been appointed an acting midshipman in the navy by President Andrew Jackson. By 1861, Maffitt had become convinced, as had many other Southern officers, that painful as it was, his first allegiance was to his state. After spending twenty-nine years in the U.S. service, he reluctantly resigned his commission when his home state of North Carolina left the Union, and offered his services to the new Confederacy. In addition to his blockade-running feats, he would become famous later in the war as the stalwart commander of the Confederate cruiser CSS *Florida*.[4]

The *Nassau* had completed her loading, and on the dark night of May 2, with all lights covered, Maffitt eased her down the Cape Fear River to its mouth and steamed for the open sea; destination — Nassau, in the Bahamas. Twenty years after the war, the running of the gauntlet was still eloquently vivid in Maffitt's mind:

*In silence Fort Caswell is passed, and a dim glimpse of Fort Campbell affords a farewell view of Dixie, as the steamer's head is turned seaward through the channel. The swelling greetings of the Atlantic billows announce that the bar is passed; over the cresting waves the good craft swiftly dashes, as if impatient to promptly face her trials of the night. Through the settled darkness all eyes on board are peering, eagerly straining to catch a view of the dreaded sentinels who sternly guard the tabooed channel. Nothing white is exposed to view; every light is extinguished, save those that are hooded in the binnacle and engine-room. No sound disturbs the solemn silence of the moment but the dismal moaning of the northeast wind and the unwelcome, but unavoidable, dashing of our paddles.*[5]

The Federals usually maintained an inner and outer ring of blockading ships off the Southern ports. At the sighting of a runner, flares and rockets would be launched and all available warships had standing orders to concentrate in the threatened area. As the war dragged on and the number of blockaders increased, the danger of their firing into each other on a dark night was an ever-increasing reality. With the runner's low profile and smokeless burning coal, a good captain with a speedy ship could pass the Union blockaders many times and never be detected. At other times, however, they were spotted by the vigilant Federals as Lieutenant Maffitt relates:

*Night-glasses scan the bleared horizon for a time in vain; suddenly an officer with bated breath announces several steamers. Eagerly pointing he reports two at anchor and others slowly cruising. Instantly out of the gloom and spindrift emerges the somber phantom form of the blockading fleet. The moment of trial is at hand; firmness and decision are essential for the emergency. Dashing between the two at anchor, we pass so near as to excite astonishment at our non-discovery; but this resulted from the color of our hull, which, under certain stages of the atmosphere, blended so perfectly with the haze as to render the steamer nearly invisible.*

The runners were usually painted a dull gray which tended to make them difficult to see in daylight as well as in darkness. Many of the steel-hulled ships built in Glasgow, Scotland, specifically for blockade running, had hinged masts and telescoping smokestacks to further reduce their silhouette.

*How keenly the grim hulls of the enemy are watched,* Maffitt continued. *How taut, like harp-strings, every nerve is strung, anxiously vibrating with each pulsation of the throbbing heart! We emerge to windward from between the two at anchor.*

*"Captain," whispered the pilot, "according to my chop logic them chaps aren't going to squint us this blessed night."*

*Ere a response could be uttered a broad-spread flash of intense light blazed from the flag's Drummond [light] for in passing to windward the noise of our paddles betrayed the proximity of a blockade runner. "Full speed!" I shouted to the engineer. Instantly the increased revolutions responded to the order. Then came the roar of heavy guns, the howl of shot, and scream of bursting shells. Around, above, and through the severed rigging the iron demons howled, as if pandemonium had discharged its infernal spirits into the air.*

Federal blockaders, while on station, were required to be constantly on the alert. Crews took turns manning their stations and when a runner was sighted, the warship had to be able to move and fire her guns within a matter of seconds. In the darkness it was impossible to aim accurately, but if enough guns could be brought to bear in the direction of the target, there was a good chance of hitting the intruder. In most cases the Federals would try to stop a blockade runner and take her captive rather than sink her. Once a runner was taken possession of and taken to a Northern port for adjudication, the crew of the Federal ship making the capture shared in the appraised value of the runner and its cargo. A sunken blockade runner meant no money for the crew.

The captain of the *Nassau* continues:

*Under the influence of a terrible shock the steamer quivers with aspen vibrations. An explosion follows; she is struck!*

*"What is the damage?" I ask.*

*"A shell, sir, has knocked overboard several bales of cotton and wounded two of the crew," was the response of the boatswain.*

*By the sheen of the Drummond lights the sea is so clearly illuminated as to exhibit the perils of our position, and show the grouping around us of the fleet, as their batteries belched forth a hailstorm of angry missiles, threatening instant annihilation.*

*In the turmoil of excitement a frightened passenger, contrary to orders, invaded the bridge. Wringing his hands in agony, he implored me to surrender and save his life and the lives of all on board. Much provoked, I directed one of the quartermasters stationed near me to take the lubber below. Without ceremony he seized the unhappy individual, and as he hurried him to the cabin, menacingly exclaimed, "Shut up your fly-trap, or by the powers of Moll Kelly I'll hould ye up as a target for the divarsion of them Yankee gunners!"*

*As perils multiplied, our Mazeppa speed increased and gradually withdrew us from the circle of danger. At last we distanced the party. Spontane-*

*ously the crew gave three hearty cheers as a relief to their pent-up anxiety, and everyone began to breathe more naturally.*[6]

For two days and a night the weather was beautiful as the *Nassau* steamed toward the Bahamas. On the third night, however, a fierce storm arose and battered the small ship with pounding waves. Florie Maffitt, Lieutenant Maffitt's twenty-one-year-old daughter who had begged him to allow her to accompany him on this trip, later wrote that she was comforted throughout this ordeal by hearing "the calm, steady voice of her father encouraging and directing his men." The next day the storm had subsided, and the sky was once again clear as the little steamer arrived in Nassau.[7]

Here Maffitt received orders to await the arrival of the *Oreto* which was inbound from England, and would later be commissioned the CSS *Florida*. He was forced, therefore, to send his daughter home on the *Nassau*, but under the command of a civilian captain. On May 28, off Fort Caswell, North Carolina, the runner came under attack as she headed into Wilmington. It was reported afterward by the pilot that Florie Maffitt sat unperturbed on the deck as the Federal shells whistled close by overhead. On learning that the ship was to be surrendered, she berated the captain and pleaded with him not to give up and to continue the run into port. On being reminded by him that he was responsible for her safety, she declared that she much preferred to be blown to bits rather than be captured by the "Yankees." The runner hove-to and surrendered, however, in spite of Florie's pleas. After the Federals took possession of the *Nassau*, Florie was taken to New York where she was later released, sent South, and returned unharmed to her family in North Carolina.[8]

Lieutenant Maffitt would return to blockade running in the dying days of the Confederacy, when in the fast steamer *Owl*, he would run one of the last loads of supplies into Galveston, Texas.[9]

In the summer of 1862, Major Benjamin F. Ficklin, an agent of the Treasury Department, approached the Secretary of the Treasury, Christopher G. Memminger, with a proposal. Knowing that the department was in need of engraving supplies, Ficklin, who had just returned from a trip abroad, offered a suggestion. On his trip home, he had passed through Glasgow, Scotland, and had noticed a sleek-looking steamer that was for sale. Ficklin proposed that he and a naval officer proceed to Glasgow, Scotland, purchase the ship, load her with the needed supplies, and run her through the blockade into a Confederate port.

The ship that Ficklin had seen in Scotland was the *Giraffe*, a sidewheel packet that was only two-years old. She had been built to operate between Glasgow and Belfast, but had lost money and her owners were forced to put her up for sale. Her graceful iron hull was

258 feet long, and she was reputed to be very fast, though she would later prove that 13.5 knots was the best she could do.

Memminger liked the idea and after discussing the plan with Secretary Mallory, directed Ficklin to proceed. The War Department ordered First Lieutenant John Wilkinson to accompany Ficklin to Scotland, purchase the *Giraffe* in the name of the Confederate government and take command.[10]

John Wilkinson, who along with Maffitt, would become one of the Confederacy's most famous blockade-runner captains, was born in Amelia County, Virginia, on November 6, 1821. The son of a career naval officer, Wilkinson entered the U.S. Navy with an appointment as midshipman in 1837 and saw duty in both the Atlantic and Pacific squadrons. Shortly before the War Between the States, Wilkinson, now a lieutenant and in command of the USS *Corwin*, spent a valuable year mapping and charting the waters off the east coast and specifically around the Florida Keys and the Bahamas.

When Virginia seceded, Wilkinson, like so many other Southern naval officers, resigned his commission and offered his services to the new Confederacy. After serving for a time at Fort Powhatan on the James, he was ordered to the New Orleans squadron where he was given command of the gunboat *Jackson*. At the time of Farragut's attack on the Crescent City in April of 1862, Wilkinson was serving as executive officer on the ironclad *Louisiana*. Taken prisoner upon the surrender of that vessel, he was transported to Boston where he was imprisoned in Fort Warren. Exchanged on August 5, 1862, Wilkinson was now available for duty, and the War Department ordered him to accompany Ficklin to England and purchase the *Giraffe*.[11]

Wilkinson, along with several subordinate officers, and Major Ficklin, departed Wilmington for Nassau on August 26, aboard the blockade runner *Kate*, under the command of Thomas Lockwood. After an uneventful trip, Wilkinson's party arrived in Nassau and continued on to Havana, Cuba, where they boarded a Spanish steamer which took them to St. Thomas. Here they boarded a British mail steamer for Southampton.

Taking the train to London, they were disappointed on their arrival to find that the *Giraffe* had already been sold in Glasgow to a company which was about to engage in the blockade-running business. Upon learning that Wilkinson was a commissioned officer in the Confederate navy, the company agreed to sell the *Giraffe* for £32,000, and her conversion to a blockade runner began at once.

Within thirty days the *Giraffe* was ready for sea. Her cargo consisted of arms and munitions for the struggling Confederate armies,

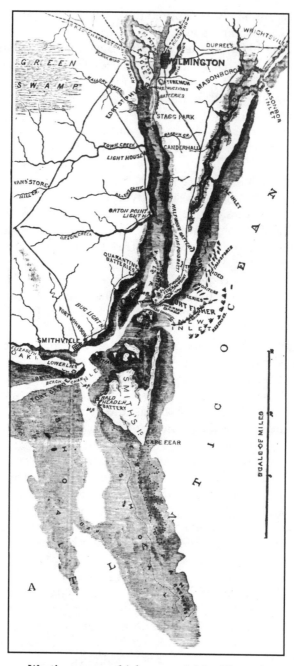

Wartime map which appeared in *Harper's Weekly*, depicting the approaches to Wilmington, North Carolina.

printing and engraving equipment for the Treasury Department, and twenty-six Scottish lithographers. After an uneventful voyage by way of Madeira and San Juan, Puerto Rico, Wilkinson recalled that: *After two days' detention at St. Johns for the purpose of coaling we got under way for that haven of blockade runners, El Dorado of adventurers, and paradise of wreckers and darkies — filthy Nassau.*[12]

The sleepy island town had been transformed into a virtual boom town since the start of the war, and Wilkinson described the scenes that met the traveler's eyes upon arrival:

*Nassau was a busy place during the war; the chief depot of supplies for the Confederacy, and the port to which most of the cotton was shipped. Its proximity to the ports of Charleston and Wilmington gave it superior advantages, while it was easily accessible to the swift, light draft blockade runners; all of which carried Bahamas bank pilots who knew every channel, while the United States cruisers having no Bank pilots and drawing more water were compelled to keep the open sea. ... Nassau is situated upon the island of New Providence, one of the Bahamas, and is the chief town and capital of the group. All of the islands are surrounded by coral reefs and shoals, through which are channels more or less intricate. ... The distance from Charleston to Nassau is about five hundred miles, and from Wilmington about five hundred and fifty. Practically, however, they were equi-distant because blockade runners bound from either port, in order to evade the cruisers lying in wait off Abaco, were compelled to give that head-land a wide berth, by keeping well to the eastward of it. But in avoiding Scylia they ran the risk of striking upon Charybolis; for the dangerous reefs of Eleuthera were fatal to many vessels. The chief industries of the islands before the war were the collection and exportation of sponges, corals, etc., and wrecking, to which was added, during the war, the lucrative trade of picking and stealing. The inhabitants may be classed as "amphibious," and are known among sailors by the generic name of "Conchs." The wharves of Nassau, during the war, were always piled high with cotton, and huge warehouses were stored full of supplies for the Confederacy. The harbor was crowded at times, with lead-colored, short masted, rak-*

First Lieutenant John Wilkinson, CSN, commander of the Confederate-owned blockade runner *Robert E. Lee* (*Giraffe*).

ish looking steamers; the streets alive with the bustle and activity during the day time and swarming with drunken revelers by night.[13]

The wages of a sailor on a blockade runner could run as high as one hundred dollars per month with a bonus for a completed trip, while captains could earn as much as $5,000 per voyage. On the Confederate owned or operated vessels, crewmen were paid the same as those on the civilian runners; however, the navy officers, and the pilots who were detailed from the army, received their normal salaries. With the prospects of easy money, Wilkinson had little trouble enlisting most of the crew who had made the trip from Glasgow, and after taking on additional coal, the *Giraffe* was ready to sail for the Confederacy.

Wilkinson, in his "Narrative of a Blockade Runner," described the *Giraffe's* first trip to Wilmington:

*Everything being in readiness, we sailed on December 26, 1862. Having on board a Charleston pilot, as well as one for Wilmington, I had not determined, on sailing, which port to attempt; but having made the land near Charleston bar during thick weather on the night of the 28th, our pilot was afraid to venture further. We made an offing, therefore, before daylight; and circumstances favoring Wilmington, we approached the western bar on the night of December 29th. We had been biding our time since twelve o'clock that day close into the shore about forty miles southwest of the bar and in the deep bay formed by the coast between Wilmington and Charleston. The weather had been so clear and the sea so smooth that we had communicated with the Confederate pickets at several points along the coast; and no sail was visible even from aloft until about three o'clock in the afternoon, when a cruiser hove in sight to the north and east. As she was coasting along the land and approaching us we turned the Giraffe's bow away from her, and got up more steam, easily preserving our distance, as the stranger was steaming at a low rate of speed. A little before sunset the strange steamer wore round, and we immediately followed her example, gradually lessening the distance between us, and an hour or more after dark we had the pleasure of passing inside of her off New River Inlet. She was evidently blockading that harbor, and had run down the coast to reconnoiter.*

*Before approaching the bar I adopted certain precautions against disaster which I ever afterwards followed. Anyone who showed an open light when we were near the fleet was liable to the penalty of death upon the spot; a cool, steady leadsman was stationed on each quarter to give the soundings; a staunch old quartermaster took the wheel and a kedge, (an iron anchor) bent to a stout hawser, was slung at each quarter. All lights were extinguished; the fire-room hatch covered over with a tarpaulin; and a hood fitted over the binnacle, with a small circular opening for the helmsman to see the compass through the aperture.*

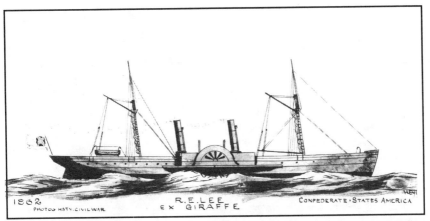

The blockade runner *Robert E. Lee,* formerly the *Giraffe.* Built in Glasgow, Scotland in 1860, she made 14 successful runs through the Federal blockade.

*About ten o'clock we passed inside the first ship of the blockading fleet, five miles outside the bar; and four or five others appeared in quick succession as the Giraffe was cutting rapidly through the smooth water. We were going at full speed when, with a shock that threw nearly everyone on board off his feet, the steamer was brought up "all standing" and hard and fast aground! The nearest blockader was fearfully close to us, and all seemed lost. We had struck upon "the Lump," a small sandy knoll two or three miles outside the bar with deep water on both sides of it. ...*

*The first order was to lower the two quarter boats; in one of them were packed the Scotch lithographers who were safely landed; and a kedge was lowered into the other with orders to the officer in charge to pull off shore and drop the kedge. The risk, though imminent, was much reduced after our panic stricken passengers had got fairly away from the ship; and the spirits of officers and crew rose to meet the emergency. The glimmer of a light, or an incautiously loud order would bring a broadside from that frowning battery crashing through our bulwarks. So near the goal (I thought) and now to fail! But I did not despair.*

*To execute the order to drop the kedge, it was necessary to directly approach one of the blockaders, and so near to her did they let it go, that the officer of the boat was afraid to call out that it had been dropped; and muffled the oars as he returned to make his report. Fortunately, the tide was rising. After twenty or thirty minutes of trying suspense, the order was given "to set taut on the hawser," and our pulses beat high as the stern of the Giraffe slowly and steadily turned seaward. In fact she swung round upon her stem as upon a pivot. As soon as the hawser "tended" right astern, the engineer was ordered to "back hard" and in a very few revolutions of the wheels the ship slid rapidly off into deep water. The hawser was instantly cut, and we headed directly for the bar channel. We were soon out of danger from the blockading fleet....*

*We passed safely over the bar; and steaming up the river, anchored off Smithville a little before midnight of the 29th of December, 1862.*[14]

A few days after her arrival, the *Giraffe* was formally commissioned as the *Robert E. Lee* and now flew the flag of the Confederate States of America. Wilkinson made several round trips in the *Lee* during the winter of 1862–63 and encountered no great difficulty. In March, the navy lieutenant switched his port of operations to St. George, Bermuda, and several runs were made between there and Wilmington. Usually the weather was good, but Wilkinson relates one trip that tested, to the limit, the *Lee's* seaworthiness, along with his own knowledge and courage:

*After discharging our cargo of cotton and loading with supplies for the Confederate government, chiefly for the Army of Northern Virginia, we sailed for Wilmington in the latter part of the month of March (1863). Our return voyage was uneventful, until we reached the coast near Masonborough Inlet, distant about nine miles north of the "New Inlet" bar. The weather had been pleasant during the voyage, and we had sighted the fires from the salt works along the coast, but before we could get hold of the land, a little before midnight, a dense black cloud made its appearance to the north and east; and the rapidity with which it rose and enlarged, indicated too surely that a heavy gale was coming from that quarter. We had been unable to distinguish any landmark before the storm burst in all its fury upon us and the rain poured in torrents. Our supply of coal was too limited to enable us, with prudence, to put to sea again; and of course, the marks or range [lights] for crossing the bar would not be visible fifty yards in such thick weather. Being quite confident of our position, however, I determined to run down the coast, and anchor off the bar till daylight.*[15]

It was in situations such as these that Wilkinson's intimate knowledge of the coastline gained while in the U.S. Navy, enabled him to be successful where other captains failed. Indicative of the Confederate navy's ability to successfully run the blockade is the fact that out of all the blockade runners captained by regular naval officers, only one was lost.[16]

*Knowing the "trend" of the land north of New Inlet bar,* Wilkinson continued, *the engine was slowed down and the lead kept going on both sides. The sounding continued quite regular three and three and a quarter fathoms, with the surf thundering within a stone's throw on our starboard beam, and nothing visible in the blinding torrents of rain. I knew that if my calculated position was correct, the water would shoal very suddenly just before reaching the bar; but a trying hour or more of suspense had passed before the welcome fact was announced by the leadsman. The course and distance run, and the soundings up to this point proved, beyond doubt, that we had now reached* the "horseshoe" north of New Inlet bar. At the moment when both leadsman almost simultaneously called out "and a quarter less three," the helm was put hard a-starboard, and the Lee's bow was pointed seaward. We could not prudently anchor in less than five fathoms (of) water, as the sea was rising rapidly; and that depth would carry us into the midst of the blockading fleet at anchor outside. It seemed an age before the cry came from the leadsman "by the mark five." The Lee was instantly stopped, and one of the bower anchors let go, veering to thirty fathoms on the chain.

The cable was then well stoppered at the "bitts," and unshackled; and two men stationed at the stoppers, with axes, and the order to cut the lashings, instantly, when so ordered; the fore-staysail was loosed, and hands stationed at the halliards; and the chief engineer directed to keep up a full head of steam. The night wore slowly away; and once or twice we caught a glimpse, by a flash of lightning, of the blockading fleet around us, rolling and pitching in the heavy sea. The watch having been set, the rest of the officers and crew were permitted to go below, except the chief engineer and the pilot. We paced the bridge, anxiously waiting for daylight. It came at last, and there right astern of us, looming up through the mist and rain, was the "Mound." (The Mound was a large gun emplacement at the south end of Fort Fisher.) We had only to steer for it, to be on the right course for crossing the bar. The stoppers were cut, the engine started ahead, and the fore stay-sail hoisted. As the chain rattled through the hawse-hole, the Lee wore rapidly around, and the Confederate flag was run up to the peak as she dashed toward the bar with the speed of a greyhound slipped from the leash. The bar was a sheet of foam and surf, breaking sheer across the channel; but the great length of the Lee enabled her to ride over three or four of the short chopping seas at once, and she never touched the bottom. In less than half an hour from the time when we slipped our chain under the guns of the fleet, we had passed beyond Fort Fisher, and were on our way up the river to Wilmington.[17]

Wilkinson continued to make regular trips with the Lee to either Nassau or Bermuda throughout the summer of 1863. On one occasion, when the need for military supplies was especially critical, a run was made on a bright, moonlit night out of Wilmington. By hugging the coastline for twelve to fourteen miles, the Lee slipped easily by the blockaders without attracting their attention. It was determined later that the Federal vigilance was much relaxed during this time, for they believed that no runner would be foolish enough to attempt a passage on a bright, moonlit night.

It was about this time that Wilkinson developed a ruse to fool the blockaders when running through their midst on a dark night. Noticing that the Federals had begun firing rockets upon sighting a runner, Wilkinson ordered his own supply of rockets from New York City (He does not say how he obtained them from New York!). When

*The Illustrated London News*

**Typical scene on board a blockade runner, as she speeds towards the Confederate coast.**

running the blockade, an officer would be stationed next to him with a supply of rockets. If they were spotted, and the Union ship fired her rockets indicating the course of the runner, Wilkinson would wait about two minutes and then launch his own rockets. These would be fired at 90 degrees to his actual course giving the impression that the Federal ship had fired them, and that the runner had changed course. Even if his immediate pursuer was not fooled, the rest of the fleet most likely would be.[18]

On the black night of August 15, 1863, the *Lee,* with Wilkinson still in command, left Wilmington with a load of government cotton on board. By the time they had passed through the ring of blockaders thirty miles off the North Carolina coast, the engineer reported that their supply of English coal was exhausted. The only coal remaining now in the bunkers was a supply of poor quality soft coal which smoked terribly. They had just begun using this inferior coal shortly after daylight, when they were spotted by a Federal cruiser. The lookout on the *Lee* shouted the alarm, and Wilkinson hurried to take a look.

*Going to the mast-head I could just discern the royal of the chaser; and before I left there, say in half an hour, her top-gallant sail showed above the horizon. By this time the sun had risen in a cloudless sky. It was evident our pursuer would be alongside of us by mid-day at the rate we were then going. The first orders given were to throw overboard the deck load of cotton and to make more steam. The latter proved to be more easily given than executed; the engineer reporting that it was impossible to make steam with the wretched stuff filled with slate and dirt.*

By turning the *Lee's* head directly away from the wind, Wilkinson was able to diminish the sailing ability of the Federal cruiser somewhat, but she continued to gain on the Confederate runner. With thirty or forty barrels of turpentine on board, Wilkinson ordered one of them broken open. Crew members began ripping apart one of the remaining cotton bales and saturating the material in buckets of turpentine. Passing these below, the contents were flung into the furnace with immediate results, and Wilkinson remembered that ... *The results exceeded our expectations.*[19]

With a full head of steam the *Lee* forged through the gray Atlantic at over fourteen knots, but the Federal ship was still dangerously near. All day the chase continued with men frantically tearing apart cotton and soaking it in the turpentine, while others took turns in the engine room swinging the contents of the buckets into the fires.

*There continued to be a very slight change in our relative positions,* Wilkinson recalled, *till about six o'clock in the afternoon, when the chief engineer again made his appearance, with a very ominous expression of countenance. He came to report that the burnt cotton had choked the flues, and the steam was running down. "Only keep her going till dark, sir," I replied, "and we will give our pursuer the slip yet." A heavy bank was lying along the horizon to the south and east; and I saw a possible means of escape. At sunset the chaser was about four miles astern and gaining upon us. Calling two of my most reliable officers, I stationed one of them on each wheel house, with glasses, directing them to let me know the instant they lost sight of the chaser in the growing darkness. At the same time, I ordered the chief engineer to make as black a smoke as possible, and to be in readiness to cut off the smoke, by closing the dampers instantly, when ordered. The twilight was soon succeeded by darkness. Both of the officers on the wheel house called out at the same moment, "We have lost sight of her, sir!" while a dense volume of smoke was streaming far in our wake. "Close the Dampers," I called through the speaking tube, and at the same moment ordered the helm "hard a starboard." Our course was altered eight points, at a right angle to the previous one. I remained on deck an hour, and then retired to my state-room with a comfortable sense of security.*

Suspecting that the Federal captain would continue on toward Abaco in the Bahamas and lay in wait for him, Wilkinson changed his destination to Bermuda, and arrived there safely two days later.[20]

When Wilkinson returned to Wilmington, he found orders awaiting him to report to Richmond for special assignment. The Confederate government wanted to make an attempt to free the 3,000 prisoners at Johnson's Island opposite Sandusky, Ohio on Lake Erie, and

Wilkinson had been chosen to lead the expedition. Selecting twenty-six officers to accompany him, Wilkinson returned to Wilmington and prepared the *Lee* for the trip to Halifax, Nova Scotia. A full load of cotton was to be carried and sold in the Canadian Province, the proceeds of which was to be used to purchase arms and clothing for the freed prisoners. Wilkinson and his men were to proceed overland through Canada, without violating Canadian neutrality. Not knowing how this would be possible, Wilkinson decided not to worry about it. After capturing the Federal steamer *Michigan*, they were to cross the lake to the U.S. side, attack the garrison, and free the prisoners. By the first part of October, all was ready.[21]

*We sailed for Halifax on the night of October 10th, 1863,* Wilkinson wrote. *The season was so far advanced, that we could not afford to lose a day; we therefore dropped down the Cape Fear River to Smithville, and although the night was very clear, I determined to attempt the passage through the fleet soon after dark, so as to get as far north along the coast as possible before daylight. We crossed the western bar about nine o'clock at night, and instead of hugging the shore, which would have carried us too far to the southward and westward, the course was shaped so as to clear Frying Pan Shoals.*

The *Lee* had been running at full speed for almost an hour when suddenly, from out of the darkness, a shell streaked by only a few feet above the ship. Quickly another shot followed, but fortunately it fell short and ricocheted over the speeding *Lee*. A third shot found its mark, and crashing through a starboard bulwark, exploded against a bale of cotton setting it ablaze. Several men were struck by flying splinters and fragments of the bursting shell. Flames, fanned by the high speed of the *Lee*, streamed to the rear threatening to set the rest of the ship on fire. In spite of the momentary confusion caused by the fire, willing hands began pushing the blazing cotton bale to the rail and finally it tumbled into the sea. Several more shots followed, but they fell wide of the mark. Because the shots came from the port side, Wilkinson surmised that the Federal blockader must have been inside the *Lee* and near the shore, but he confessed that they never saw the Union ship. Sending up two rockets to confuse the attacker, the *Lee* continued on her course.[22]

Arriving in Halifax on October 16, arrangements were made to dispose of the cotton and purchase the needed arms and clothing. After unloading, the *Lee* was quickly made ready for the outbound trip, and under the command of John Knox, departed Halifax and headed for Bermuda to take on a load of arms and equipment.

On November 5, the *Robert E. Lee* left St. George for the last time and plowed toward the North Carolina coast. She had made fourteen successful runs through the blockade under the capable hands of Lieutenant Wilkinson. Three days later, however, the courage and intelligence of the wise Confederate navy lieutenant was not present on her bridge, and she fell easy prey to a Federal blockader. Knox seems to have lost heart while approaching the bar at Wilmington and turned around and steamed toward the open sea, where he was quickly captured the next morning.[23]

Wilkinson, whose mission in Halifax by this time had been aborted, relates a sad postscript to the story of the *Robert E. Lee:*

*My staunch old helmsman, who had been released in New York by claiming British protection, and who started at once in search of me, met me in Halifax on our return from the Johnson's Island expedition. He actually shed tears as he narrated the train of circumstances which led to the capture. "She would have gone in by herself," he said, "if they had only let her alone."*[24]

Blockade running during the war was indeed, as some have said, the "lifeline of the Confederacy." Because of dedicated men such as Maffitt, Wilkinson, and many others, along with the sleek, fast steamers they guided, the Southern armies were never without the means to fight. In addition to munitions and supplies, the Army of Northern Virginia depended almost entirely, during the last winter of the war, upon the gray-colored phantoms that slipped into Wilmington for the bulk of its food supply. By the crushing end of the conflict, blockade runners had supplied almost everything for the struggling Confederacy except what it needed most — manpower.

# Chapter *Five*

## Greyhound of the Seas

One of the most successful aspects of the Confederate navy during the War Between the States was the activities of her commerce-raiding cruisers. Faced with the reality of an inferior naval force that could never hope to challenge the U.S. Navy on anything approaching an equal footing, the Confederate government sought the most expedient way of damaging the Northern economy. During the war, more than half of Northern shipping disappeared from the world's oceans as Confederate raiders destroyed 110,000 tons of shipping and drove an additional 800,000 tons to foreign flags. As a result, American leadership in maritime commerce remained crippled until the advent of World War II. The Confederacy accomplished this by commissioning sea-going cruisers to hunt down and destroy Northern-owned merchant ships and their cargoes. The Confederate navy commissioned and put to sea eight cruisers during the war, the most renowned of these being three ships built in England: the *Florida*, the *Shenandoah*, and the *Alabama*. Of these three, the cruise of the CSS *Alabama* was by far the most successful and damaging to the Federal economy.[1]

One of the most fortuitous decisions that Stephen R. Mallory ever made as secretary of the navy was the selection of James Dunwoody Bulloch to be the navy's procurement agent in Great Britain. After twenty-two years of service in the U.S. Navy, Bulloch resigned his com-

**Commander James D. Bulloch, CSN, special financial agent in England for the Navy Department, and genius behind the design and construction of the CSS *Alabama*.**

mission at the outbreak of war and was appointed a commander in the Confederate navy. Bulloch's efforts to provide the Confederacy with the means and materials to conduct a naval war against the United States is a classic example of one person's struggle against overwhelming odds. Because of the secret nature of his work, his contribution to the Confederate effort remains generally unknown and under appreciated even to this day. Tactful, intelligent, and totally devoted to the cause of his beloved Southland, he spent the entire war laboring for his country far from her troubled shores. One of Bulloch's many accomplishments, while operating within the realm of British neutrality, international intrigue, and Union espionage, was the building and launching on the oceans of the world, one of the finest cruisers ever built.[2]

On August 1, 1861, Bulloch signed a contract with John Laird and Sons of Birkenhead across the Mersey from Liverpool for the construction of their 290th hull. Despite the fact that an iron ship could be built faster and more economically, Bulloch insisted that the 290 be a wooden ship. An iron ship, he reasoned, could not be repaired in remote ports, whereas a wooden ship could be repaired by most facilities and even by the ship's carpenter while at sea. Wooden decks were also stronger than iron when subjected to stress caused by the firing of heavy ordnance. Bulloch designed the 290 to be self-sustaining at sea by allocating extra space below decks for the storage of tools, provisions, and 350 tons of coal. A condensing unit, attached to the boilers, could supply fresh water for the crew.

The 290, which would become the *Alabama*, was the largest cruiser ever built for the Confederacy. Her slim, graceful hull, built of the finest materials available, was 220 feet long and copper-clad below the water line. Weighing 1,040 tons, she was bark-rigged with long lower masts which accommodated oversize fore and aft sails, while her two horizontal engines, each rated at 300 horsepower, developed a total of 1,000 horsepower during trial runs. She had a retractable funnel, and a propeller that could be raised out of the water and into a well in the stern in fifteen minutes, thus eliminating drag when the vessel was under sail. Fast under steam or sail, the *Alabama*, under the right conditions, could make almost fifteen knots when under both. She was the perfect cruiser, and by living off her prizes, could literally stay at sea indefinitely.[3]

While the *Alabama* was designed for speed and was supposed to avoid combat with enemy warships, she was nevertheless equipped with a formidable battery. Her armament included a 100-pounder Blakely rifle mounted on a forward pivot; an 8-inch smoothbore pivoted abaft the main mast; and six 32-pounders in broadside. To service and man these guns, she carried a crew of 120 men and 24 officers.[4]

In spite of the suspicion and efforts by Federal agents to stop her construction, number 290, now named the *Enrica*, slid down the ways on May 15, 1862. Towed to a graving dock, huge cranes began lowering her engines and boilers in place, and by June 15, she was ready for her first trial run. [5]

Because the *Enrica* could not be armed in English waters without violating the British Foreign Enlistment Act, Bulloch purchased the bark *Agrippina* which could be used as a supply vessel. Loading her with guns, ordnance, stores, clothing and 350 tons of coal, Bulloch contracted with a British captain to command her and rendezvous with the *Enrica* in the Azores.

Meanwhile, on June 13, the British steamer *Melita* was pulling into the harbor of Nassau in the Bahamas with a group of Confederate naval officers on board headed by Commander Raphael Semmes. After a successful cruise destroying Federal commerce, Semmes and his officers were returning to the Confederacy after leaving the worn out CSS *Sumter* at Gibraltar. Waiting for Semmes was a dispatch from Mallory promoting him to captain and ordering him to return to England and take command of the *Alabama*.

Raphael Semmes would become one of the most famous commanders in Confederate naval history,

Scharf's *History of the Confederate States Navy*

**Captain Raphael Semmes, commander of the CSS *Alabama*. On February 10, 1865, Semmes was promoted to rear admiral for "gallant and meritorious conduct in command of the steam sloop *Alabama*."**

and his exploits on the *Alabama* would become legendary. He was born in Charles County, Maryland, on September 27, 1809, and entered the U.S. Navy at the age of sixteen as a midshipman. During his term in the "old" navy, Semmes studied law, particularly international law, and while on an extended leave, passed the bar exam and opened a law office in Cincinnati, Ohio. Recalled to active duty, Semmes, now a lieutenant, was assigned to the Pensacola Navy Yard in Florida. Moving his family to nearby Alabama, he ever after considered himself a citizen of that state. By the time of Alabama's secession from the Union, Semmes was a commander serving as secretary of the Lighthouse Board. Resigning his commission, he hurried to Montgomery in February of 1861 to offer his services to the Confederacy.[6]

Mallory sent Semmes to the Northern states to purchase arms and equipment and to look for vessels that could be acquired for conversion into warships. Finding none, Semmes returned to Montgomery, where Mallory mentioned that a worn-out steamer at New Orleans might be suitable for commerce raiding. Given the steam packet *Havana* (a former mail steamer on the Havana to New Orleans run), Semmes had her reconditioned and commissioned into the Confederate navy as the CSS *Sumter*. On June 30, Semmes took the little *Sumter* on a mad dash down the Pass a L'Outre, past the Union frigate *Brooklyn*, and out into the Gulf of Mexico. For the next six months the Confederate commander roamed the seas capturing eighteen ships, seven of which he destroyed.[7]

In need of repairs, he arrived at Gibraltar only to be frustrated by delays and the arrival of three Federal warships outside of the harbor. Feeling that the *Sumter* had outlived her usefulness, Semmes left her at Gibraltar and traveled to London, where he met with Bulloch. Now on his way back to the Confederacy, the message from Mallory ordered Semmes to return to England and take command of the *Alabama*.

Arriving in Liverpool on the British steamer *Bahama* from Nassau, Semmes and his officers were disappointed to find that the *Enrica* had already left port. Warned by an informant that British authorities, under pressure from U.S. officials, were about to confiscate the *Enrica*, Bulloch acted quickly. Having previously contracted with Matthew J. Butcher, a British captain, to command the *Enrica*, enlist a crew, and sail her to the Azores, Bulloch scheduled an elaborate "trial run" to get the ship out of Liverpool. On Monday morning, July 28, the *Enrica* left her dock and anchored off Seacombe. Bulloch had invited a distinguished group of ladies and gentlemen to go along and enjoy the trial run. The next morning, with all the excited passengers aboard, and with flags and pennants flying, the *Enrica* steamed for the open sea. Bulloch and his wife played the perfect host and hostess as champagne corks popped and a bountiful lunch was served, while everyone enjoyed the ocean breeze and the splendid new ship that sped them across the waves.[8]

Later, in the afternoon, Bulloch regretfully announced that the passengers would have to return to port on board the tug *Hercules*, for it had become "necessary" to keep the *Enrica* out overnight to complete her trials. Accompanying the merry passengers on board the tug, which had followed the *Enrica* on her trial run, Bulloch left instructions for Captain Butcher to meet him the following morning with the *Enrica* at Moelfra Bay.

Shortly after dawn on July 30, Bulloch was about to board the *Hercules* when he was handed an urgent telegram from his confidant in Southampton. It informed him that the steam sloop USS *Tuscarora* had sailed and was thought to be headed for Queenstown on the south coast of Ireland. It seemed evident that she meant to intercept the *Enrica* if she followed the normal route down the Irish Sea and through St. George's Channel. Captain Butcher, reasoned Bulloch, would now have to take the more dangerous and lengthy route around the rocky north coast of Ireland.[9]

Late in the afternoon, with scattered showers and lowering weather, the *Hercules* with Bulloch on board arrived in Moelfra Bay where the *Enrica* was anchored. After enlisting thirty to forty seaman whom Bulloch had brought out with him on the tug, Butcher made ready to sail. As night fell the weather worsened, and by midnight, rain was falling in torrents, and a strong gale was blowing from the southwest. Finally, by 2:30 a.m. all was ready, and Bulloch ordered the British captain to get under way and head northward into the Irish Sea. George Bond, a pilot Bulloch had entrusted, carefully guided the rolling *Enrica* through the driving wind and rain along the coast of Ireland. By daybreak, the rain had stopped and the wind had diminished, allowing the *Enrica* to spread her canvas, and majestically she swept across the waves at thirteen and one-half knots.

Near the end of the day, Bulloch hailed a fishing boat, and he and Bond went ashore near Giant's Causeway. As they stood on the rocky coast, the *Enrica's* graceful sails disappeared in the gathering darkness as she sped onward toward Terceira in the Azores and her rendezvous with history. Taking rooms at a local Inn, Bulloch recorded his thoughts later that night:

*During the evening it rained incessantly, and the wind skirled and snifted about the gables of the hotel in fitful squalls. Bond and I sat comfortably enough in the snug dining-room after dinner, and sipped our toddy, of the best colerain malt; but my heart was with the little ship buffeting her way around that rugged north coast of Ireland. I felt sure that Butcher would keep his weather-*

*eye open, and once clear of Innistrahull, there would be plenty of sea room; but I could not wholly shake off an occasional sense of uneasiness.*[10]

Bulloch re-chartered the *Bahama* for a "trip to Nassau," and Semmes and his party, along with Bulloch, sailed from Liverpool on August 12. The man and his ship were about to meet.

On August 20, the *Bahama* arrived at Porto Praya, the location designated for rendezvous in the Azores, and Semmes recalled this moment: *At half past eleven A. M., we steamed into the harbor, and let go our anchor. I had surveyed my new ship, as we approached, with no little interest, as she was to be not only my home, but my bride, as it were, for the next few years, and I was quite satisfied with her external appearance. She was indeed, a beautiful thing to look upon. ... Her model was of the most perfect symmetry, and she sat upon the water with the lightness and grace of a swan.*[11]

Butcher had already lashed the *Agrippina* and the *Enrica* together and was busy transferring guns and stores to the cruiser. A strong wind forced Semmes to move the three ships to a protected cove, and there, for the next two days, the work of converting the *Enrica* into the *Alabama* continued. Semmes was pleased with the interior of the ship but relates a picture of chaos on her decks where ... *everything was in a very uninviting state of confusion, guns, gun-carriages, shot, and shell, barrels of beef and pork, and boxes and bales of paymaster's, gunner's and boatswain's stores lying promiscuously about the decks; sufficient time not having elapsed to have them stowed in their proper places.*

Semmes, who soon would be referred to behind his back as "Old Beeswax" because of his handle-bar mustache, was not overly impressed with the crew he was about to inherit, but felt they had potential. The sixty odd men had been recruited off the docks of Liverpool and *were as unpromising in appearance, as things about the decks. What with faces begrimed with coal dust, red shirts, and blue shirts, Scotch caps, and hats, brawny chests exposed, and stalwart arms naked to the elbows, they looked as little like the crew of a man-of-war, as one can well conceive. Still there was some 'physique' among these fellows, and soap, and water, and clean shirts would make a wonderful difference in their appearance.*[12]

It was a beautiful Sunday morning, August 24, 1862, when the *Bahama* and the *Enrica* raised their anchors and steamed toward the open sea. Once past the three mile limit, the two steamers hove to near each other and Semmes called the crews together for a momentous ceremony. *The officers were all in full uniform, and the crew neatly dressed, and I caused "all hands" to be summoned aft on the quarter-deck, and mounting a gun-carriage, I read the commission of Mr. Jefferson Davis, appointing me a captain in the Confederate States Navy, and the order of Stephen R. Mallory, the Secretary of the Navy, directing me to assume command of the Alabama. Following my example, the officers and crew had all uncovered their heads, in deference to the sovereign authority, as is customary on such occasions; and as they stood in respectful silence and listened with rapt attention to the reading, and to the short explanation of my object and purposes, in putting the ship in commission which followed, I was deeply impressed with the spectacle.*[13]

While Semmes was reading his commission to his officers and men, two small spheres, unnoticed by the crew, were slowly being hoisted to the mastheads. Quartermaster Henry Marmelstein, a Southern coast pilot, stood by the English colors which still fluttered in the breeze, ready to strike them upon command, while a gunner, lock-string in hand, stood at attention by the weather-bow gun. Semmes finished reading, and with a wave of his hand, the halyards connected to the spheres were pulled and out streamed the Stars and Bars and a commission pennant. The English colors came down, the gun was fired, and the band assembled on the quarterdeck struck up an exhilarating chorus of "Dixie." The air was rent with thunderous cheers from officers and men, and thus, amid the beauty of this tranquil scene of sky and ocean, the *CSS Alabama* was born.[14]

There remained one final act necessary to complete the transformation of the *Alabama* into a fighting "man-of-war" — the enlistment of the crew. Semmes gave his last speech of the two-year cruise, appealing to the English sailors of the *Bahama* and former *Enrica* to cast their lot with the young, new nation whose flag floated above their heads. In the end, 80 young men signed the Articles of Enlistment, forfeiting any protection by the British Crown and entrusting their fates with those of the Confederacy. The remainder of the crew would eventually come by the enlistment of volunteers from the ships the *Alabama* would capture. It had been an impressive moment, and Bulloch and others worked long into the night preparing papers and pay vouchers for each new recruit.[15]

It was past midnight before Bulloch, accompanied by Butcher and the twenty sailors who had refused to sign the Articles of Enlistment, returned to the *Bahama*. As she lifted her anchor and steamed away to return to Liverpool, it must have been with mixed feelings that Bulloch watched the graceful silhouette of the *Alabama* fade into the darkness. He could be extremely proud of his efforts, for she was at this moment the finest cruiser of any nation afloat. And yet, she was commanded not by him, but by another. Bulloch knew, however, that his duty still lay among the intrigues of Liverpool and London. While he would follow her career with satisfaction and pride, it would be his fate never to see the *Alabama* again.[16]

There was still much work to be done. *The day after the Bahama left us, was cloudy, and cheerless in aspect, with a fresh wind and a rough sea,*

Semmes wrote. *The ship was rolling and tumbling about, to the discomfort of every one, and confusion still reigned on board. Below decks everything was dirt and disorder. Nobody had as yet been berthed or messed, nor had any one been stationed at a gun or a rope. Spare shot-boxes and other heavy articles were fetching way, and the ship was leaking considerably through her upper works. ... I needed several days yet to put things "to rights," and mold the crew into a little shape. I withdrew, therefore, under easy sail, from the beaten tracks of commerce; and my first lieutenant went to work berthing, and messing, and quartering, and stationing his men.*[17]

Executive officer on the CSS *Alabama*, First Lieutenant John McIntosh Kell, from Georgia.

Semmes' first "Luff" (lieutenant) and executive officer was John McIntosh Kell from Georgia, who had twenty years of experience in the "old" navy. Remaining distant and aloof from the men and most of his officers during the cruise, Semmes preferred to command the *Alabama* with a firm hand through his first lieutenant. Kell, who was 39-years old, was a commanding figure and just the officer Semmes needed to bring order out of chaos. Standing six feet two inches tall, he was stalwart in frame and carried himself so as to command respect. With piercing blue eyes and a massive auburn beard, he would come to be respected, instantly obeyed, and loved by most of the crew.[18]

The *Alabama's* second lieutenant was Richard F. Armstrong, a recent graduate of the Naval Academy at Annapolis and also a native of Georgia. Skilled in gunnery, Armstrong was in charge of the 100-pounder Blakely pivot gun and two of the 32-pounders.

The third lieutenant was Joseph D. Wilson, who was nicknamed "Fighting Joe" because of his aggressiveness. Appointed to the Naval Academy in 1857, Wilson resigned when his home state of Florida seceded, and after serving with Semmes on the *Sumter*, was now in charge of the after-gun division.

British-born John Low was fourth lieutenant and was often used by Semmes as boarding officer, for his English accent helped convey the impression that the *Alabama* was a British man-of-war.

Arthur Sinclair, the fifth lieutenant, was on board the CSS *Virginia* during her battles in Hampton Roads and was the scion of an old Virginia family. Sinclair was in charge of one of the *Alabama's* gun divisions.

Others included Midshipman Irvine S. Bulloch from Georgia, younger brother of James D. Bulloch; Surgeon Francis L. Galt, who was from Virginia and never lost a man to disease while on the *Alabama*; and D. Herbert Liewellyn, assistant surgeon, who hailed from Witshire, England, and had been the surgeon on board the *Bahama* until her rendezvous with the *Alabama*. Miles J. Freeman from Louisiana was chief engineer and Beckett K. Howell, brother-in-law of Jefferson Davis and also a Louisiana native, was lieutenant of marines and the only representative of the Marine Corps on board. An impressive array of steerage and warrant officers rounded out the *Alabama's* complement and they would prove themselves more than equal to their tasks over the next two eventful years.[19]

The CSS *Alabama*, sketched by Captain Hagar of the *Brilliant*, and published in *Harper's Weekly*, 1862.

The first order of business was to mount the battery of guns, assign the men to their stations, and train them in the art of naval gunnery. Kell, with the help of the other officers, got to work and soon conditions improved considerably. Semmes wrote that: *We now devoted several days to the exercise of the crew, as well at general, as division quarters. Some few of the guns' crews had served in ships of war before, and proved capital drill-sergeants for the rest. The consequence was, that rapid progress* was made, and the Alabama was soon in a condition to plume her wings for her flight. I only remained to caulk our upper works, and this occupied us but a day or two longer.[17]

Eleven days after the commissioning of the *Alabama*, the first prize was captured not more than a hundred miles from were her flag first unfurled. The lookout had spotted a distant sail, and after giving up the chase, Semmes came upon the 454-ton whaler *Ocmulgee* out of Edgartown, Massachusetts. She was lying to with a large sperm whale lashed to her side, which the crew was busy working on, when the *Alabama* approached flying United States colors. Semmes wrote that her captain *was a genuine specimen of the Yankee whaling skipper; long and lean, and as elastic, apparently, as the whalebone he dealt in.* The whaling captain stared in blank astonishment as the Confederate ensign replaced the Stars and Stripes at the *Alabama*'s masthead.

After removing her crew of 37 and taking some provisions from her hold, Semmes decided, since it was now dark, to wait until morning to burn her. Hoisting a light to the peak of the prize, the two vessels anchored for the night. At the first rays of the morning sun, on September 6, 1862, the *Ocmulgee* was set ablaze. The thick, black smoke that mushroomed skyward was the first of many which would mark the path of the *Alabama*.[21]

The next day being Sunday, Semmes held a general muster and inspection. *With clean, white ducks,* he wrote, *with the brass and iron work glittering like so many mirrors in the sun, and with the sails neatly trimmed, and the Confederate States flag at our peak, we spread our awnings and read the Articles of War to the crew.* A great change had come over the men, Semmes noted. *Their parti-colored garments had been cast aside, and they were all neatly arrayed in duck frocks and trousers, well-polished shoes, and straw hats.* With the muster and inspection completed, Kell paroled the prisoners from the *Ocmulgee*, and loading them in their whale boats, directed them to pull for the island of Flores not far distant.[22]

No sooner were the prisoners landed than the cry, "Sail Ho!" came from the masthead. A schooner was approaching the island and straining every inch of canvas to reach the marine league where she would be safe from capture. Semmes set a course to intercept her and fired a blank cartridge, but the schooner refused to stop. The next shot was from one of the 32-pounders which streaked between the schooner's masts a few feet over the deck. Semmes commented that if anyone *has heard a 32-pounder whistle, in such close proximity, he knows very well what it says, to wit, that there must be no more trifling.* The schooner luffed into the wind, bringing her to a stop, and the American colors were run up to her peak. She proved to be the *Starlight* inbound to Boston with a stopover at the island of Flores.

Semmes reluctantly placed the captain and his crew of seven in irons, in retaliation for the humiliation suffered by his paymaster, Henry Myers of the *Sumter*. Myers, who had been trapped in Tangiers when the *Sumter* stopped there for coal, was shackled in irons and thrown into a dark cell. Handed over to American officials later, with a shaven head, he was spirited out of Morocco and imprisoned in Boston. To be sure that word of his actions reached American officials, Semmes practiced this bit of retaliation for the next seven or eight captures. Within 24 hours, though, the *Starlight's* captain and men were paroled and standing on the shores of Flores.[23]

Hauling off from the island of Flores and gaining the open sea, Semmes stopped another whaler which turned out to be Portuguese, a rarity among an American dominated industry. Sending the Portuguese captain on his way with an apology, another sail was spotted late in the day toward the northwest, and the *Alabama* gave chase. Thinking the *Alabama* was a U.S. gunboat sent out to protect the whalers, the *Ocean Rover* of New Bedford, Massachusetts, fell an easy prey.

Darkness had arrived by the time the *Ocean Rover* was secured, so Semmes again decided to hold the prizes until morning before burning them. During the night another ship was seen heading for Flores and the *Alabama* gave chase. It was daylight before Semmes drew close enough to use one of his 32-pounders. Lieutenant Armstrong dropped a shot *near enough to her stern to give the captain a shower-bath,* Semmes related, and the *Alert* out of New London hove to. After taking from her what supplies were needed and securing her chronometer and charts, Semmes ordered her, along with the *Starlight* and the *Ocean Rover,* put to the torch. Their crews were given the whalers' boats, paroled and sent on their way toward Flores.[24]

Late in the afternoon, another ship approached, attracted by the three plumes of smoke from the burning whalers, and she, too, became an easy victim. She was the *Weathergauge,* a whaling schooner and only six weeks out of Provincetown. She was the fifth prize taken so far, and Lieutenant Kell described, in rather matter-of-fact terms, the method worked out by now of capturing prizes:

*As soon as we sighted a ship we would hail her. If she didn't stop we fired a blank cartridge across her bow. If she still refused to respond, we would send a shot in front of her, and that would bring her to. Our long range guns were of invaluable service in this business. When we hailed a ship we generally had the U.S. flag flying and kept it up until we were alongside. Then we would lower a boat and send an officer on board; but just before he boarded her the U.S. flag would come down and up would go the Confederate flag. Our officer would go to the captain of the ship we had caught, demand his papers, order him into the boat and bring him on board. Admiral Semmes always remained in his cabin when a capture was made and the captains of our prizes were taken before him there. He examined their papers and questioned them closely. If the ship was found to belong to a citizen of a neutral country, a fact which the captain's papers would always reveal, she was at once released. When we discovered that we had the property of a citizen of the United States we took her officers, crew and passengers (if she had any) on board. We then went through her cargo and appropriated what we needed, for we lived almost entirely on our prizes. When we had all we wanted, we set fire to the captured ship and sailed away to look for another.*[25]

The *Weathergauge* had no more than surrendered, when the cry "Sail Ho" echoed from the masthead. Throwing a prize crew on the *Weathergauge* with instructions to "hold onto" the island of Corvo until they returned, Semmes started in pursuit. This was a fast one and he wrote that she *...seemed determined to run away from us; and as she was fast, and we were as determined to overhaul her as she was to run away, she led us a beautiful night-dance over the merry waters. The moon rose bright, soon after the chase commenced, and, striking upon the canvas of the fleeing vessel, lighted it up as though it had been a snow-bank. ... The cut of the sails, and the taper of the spars of the chase looked American, and then the ship was cracking on every stitch of canvas that would draw, in the effort to escape — she must surely be American, we thought. ... The speed of the two ships was so nearly matched, that, for the first hour or two, it was impossible to say whether we had gained on her an inch. We were both running dead before the wind, and this was not the Alabama's most favorable sailing point. With her tall lower masts, and large fore-and-aft sails, she was better on a wind, or with the wind abeam. The chase was leading us away from our cruising ground, and I should have abandoned it, if I had not had my pride of ship a little interested. It would never do for the Alabama to be beaten in the beginning of her cruise, and that, too, by a merchantman; and so we threw out all our "light kites" to the wind, and gave her the studding-sails "alow and aloft." To make a long story short, we chased this ship nearly all night, and only came up with her a little before dawn; and when we did come up with her, she proved to be a Dane!*[26]

During the next five days, four more whaling schooners, the *Altamaha, Benjamin Tucker, Courser,* and *Virginia* became easy victims to the *Alabama*. While their ships were being burned, the crews were all paroled and sent pulling for shore in their own whaleboats. It was now September 17, and with a rising sea running, Semmes turned the *Alabama*'s head toward the northwest.

The next morning dawned cloudy, and with an increasing wind the *Alabama* began to pitch and roll as the lookouts gripped the rigging to keep from being flung overboard. After chasing a brig which turned out to be a Frenchman, another sail was sighted from the swaying masthead. *It was blowing half a gale of wind*, Semmes relates, *and it re-*

mained to be proved whether the Alabama was as much to be dreaded in rough whether as in smooth. ... I had the wind of the chase, and was thus enabled to run down upon her, with a flowing sheet. I held onto my topgallant sails, though the masts buckled, and bent as though the sticks would go over the side. The chase did the same.

Semmes was pleased. The *Alabama* sped across the turbulent waves like a racer, and within three hours the chase was within range of Armstrong's guns. The casting loose of a gun on the pitching and rolling deck of the Confederate cruiser was dangerous in the extreme, but Armstrong managed to get a shot off in the direction of the fleeing ship. It had the desired effect for she hoisted the U.S. colors, clawed up her topgallant sails, and hove to. She was the *Elisha Dunbar,* but by now the wind was whistling through the *Alabama's* wire rigging, and the ocean was boiling with angry waves. Semmes hesitated dispatching a boat to the captive, but recalled that he *had a set of gallant, and skillful young officers around me, who would dare anything I told them to dare, and some capital seamen, and with the assistance I could give that, by maneuvering the ship, I thought the thing could be managed.*

Sending two of his best boats with hand-picked crews, Semmes gave instructions to bring back, after dispatching her crew to the *Alabama,* only her chronometer and flag. Before returning, they were to burn her. The *Elisha Dunbar* became the only prize taken by the *Alabama* where Semmes did not examine the ship's papers prior to destroying it. By the time the boarding party reached the side of the *Alabama,* the *Elisha Dunbar* was a mass of flames. Semmes eloquently described the scene:

*This burning ship was a beautiful spectacle, the scene being wild and pic-turesque beyond description. The black clouds were mustering their forces in fearful array. Already the entire heavens had been overcast. The thunder be-gan to roll, and crash, and the lightening to leap from cloud to cloud in a thousand eccentric lines. The sea was in a tumult of rage; the winds howled, and the floods of rain descended. Amid this turmoil of the elements, the Dunbar, all in flames, and with disordered gear and unfurled canvas, lay rolling and tossing upon the sea. Now an ignited sail would fly away from a yard, and scud off before the gale; and now the yard itself, released from the control of the braces, would swing about wildly, as in the madness of despair, and then would drop into the sea. Finally the masts went by the board, and the hull rocked to and fro for a while, until it was filled with water, and the fire nearly quenched, when it settled to the bottom of the great deep, a victim to the pas-sions of man, and the fury of the elements.*[27]

In eleven days Semmes had captured and destroyed ten Northern whalers worth an estimated $232,000. Considering that Bulloch had spent $228,000 for the cruiser, she had paid for herself already. With the whaling season drawing to a close around the Azores, Semmes set a course for the stormy banks off the coast of Newfoundland. It had been a good beginning.

Though Semmes, Kell, and the other officers demanded strict obedience from the crew while they were on duty, life was not all hard work on the *Alabama*. In the evenings the rigid routine and incessant duties would be purposely relaxed, and the men would gather on the forecastle where music, boisterous songs, and laughter would echo across the dark ocean waters. Sometimes an extemporized "ballroom" would be set up; shot-racks, ropes and tackle would be moved out of the way, and with some playing the part of the ladies, high-stepping dancers would swirl across the *Alabama*'s deck.

Even for Semmes and his officers this was a time of relaxation. *It was my custom, on these occasions,* Semmes reflected, *to go forward on the bridge — a light structure spanning the deck, near amidships — which, in the twilight hours, was a sort of lounging place for the officers, and smoke my single cigar, and listen to whatever might be going on, almost as much amused as the sailors themselves. So rigid is the discipline of a ship of war, that the captain is necessarily much isolated from his officers. He messes alone, walks the quarter-deck alone, and rarely, during the hours of duty, exchanges, even with his first lieutenant, or officer of the deck, other conversation than such as relates to the ship, or the service she is upon. I felt exceedingly the irksomeness of my position, and was always glad of an opportunity to escape from it. On the "bridge," I could lay aside the "captain," gather my young officers around me, and indulge in some of the pleasures of social intercourse; taking care to tighten the reins gently, again, the next morning. When song was the order of the evening, after the more ambitious of the amateurs had delivered themselves of their solos and cantatas, the entertainment generally wound up with "Dixie," when the whole ship would be in an uproar of enthusiasm, sometimes as many as a hundred voices joining in the chorus; the unenthusiastic Englishman, the stolid Dutchman, the mercurial Frenchman, the grave Spaniard, and even the serious Malyan, all joining in the inspiring refrain, — "We'll live and die in Dixie!"*[28]

At 8:00 p.m., all merriment came to an abrupt end as the shrill cry of the boatswain's whistle pierced the night, and the call was heard for the port and starboard watches to report to their stations. ...*Pretty soon,* Semmes continued, *the watch, which was off duty, would "tumble" below to their hammocks, and the midshipmen would be seen coming forward from the quarter-deck, with lantern and watch-bill in hand, to muster the watch whose turn it was to be on deck. The most profound stillness now reigned on board during the remainder of the night, only broken by the necessary orders and movements, in making or taking in sail, or it may be, by the whistling of the gale, and the surging of the sea, or the cry of the look-outs, at their posts, every half hour.*[29]

The *Alabama* continued to fight its way westward against gale-force winds and surging seas until, when about 200 miles from Newfoundland on October 3, two ships were seen approaching from dead ahead. They were the *Brilliant* and the *Emily Farnum* out of New York, heavily laden with flour and grain for the mills of London and Liverpool. As the two vessels were about to pass, the *Alabama* wheeled around, fired a gun, and hoisted the Confederate colors. The two merchantmen, knowing there was no escape, rounded into the wind and resigned themselves to their fate. The *Emily Farnum's* papers documented her cargo as definitely being owned by neutrals and Semmes placed her on ransom bond and unloaded on her all his prisoners, including the crew of the *Brilliant*. The *Brilliant* was not so fortunate, and she was soon a mass of flames.[30]

On October 7, two more ships loaded with flour and grain for the English market were intercepted and captured. After taking what supplies they needed from the 409-ton bark *Wave Crest* out of New York, Semmes gave his gunners some target practice and then burned her. Continuing westward toward the northeast coast of the U.S., the 293-ton brig *Dunkirk* was spotted, and after several hours of a moonlight chase, she too was captured and destroyed. Found among the crew of the *Dunkirk* was a seaman, George Forrest, who had deserted from the *Sumter* when it was at Cadiz. A court-martial convened the next morning, and Forrest, who had been placed in double irons, was sentenced to be dishonorably discharged from the Confederate navy and ordered to serve during the remainder of the *Alabama's* cruise without pay. Forrest probably felt fortunate that he was not sentenced to be hanged.[31]

While the court-martial was in progress, the 1,300-ton *Tonawanda*, loaded with grain and 75 passengers, was chased and captured. Not having room on board the *Alabama* for the *Tonawanda's* crew and passengers, Semmes placed the prisoners from the *Wave Crest, Dunkirk,* and the *Manchester,* (which had been captured on the 11th) on board her and released her on a $80,000 bond. Two crew men enlisted from the *Tonawanda,* one of whom was David White, a 17-year-old slave from Delaware who was accompanying his master on a voyage to Europe. Considering White the property of an enemy, Semmes brought him on board and assigned him to duty as a wardroom mess steward. White's name was entered on the books of the *Alabama* as a crew member and he was given the pay that his grade demanded. Lieutenant Sinclair fondly remembered David White:

*Dave became a great favorite with the officers, his willing, obliging manners, cheerful disposition, and untiring attention winning for him the affection of not only the officers, but of the entire ship's company. ... It was his privilege to go on shore with the ward-room steward to market; and on all occasions the American consul or his satellites would use all their eloquence to persuade Dave to desert his ship, reminding him of his present condition of slavery and the chance presented of throwing off his shackles, but Dave remained loyal in the face of all temptation.*[32]

David White, after performing his duties faithfully, drowned when the *Alabama* went down off Cherbourg.

On October 15, with a rising sea and winds approaching gale force, the bark *Lamplighter* was intercepted and boarded. She proved to be an American vessel on her way from New York to Gibraltar with a cargo of tobacco. After removing the crew and setting her on fire, the boarding party barely made it back to the heaving deck of the *Alabama*. *For the next few days,* Semmes wrote, *we had as much as we could do to take care of ourselves, without thinking of the enemy, or his ships.*[33]

On the morning of October 16, the barometer began to fall steadily, and gale-force winds built rapidly to hurricane force. Semmes explained the hasty preparations that took place to prepare the *Alabama* for the storm: *We had been under short sail before, but we now took the close reefs in the topsails, which tied them down to about one third of their original size, got up, and bent the main storm-sail, which was made of the stoutest No. 1 canvas, and scarcely larger than a pocket handkerchief, swung in the quarter-boats, and passed additional lashings around them; and, in short, made all the requisite preparations for the battle with the elements which awaited us.*[34]

Sinclair gives a vivid, and frightening, description of the fierceness of the storm as it battered the *Alabama*: *Its fury was so great that no sea could get up, the ocean surface having the appearance rather of a mill-stream. The air was white with "spoon-drift," giving the appearance of a heavy snowstorm. The officers and men were cowering under the weather bulwarks, or lashed at important stations. The wheel doubly manned, and in spite of this precaution it at one time, during the violent laboring of the vessel, got away from control, and, with a whirl, threw a man completely over it to leeward. For two hours this mad play of the ocean devils continued. The dark green clouds nearly met the water, twisting and squirming between each other like snakes or loathsome reptiles as the whirlwinds direct them in their play.*[35]

The *Alabama* was pushed over so far that her lee guns were hidden beneath the waves and the lee quarter-boats, in spite of the extra lashings, were twisted from their devits and smashed to pieces. Though groaning as if in agony, her hull was holding tight and very little water was finding its way into her hold. Lifelines had been stretched across the deck fore and aft to prevent the men from being swept overboard and it was all each man could do to look out for himself.

With the barometer hovering at 28.64, it suddenly became deathly calm and Semmes knew, *... that we were in the terrible vortex of a cyclone, from which so few mariners have ever escaped to tell the tale! ... The ship,* *which had been pressed over only a moment before by the fury of the gale as described, had now righted,* Semmes continued, *and the heavy storm staysail, which, notwithstanding its diminutive size, had required two stout tackles to confine it to the deck, was now, for want of wind to keep it steady, jerking these tackles about as though it would snap them to pieces, as the ship rolled to and fro! The aspect of the heavens was appalling. The clouds were writhing and twisting, like so many huge serpents engaged in combat, and hung so low, in the thin air of the vortex, as almost touch our mastheads. ... The waves seemed now, in the diminished pressure of the atmosphere in the vortex, to jut into the sky, and assume a conical shape — (and) were dancing an infernal reel, played by some necromancer. They were not running in any given direction, there being no longer any wind to drive them, but were jostling each other, like drunken men in a crowd, and threatening every moment, to topple one upon the other.*[36]

With pocket watch in hand, Semmes timed the passing of the vortex. In exactly 30 minutes the fury began anew. The men of the *Alabama* could see it coming, — a giant black wall of torrential rain driven by horrific winds which whipped the waves into sheets of blinding spray. Again, the *Alabama* was blown over until her quivering masts were almost lying on the waves. *It was impossible to raise one's head above the rail,* Semmes recounted, *and difficult to breath for a few seconds. We could do nothing but cower under the weather bulwarks, and hold on to the belaying pins, or whatever other objects presented themselves, to prevent being dashed to leeward, or swept overboard. The gale raged, now, precisely as long as it had done before we entered the vortex — two hours — showing how accurately Nature had drawn her circle.*[37]

For the next several days, the *Alabama* was tossed about on the rough seas which followed in the track of the storm, while the men went about repairing the damage. Promptly, the shredded sails were replaced, the broken main-yard spliced, and the guns put in order; and presently was heard the cry from the mast-head, "Sail Ho!"[38]

It was now October 23, and to the northwest a large ship was spotted running before the wind and approaching the *Alabama* at great speed. Semmes called Master's Mate James Evans to his side and asked him to take a look at the distant oncoming vessel. Evans had been a pilot out of Savannah and had become an expert in identifying the nationalities of the ships that were sighted. Lowering his marine glass, Evans said, "She is a Yankee, sir," and with the firing of a blank cartridge, the *Lafayette* out of New York, loaded with grain for the Irish market, was brought to the wind. Her papers indicated her cargo was owned by neutrals but Semmes pronounced them fraudulent and the ship was burned. From this period on, Semmes was to find that almost every American merchantman attempted to protect his cargo by bogus certificates of ownership.[39]

During the remainder of October, three more vessels were added to the growing list of victims. Now, however, while only 250 miles off the coast of New York, the *Alabama* was down to only four days supply of coal and Semmes ordered her course set to the south. Upon leaving the *Agrippina* in the Azores, Semmes had ordered her captain, Robert McQueen, to rendezvous with him at Fort-de-France on the island of Martinique, and it was toward this island in the Caribbean that the *Alabama* now set her course.

As the *Alabama* sailed south, Bermuda was passed on November 5, and two more vessels were boarded and destroyed. One of these was the 599-ton *Thomas B. Wales*, an East India trader from Calcutta bound to Boston with a cargo of jute, linseed, and 1,704 bags of saltpeter. Semmes was confident that the saltpeter was destined for the powder mills of the North, and with no hesitation, applied the torch. The *T. B. Wales* was a fortunate capture in several respects. Eleven seamen volunteered for enlistment on the *Alabama* bringing her complement to 110 which was just ten short of a full crew. Now all her guns could be manned at one time. In addition, several of the *Wales'* spars were almost an exact match for those damaged by the hurricane on the *Alabama*, and these were quickly appropriated and put in place. On board the prize was George H. Fairchild, the U.S. Counsel to Mauritius, his wife, and three young daughters. Brought on board the *Alabama*, the ladies soon made themselves very much at home among Semmes' handsome officers. After the war, when Semmes was arrested for "war crimes," Fairchild voluntarily testified on his behalf, and the charges of inhuman treatment were dismissed.[40]

November 16 found the *Alabama* approaching the island of Dominica on her way to Martinique. Preparations had been made on board the *Alabama* to enter the French-governing port of Fort-de-France, and Semmes describes the result: *It is Sunday, and muster-day, and the Alabama has once more been put in perfect order. She has had a coat of paint, inside and out, her masts have been freshly scraped, and her rigging re-rattled, and tarred down. Her guns are glistening in the new coat of "composition" which the gunner and his mates have put upon them; her engine-room is all aglow with burnished brass and steel; her decks are white and sweet, and her awnings are spread. The muster is over, the men are lying listlessly about the decks, and our lady passengers are comfortably seated on the quarter-deck, with several of the young officers around them, and with the children playing at their feet. Such was the contrast which the Alabama presented, on that quiet Sabbath day, with her former self only a few weeks back, when we had been rolling and tumbling in the Gulf Stream, with crippled yards, torn sails,*

Sketch appeared in *Harper's Weekly*

A romantic drawing by Winslow Homer depicting the fear and trepidation among the passengers of a Northern merchant vessel upon sighting the *Alabama*.

*and her now bright sides seamed and defaced with iron rust from her corroding chains.*[38]

Two days later found the *Alabama* passing through the Dominica Channel, and Semmes ordered steam raised and the propeller lowered. About 10:00 a.m. she steamed into the harbor of Fort-de-France, the first port she had seen since leaving Terceira in the Azores, and dropped anchor. Anchored nearby was the *Agrippina*, heavily laden with a full cargo of English coal.

Sending Kell on a courtesy call to French Admiral Conde', who was governor of the island, Semmes began unloading his prisoners and sent his paymaster along with David White into the city for fresh provisions. Shortly, however, Kell returned on board with some discomforting news. The governor had informed him that McQueen of the *Agrippina*, influenced by a readily consumed bottle of whiskey, had told everyone within hearing distance for what ship he was waiting. The admiral suggested that Semmes move the *Alabama* under the protection of the guns of the French fort in case American warships should arrive. The *Agrippina* had been in port for eight days, and Semmes could not risk coaling at Martinique now. Reprimanding McQueen for his indiscretion, Semmes ordered him to leave Martinique immediately and meet him at the desolate island of Blanquilla farther to the south.

Meanwhile, the *Alabama*'s decks were soon crowded with curious Frenchmen who came on board eager to get a look at the famous "pirate" ship and her "pirate" captain. Semmes was amused at their display of disappointment as they were shown around the pristine ship by his dashing and smartly uniformed officers. During the afternoon, native "bum-boats" surrounded the *Alabama* and a brisk trade ensued between the islanders and the crew. Fruit, tobacco and pipes were especially sought after, as well as one other commodity. Seaman Forrest, who was still serving his sentence on board, managed to obtain a supply of rum and distributed it secretly among some of the crew.

Early in the evening a disturbance was heard on the forecastle, and Kell went forward to investigate, only to be met by curses and a hurled belaying pin which barely missed his head. A score of the crew were drunk and Kell, standing his ground, ordered other crew members to seize them, but no one moved. Shortly, Semmes arrived on deck and seeing that the men were armed only with sheath-knives and belaying-pins, and all his officers well armed with revolvers, he turned to his first lieutenant and said, "Mr. Kell, give the order to beat to quarters." The months of training and discipline paid dividends when at the sound of the fife and drum, the men instinctively stumbled to their stations. With the men standing at rigid attention at their guns, Semmes and Kell slowly moved among them eyeing each one carefully as they passed. When an intoxicated man was found, Semmes had him seized and put in double irons. Twenty men were identified in this manner and Semmes ordered them taken to the gangway and doused with buckets of sea water. At first, they laughed, cursed and chided those heaving the buckets, but after two hours of non-stop dousing, coughing and sputtering, they begged for mercy. With their irons removed, they were permitted to go below to "sleep it off," while Semmes ordered Kell to sound the retreat, and the rest of the crew was finally allowed to stand down from their stations. For the ringleader, Forrest, there was no such reprieve. Semmes ordered him "spread eagled" in the rigging for periods of four hours at a time.[42]

The *Alabama's* commander wrote that this was the first and only "mutiny" on board the Confederate cruiser and that ... *It became a saying afterward among the sailors, that "Old Beeswax was h-ll upon watering a fellow's grog."*[43]

McQueen's loose tongue had reached the ears of Federal authorities on the island, and the next morning the USS *San Jacinto* arrived and blockaded the harbor. The Union ship carried a battery of fourteen 11-inch guns and was more than a match for the *Alabama*, and Semmes contented himself by watching her make preparations for snaring him when he tried to escape. That night it became cloudy, and rain began to fall. Building steam, Semmes raised the anchor and steamed out of Fort-de-France with no lights showing and no glimpse of the *San Jacinto*. It was not until the next morning that the Federal captain discovered that the *Alabama* was gone.[44]

On November 21, the *Alabama* overtook the *Agrippina*, and together they continued on to an anchorage off the beach of Blanquilla. Inhabited only by a small herd of goats, Blanquilla was a sandy coral island a few miles off the coast of Venezuela. Semmes was surprised, as they dropped anchor, to see an American whaling vessel lying close to the beach, and her captain, seeing the U.S. colors at the *Alabama's* mast, rowed over to pay a visit. Once on board, the captain expressed how pleased he was to have this sparkling "U.S. gunboat" in the area to protect him, and that she was just the ship to "give the pirate Semmes fits." The "Pirate Semmes" then gently informed him of his true identity and wrote later that, *A terrible collapse awaited him. ... An awful vision seemed to confront him. His little Schooner, and his oil, and the various little ventures which he had on board, ... were all gone up the spout! And then he stood in the presence of the man whose ship he had characterized as a "pirate," and whom he had told to his face, he was no better than a freebooter.* Semmes assured the frightened captain that because they were both in Venezuelan territorial waters, neither he nor his vessel would be harmed.[45]

With the coaling operations continuing, Semmes settled his account with Seaman Forrest. He was banished to the island with only the clothes on his back where in the coming days, in desperation, he joined the crew of the whaling schooner.

With all hands not needed for the coaling, part of the crew were issued arms for hunting and given liberty on the island where there was an abundance of everything except rum. Unknown to Semmes, however, was the great sport the sailors found in shooting the farmers' goats. It was probably a good thing that "Old Beeswax" never found out.[46]

With coaling completed, Semmes weighed anchor and set his course for the Windward Passage, a shipping lane between Cuba and Haiti. He hoped to capture a clipper ship inbound from California loaded with gold for the U.S. mint. Newspapers that Semmes had taken from his prizes illustrated the extent to which he was hurting the Northern commerce. The *New York Shipping and Commercial List* for October 8th noted that "Vessels under foreign flags command higher rates, in consequence of the reported seizure and destruction of American vessels by the Rebel Steamer 290." Another issue of this paper noted that shipments were being made almost entirely in foreign bottoms, "American vessels being in disfavor."[47]

Not finding the California treasure ship, but overtaking and destroying three other vessels along the way, the *Alabama* arrived at the desolate Las Arcas Islands off the Yucatan peninsula on December 22. Here she remained during the latter days of December, while details from her crew were busy coaling, painting, and caulking. Semmes described this desolate island paradise as the year 1862 slipped away: *The naturalist would have reveled at the Arcas, in viewing the debris of sea-shell, and coral, and the remains of stranded fish, that lay strewn along the beach; and in watching the habits of the gannet, man-of-war bird and a great variety of the sea-gull, all of which were laying, and incubating. As the keel of one of our boats would grate upon the sand, clouds of these birds would fly up, and circle around our heads, screaming in their various and discordant notes at our intrusion. Beneath our feet, the whole surface of the islands was covered with eggs, or with young birds, in various stages of growth. Here, as at Blanquilla, all our boats were hoisted out, and rigged for sailing; and fishing, and turtling parties were sent out to supply the crew, and in the evening sailing and swimming matches, and target-shooting took place. This was only the by-play, however, whilst the main work of the drama was going forward, viz., the coaling, and preparations of the Alabama for her dash at the enemy.*[48]

The Greyhound of the seas was indeed about to make "her dash at the enemy," as Semmes had a reason other than enemy commerce for being in the Gulf of Mexico. It concerned a pompous Massachusetts general and an expedition that was about to sail for Galveston, Texas.

# *Chapter Six*

## From Galveston to Cape Town

Northern newspapers, found on several prizes seized by the *Alabama*, had spelled out, in great detail, the plans for the sailing of a large expeditionary force with the intent of invading Texas. This force, led by General Nathaniel P. Banks, was to consist of 30,000 troops transported in 100 transports, and was scheduled to arrive off Union-held Galveston, according to the papers, on January 10, 1863. No Federal warships were being dispatched with the invading force, for Union authorities felt there was little danger of interference by Confederate naval forces. Semmes' plan was to surprise the transports in a night attack, steam through their midst firing at every target, and then make his escape.[1]

On January 5, the *Alabama* left the pristine waters and island paradise of Las Arcas off the Yucatan and headed north. Semmes felt confident of success: *We had an abundant supply of coal on board, the ship was in excellent trim, and as the sailors used to say of her, at this period, could be made to do anything but "talk." My crew were well drilled, my powder was in good condition, and as to the rest, I trusted to luck, and to the "creek's not being too high."*[2]

Semmes allowed five days of easy sailing to reach the Texas coast and at about mid-day on the 11th, the cry of "Land Ho" came from the masthead. Instead of an immense fleet of transports, the lookouts re-

96

ported within a few minutes, five steamers in sight which looked suspiciously like men-of-war. *Here was a damper!* Semmes exclaimed, *What could have become of Banks, and his great expedition, and what was this squadron of stream ships-of-war doing here?* Presently, a distant shell, fired by one of the Federal steamers was seen to explode over Galveston. Semmes reasoned that the city must have been recaptured by the Confederates, for Union forces surely would not be shelling their own troops. General Magruder's forces had, indeed, recaptured Galveston on January 1, and Bank's expedition was forced to stop at New Orleans.

As the officers and men on the *Alabama* continued to watch, the lookout called down from the masthead, *One of the steamers, sir, is coming out in chase of us.* The steamer that pulled away from the Union fleet to investigate the "suspicious sail" to the southeast was the iron side-wheel steamer USS *Hatteras* commanded by Lieutenant Homer C. Blake. The *Hatteras* was a converted Delaware River passenger steamer of 1,126 tons and carried four 32-pounders, two 30-pounder rifles, one 20-pounder rifle, and one 12-pounder howitzer. Though her armament was respectable, her engines were exposed and unprotected above deck, and her immense side-wheels were vulnerable to enemy fire. Slower than the *Alabama* as well, she would prove to be no match for the Confederate cruiser.[3]

Semmes ordered the *Alabama* to sail slowly away from the distant oncoming Federal, and at the same time called the engine room and ordered steam raised and the propeller lowered. His plan was to draw the Union ship away from the rest of the fleet and delay the action until darkness. As evening approached, the crew, excited by the impending contest, was already at their stations with guns loaded and lock-strings in hand. In the fading light the pursuing Federal warship was still visible off the stern, black smoke pouring from her stacks and her side-wheels churning the Gulf waters, as she strove to catch the *Alabama*.

*At length, when I judged that I had drawn the stranger out about twenty miles from his fleet,* Semmes wrote, *I furled my sails, beat to quarters, prepared my ship for action, and wheeled to meet him. The two ships now approached each other, very rapidly. As we came within speaking distance, we simultaneously stopped our engines, the ships being about one hundred yards apart. The enemy was the first to hail. "What ship is that?" cried he. "This is her Britannic Majesty's steamer 'Petrel',"* we replied. *We now hailed in turn, and demanded to know who he was. The reply not coming to us very distinctly, we repeated our request, when we heard the words, "This is the United States ship ———" the name of the ship being lost to us. But we had heard enough. All we wanted to know was, that the stranger was a United States ship, and therefore our enemy. ... Presently, the stranger hailed again, and said, "If you please, I will send a boat on board you." ... We replied, "Cer-*

*tainly, we shall be happy to receive your boat;" and we heard a boatswain's mate call away a boat, and could hear the creaking of the tackles, as she was lowered into the water.*

The deception could not be carried on much longer. I turned to my first lieutenant, Semmes continued, *and said, "I suppose you are all ready for action?" "We are," he replied; "the men are eager to begin, and are only waiting for the word." I then said to him, "Tell the enemy who we are, for we must not strike him in disguise, and when you have done so give him the broadside." Kell now sang out, in his powerful, clarion voice, through the trumpet, "This is the Confederate States steamer 'Alabama'!" and turning to the crew, who were all standing at their guns — the gunners with their sights on the enemy, and lock-strings in hand — gave the order, fire!* [4]

The *Alabama* shook and trembled as her five heavy guns roared in unison into the night. Flames enveloped her graceful hull, lighting the Confederate cruiser up like a volcano, as five deadly shells streaked toward the *Hatteras*. The Federal sailors, also standing ready at their guns, returned the fire in an instant, and the peaceful Gulf air was rent with the deafening sound of bellowing cannon and bursting shells. The two ships were now steaming parallel to each other, the distance varying between 40 and 100 yards. Semmes' men were quickly re-loading and soon, one by one, each of her guns fired again sending their destructive missiles crashing into the already battered *Hatteras*. Iron fragments flew from the Federal's hull as the *Alabama's*'s shells exploded low against her side. At times, when the vessels drew near each other, the crack of musket and pistol shots could be heard above the roar of the heavy guns. Again and again, the *Alabama's*'s guns thundered at the enemy, while the *Hatteras* bravely returned her fire, though many of the Federal's shots were aimed high.

Within a very few minutes, the *Hatteras* was in serious trouble. One of the *Alabama's* shells crashed through her side and exploded with a dull roar in her hold, setting the ship on fire. Within seconds, another shell tore through her sick bay and exploded in an adjoining compartment igniting another fire. With great sheets of iron plate ripped from her side, water was pouring into her in unstoppable torrents causing her to list to port. Another shell exploded in her boiler, and scalding steam filled the engine room as her giant side-wheels slowly came to a stop.

The *Hatteras* was on fire in two places. Her engines were disabled, her pumps could not be run for lack of steam, and her hold was quickly filling with water. Lieutenant Blake, realizing the *Hatteras* was rapidly sinking, ordered the magazine flooded to prevent an explosion, hoisted a light to the masthead, and had a lee gun fired as a token of surrender. It had been only thirteen minutes since the *Alabama's* guns fired their first salvo.

The CSS *Alabama* sinks the *Hatteras*. Engraving incorrectly depicts the two vessels steaming in opposite directions.

Semmes, who had been directing the action standing on the horse-block, shouted: *Mr. Kell, the enemy has fired a gun to leeward; cease firing!* The *Alabama* now steamed close to the *Hatteras*, and Kell inquired of Blake if he had surrendered and did he need assistance. Receiving an affirmative answer to both questions, and seeing the Union ship was settling rapidly by the bow, Kell gave the order, *All hands out (with) boats to save life.*[6]

Within 45 minutes, all seventeen officers and 101 men of the *Hatteras* had been rescued and brought safely to the deck of the *Alabama*. Two minutes after Blake left his ship, she slipped beneath the dark waters of the Gulf. Two men on the *Hatteras* had been killed and five wounded, while six men, who were in the lowered boat when the action began, escaped to the Federal fleet offshore.[7] It had been a remarkably easy and bloodless victory for the *Alabama*, with only one of her crew being slightly injured, and only seven minor hits along her starboard side. Master's Mate George T. Fullam described the *Alabama's* damage: *One shot struck under the counter, penetrating as far as a timber, then glancing off. A second struck the funnel, a third going through the side, across the berth deck and into the opposite side, another raising the deuce in the lamp room, and the others lodging in the coal bunkers ... the enemy's fire being chiefly to our stern, the shots flying pretty thick over the quarter-deck near to where our captain was standing. As they came whizzing over him, he with usual coolness, would exclaim, "Give it to the rascals;" "Aim low men;" "Don't be all night sinking that fellow."*[8]

As the other Union warships hurried in the direction of the gun flashes on the dark horizon, the *Alabama* with all lights extinguished, steamed away to the southeast leaving an empty ocean behind her.

With the *Alabama's* decks crowded with prisoners and her cabins overflowing with Federal officers, Semmes set a course for Kingston, Jamaica. The passage was rough and stormy — the Confederate cruiser being buffeted by one southerly gale after another. Lieutenant Sinclair describes this tiring voyage: *The weather soon after leaving the coast sets in squally with rain, the wind veering ahead. We let steam go down, and battle with it under sail. This is bad, as we have in prisoners a force fully equal to our own, and though on parole, we are anxious to land them as quickly as possible. The strict watch kept over them is very wearing to officers and men, who must sleep at all times on their arms.*[9]

It took nine days to reach the west coast of Jamaica, and along the way the *Alabama* chased a sail which turned out to be McQueen and the *Agrippina*. Hoisting the Stars and Bars, Semmes sailed by without revealing the connection between the two ships to the Federal prisoners on board. On January 20, the storm-tossed *Alabama* finally entered the harbor of Port Royal at Kingston and dropped her anchor.[10]

Semmes' first order of business, after a courtesy call to the local authorities, was to land his prisoners in care of the American consul. With this accomplished, the *Alabama* was again inundated with curious visitors, only this time they were officers from Her Britannic Majesty's English Squadron which was anchored in port. Soon a warm and cordial relationship developed as the *Alabama's* officers played host to the officers of the British fleet. Semmes, who had been feeling

*The Illustrated London News*

**The CSS *Alabama* in the harbor of Port Royal, Jamaica, after dropping off prisoners taken from the *Hatteras*.**

the strain of the past several months, accepted the invitation of an English friend to spend some time at his retreat in the mountains of the island, and turning the ship over to Kell, departed for four days of relaxation. Kell would have a busy time of it. With coaling in progress and carpenters and mechanics busy repairing the damage from the battle with the *Hatteras*, the officers remained on board, but the crew was given liberty one watch at a time. Soon, Confederate sailors in various stages of intoxication were making the rounds of all the bars and dance halls in the town arm and arm with the tars from the British fleet. Many "adopted" the destitute Federal sailors from the *Hatteras* who had lost all their funds, and soon "Yankees" and "Rebels" could be seen making the rounds together, with the gray clad sailors paying the bill![11]

Semmes returned on January 24 to find the *Alabama* coaled, the repairs completed, and Lieutenant Kell and the other officers trying to scrape the crew out of the bars and brothels of Kingston. Lieutenant Sinclair explained how ... *officers with armed boat's crews are scouring the streets and dens. One is reminded of the old problem of ferrying over the river the goose, the fox, and the bag of corn; for no sooner is one lot delivered at the boat and another raid made up-town, than the prisoners break guard somehow and are up-town again.* Sinclair, attempting to enter a dance hall to look for his men, was stopped at the door where ... *One of the ladies remarked, "Say, middy, come some other time. The tickets are limited at this ball; and besides, the company is select!" "Tell old 'Beeswax,'" said another persuasive maiden, "your old piratical skipper, to go to sea, burn some more Yankee ships, and come back. We'll give up the boys then, and you shall have your turn." It took much diplomacy to carry our point; and it was only accomplished by reasoning most earnestly with the soberer of the crew, and a generous amount (on my part) of treating among the fair hosts.*

As the boatloads of frolicking sailors arrived at the *Alabama's* gangway, those who were especially drunk were placed in single irons and hustled below. Finally, everyone was on board with the exception of seven men who could not be found, and on the evening of the 25th, the *Alabama* steamed out of Kingston and set her course for the coast of Brazil. The seven trained men would be missed, and they were listed as deserters on the ship's rolls, but this was really a misnomer. Sinclair explained that they would no doubt awaken from their drunken state to find that their ship had sailed, their accumulation of pay gone, *and (their) 'quasi' friends knowing them no more.*[12]

The day after leaving Kingston the *Alabama* stopped the 255-ton bark *Golden Rule* loaded with a cargo of food and medicine for the Panama Railroad Company and the Pacific Mail Steamship Company. Finding no absolute proof of neutral ownership of her cargo among the ship's papers, Semmes transferred the crew to the *Alabama* and set the *Golden Rule* ablaze. Within two days, the brig *Chastelaine* of Boston was also captured and suffered a similar fate.

With two additional crews on board, Semmes made a quick stop at Santo Domingo, dropped off his prisoners, and sailed on the morning of January 29, for the Mona Passage.

On Sunday, February 1, Semmes held the first muster since leaving Jamaica. *We had been out now a week,* he explained, *and in that time I had gotten my crew straightened up again. The rum had pretty well worked out of them; most of the black rings around the eyes had disappeared, and beards had been trimmed, and heads combed. The court-martial which had been trying the few culprits, that had been retained for trial, had gotten through its labors, and been dissolved, and Jack, as he answered to his name, and walked around the capstan, was "himself again," in all the glory of white "ducks," polished shoes, straw hats, and streaming ribbons.*

During the month of February, only four prizes were captured: the *Palmetto*, the *Golden Eagle*, the *Olive Jane* and the *Washington*. The *Olive Jane* was loaded with casks of wine and brandy bound for New York, and Semmes, not giving his thirsty crew the opportunity to smuggle any on board, took nothing from her but immediately set the ship on fire. The *Washington*, out of New York, was loaded with fertilizer which was owned by Peruvian agents in Antwerp, so a disappointed Semmes bonded the vessel for $50,000, and after unloading his prisoners, allowed her to continue.[13]

The *Alabama* had now crossed the 30th parallel and stood, as Semmes described it, "like a toll-gate" for all the ships that had rounded the Capes and were plodding northward. At times as many as seven or eight sails would be in sight at one time.

As daylight approached on the morning of March 1, a ship was discovered not more than a half mile away. Without disturbing the morning scrubbing of the *Alabama*'s decks, the 1,047-ton *John A. Parks*, laden with a cargo of lumber, was easily captured. The *Alabama*'s carpenter, ecstatic over finding a prize loaded with lumber, appropriated what was needed, and then the ship was destroyed. The *John A. Parks* also supplied a piece of exciting information. From newspapers found on board, Semmes learned that he was no longer the only Confederate cruiser prowling the oceans; the CSS *Florida*, under the command of John Newland Maffitt, had escaped from Mobile on January 16. While the Northern merchant ship was burning, a passing English bark was hailed and agreed to take all of the *Alabama*'s prisoners.[14]

As the *Alabama* approached the equator, the weather began to deteriorate with squalls and rain showers bringing the line of sight for the lookouts down to just a few miles. The night of March 15 was especially thick and murky with low visibility, when a few minutes after mid-night, the lookout suddenly cried, "Sail ho! Close aboard!" Within a few minutes a ship sailed by like a ghost headed in the opposite direction; the only light visible being the one in the binnacle. Quickly, the *Alabama* turned to take up the pursuit, but by then the prey was almost out of sight. *Both ships were on a wind, however,* Semmes explained, *and this ... was the Alabama's best point of sailing. Our night-glasses soon began to tell the usual tale. We were overhauling the chase; and at quarter past three, or a little before dawn, we were near enough to heave her to with a gun.*

She proved to be the *Punjab* of Boston, bound from Calcutta to London with a properly certificated English cargo of jute and linseed oil. Semmes unloaded what few prisoners he had on board and released her on a ransom-bond.[15]

During the remainder of March, four ships were taken: the *Morning Star*, the *Kingfisher*, the *Nora*, and the *Charles Hill*. The *Morning Star's* cargo proved to be properly certificated as belonging to a neutral so she was bonded and released for $61,750. The whaling schooner *Kingfisher* was not as fortunate, however, and was promptly set ablaze. The *Charles Hill* and the *Nora*, both from Boston out of Liverpool, were also found to be carrying Northern-owned cargo, and they, too, were burned.[16]

On the 29th, the *Alabama* crossed the Equator and continued south along the coast of Brazil. Five days later she was still groping her way through thick and rainy weather when, ... *During the morning watch,* Semmes wrote, *the dense clouds lifted for a while, and showed us a fine, tall ship steering, like ourselves, to the southward. We immediately made sail in chase. The wind was blowing quite fresh from the southwest at the time, and we gained very rapidly upon the stranger. At twelve o'clock the wind died away, and the heavy rains being renewed, she was entirely shut out from view. We continued the chase all day; now being sure of her, and now being baffled by the ever shifting clouds, and changing wind and weather.*[17]

With darkness approaching and the wind having died away, Semmes dispatched a boat whose crew boarded the becalmed vessel. She proved to be the *Louisa Hatch* of Rockford, Maine and was loaded with a 1,100-ton cargo of Welsh smokeless coal. Semmes had been heading for the island of Fernando de Noronha and had informed McQueen of the *Agrippina*, prior to their departure from Las Arcas, that he was to meet him there. Not entirely trusting the old Scottish captain, Semmes decided to put a prize crew on the *Hatch* and take her with him in case the *Agrippina* did not make the rendezvous. It was a fortuitous decision, for McQueen had sold his load of coal, pocketed the money, and returned to England with, as Semmes related, "some cock and bull story."

On April 10, the *Alabama* and the *Louisa Hatch* dropped anchors in the open roadstead of Fernando de Noronha, a rugged and rocky island used as a penal colony by Brazil. Presenting his compliments to the governor, Semmes began transferring 300 tons of coal from the *Hatch* to the *Alabama*. With the governor enjoying the visit of the famous Confederate cruiser, little attention was paid to the fact that Semmes, in violation of Brazilian neutrality, had brought a prize into port.[18]

On April 15, two American whalers anchored approximately five miles out, and lowering a boat, soon pulled along side the *Louisa Hatch*. Master's Mate Fullam, who was in his shirt sleeves with no uniform being visible, met them at the rail, and the whalers, pointing to the *Alabama*, wanted to know "what steamer was that?" Fullam told them it was a Brazilian packet-steamer, but suddenly, with a splashing of oars, the whalers began rowing frantically for their ships. Looking around, Fullam discovered the reason: a small Confederate flag, a boat ensign, had been thrown over the spanker-boom to dry and a puff of wind had billowed out the folds. The "Brazilian packet-steamer" raised steam and easily captured both whalers. Soon the *Lafayette* and the *Kate Cory* were in flames, and after transferring his prisoners to a Brazilian schooner, the *Louisa Hatch* was also burned.[19]

Giving up all hope of ever seeing the *Agrippina* again, Semmes put to sea on April 22, 1863, and before the month was out, he had resumed his war against Northern commerce. On May 3, cruising off Bahia (present day Salvador), Brazil, two more American merchant ships, the *Sea Lark* of New York bound for San Francisco, and the *Union Jack* out of Boston bound for Shanghai, were intercepted and captured. On board the *Union Jack* were several lady passengers who were transferred to the *Alabama* by a "whip," which was similar to a boatswain's chair, which was slung between the yardarms of the two ships. One of the ladies, an Irish servant, was livid with rage and denounced Semmes to his face calling him a "Rebel" and a "Pirate," and Semmes was forced to order a bucket of water dashed on her to calm her down.[20]

With the crews of four prizes on board, the *Alabama's* decks were becoming especially crowded, and Semmes resolved to run into Bahia and unload them in care of the Brazilian authorities. On May 11, at 5:00 p.m., the *Alabama* arrived at this second largest city on the coast of Brazil and dropped anchor. The harbor was crowded with vessels, but the only warship present was a Portuguese man-of-war. The next morning, after gaining permission from the local governor, Semmes landed his prisoners, which numbered close to 100, and taking on a few boatloads of coal and various other provisions, allowed the crew to go on liberty.[21]

Early on the morning of the May 13, the *Alabama's* watch reported that a strange steamer had entered the harbor and anchored during the night. Semmes ordered the Confederate flag hoisted to the *Alabama's* peak and was pleasantly surprised to see the newly arrived steamer also hoist the Stars and Bars. Sending a boat, Semmes learned that she was the CSS *Georgia* under the command of an old friend, Lieutenant William L. Maury. The *Georgia* had been purchased in England by Maury's cousin, Matthew F. Maury, outfitted off the coast of France, and commissioned as a Confederate cruiser on April 9, 1863. For the next four days while the *Georgia* loaded coal, the officers of the two Confederate cruisers exchanged visits, and, as guests of an English company, were taken on a railroad excursion into the interior.

During this time, a telegram was received informing them that the *Florida* had also arrived at Pernambuco farther up the coast and was busy re-coaling and taking on supplies. Lieutenant Sinclair, with a little "tongue in cheek," was justifiably proud of this moment: *We can straighten up now and put on airs, boast of the "Confederate Squadron of the South American Station," and await the arrival of any vessel of the enemy's navy in perfect security.* With the two Confederate cruisers in port and the *Florida* within telegraphic communications, Sinclair bubbled with enthusiasm: *We cannot avoid the felling of pride and satisfaction that our struggling little Confederacy has actually been able to overmatch the enemy in cruisers, at least for the time being, and put them on the defensive so far as the Brazilian coast goes.*[22]

Unknown to Sinclair and to the rest of the "Confederate Squadron" at Bahia, was the fact that there were actually four Confederate cruisers now prowling the oceans. On May 6, John Newland Maffitt of the *Florida* had commissioned one of his prizes as the Confederate cruiser CSS *Clarence*. Her commander, Lieutenant Charles W. Read, the dashing young officer from the destroyed ironclad CSS *Arkansas*, was at that moment busily burning American shipping along the Northern seaboard.

On the 21st, the *Alabama* steamed out of Bahia and headed south looking for any American vessels rounding Cape Horn. The *Georgia* would depart in a few days, and one year later, the *Florida*, in a gross violation of Brazilian neutrality, would be seized at Bahia by the Federal warship USS *Wachusett*. Within the next ten days, five vessels were overtaken including the 1,237-ton clipper *Talisman*, bound from New York to Shanghai. Part of the *Talisman's* cargo included four brass 12-pounder howitzers which Semmes would find useful later.[23]

Continuing to sail toward the south, the *Alabama* on June 20, intercepted the bark *Conrad* bound from Buenos Aires to New York with a cargo of wool. Semmes related that, ... *The Conrad being a tidy little bark, of about three hundred and fifty tons, with good sailing qualities, I resolved to commission her as a cruiser.* Assigning his boarding officer, Lieutenant John Low as her commander, and Midshipman George T. Sinclair as the first lieutenant, Semmes transferred two of the 12-pounders to the *Conrad* along with twenty rifles, a half dozen revolvers, and eleven crewmen. The next day at approximately 5:00 p.m., with little ceremony, the *Conrad* hoisted the Confederate flag and was commissioned the CSS *Tuscaloosa*. The crew of the *Alabama* climbed into the rigging, gave three hearty cheers, and Low and the *Tuscaloosa* set sail for their own cruise against American shipping. As the *Tuscaloosa's* sails faded over the distant horizon, Charles Read, thousands of miles to the north, was burning Northern merchant ships within sight of the Federal coast. Above the equator, Maffitt and the *Florida* were headed toward the Caribbean, leaving a smoking trail of burning ships behind, and Maury, with the *Georgia*, was also prowling the Atlantic. At this moment during the month of June, 1863, five Confederate cruisers were roving the high seas and putting the torch to anything flying a United States flag.

Semmes and the *Alabama* had been cruising the shipping lanes off the coast of South America now for almost three months, and it was time to think about leaving, for Secretary Welles and the Union Navy had had enough time to learn of his whereabouts. Enemy cruisers could be expected at any time. In addition, Semmes, weary and fighting a nagging fever, needed some well earned rest. Directly across the Atlantic was Cape Town, South Africa, and Semmes ordered the *Alabama* turned to the east.[24]

Shortly after setting the course for Cape Town, however, officers discovered that the ship's entire bread supply had been destroyed by weevils. Crossing the Atlantic without an adequate supply of fresh bread for the officers, the crew and any prisoners they might have on board, was out of the question. Semmes, seeing no alternative, reluctantly gave the order to turn about and head for Rio de Janeiro, 825 miles away. Fortune smiled on the *Alabama*, however, for on July 2, the *Anna F. Schmidt* was captured and included in her cargo was a thirty day's supply of fresh bread.

By 9:00 p.m. that evening, the *Schmidt* was a mass of flames and the *Alabama* was just beginning to pull away when, *a large, taunt ship, with exceedingly square yards,* Semmes explained, *passed us at rapid speed, under a cloud of canvas from rail to truck, and from her course seemed to be bound either to Europe or the United States.* The strange vessel paid no attention to the burning ship but sped past and was rapidly disappearing into the darkness by the time the *Alabama* could give chase. Semmes thought she might be one of the giant clipper ships that had just rounded the Horn, and eager to capture such a prize, ordered the propeller lowered and added steam to the power of the *Alabama's* sails.

*It was blowing half a gale of wind,* Semmes reported, *but the phantom ship, for such she looked by moonlight, was carrying her royals and top-gallant studding-sails. This confirmed my suspicion, for surely, I thought, no ship would risk carrying away her spars under such a press of sail, unless she were endeavoring to escape from an enemy. By the time we were well under way in pursuit, the stranger was about three miles ahead of us. I fired a gun to command him to halt. In a moment or two, to my astonishment, the sound of a gun from the stranger came booming back over the waters in response. I now felt quite sure that I had gotten hold of a New York and California clipper-ship. She had fired a gun to make me believe, probably, that she was a ship of war, and thus induce me to desist from pursuit. But a ship of war would not carry such a press of sail, or appear to be in such a hurry to get out of the way — unless, indeed, she were an enemy's ship of inferior force; and the size of the fugitive, in the present instance, forbade such a supposition.*

Although Semmes was concerned that he might have grabbed a "tiger by the tail," he resolved to continue the chase to determine the identity of this mysterious stranger. With the help of her engines, the *Alabama* pounded over the dark waters, her huge sails billowing in the moonlight. Semmes ... *sent orders below to the engineer, to stir up his fires, and put the Alabama at the top of her speed. My crew had all become so much excited by the chase, some of the sailors thinking we had scared up the "Flying Dutchman," who was known to cruise in these seas, and others expecting a fight, that the watch had forgotten to go below to their hammocks.*

She was fast, but the *Alabama* steadily gained on her. *About midnight,* Semmes continued, *we overhauled the stranger near enough to speak (to) her. She loomed up terribly large as we approached. She was painted black, with a white streak around her waist, man-of-war fashion, and we could count, with the aid of our night-glasses, five guns of a side frowning through her ports. "What ship is that?" now thundered my first lieutenant through his trumpet. "This is her Britannic Majesty's ship, Diomede!" came back in reply very quietly. "What ship is that?" now asked the Diomede. "This is the Confederate States steamer Alabama." "I suspected as much," said the officer, "when I saw you making sail, by the light of the burning ship."*

*A little friendly chat now ensued, when we sheared off, and permitted her Britannic Majesty's frigate to proceed, without insisting upon an examination of "her papers;" and the sailors slunk below, one by one, to their hammocks, disappointed that they had neither caught the "Flying Dutchman," a California clipper, or a fight.*[25]

Learning from an English ship that another steamer had been sighted headed eastward, Semmes decided to put into Saldanha Bay, sixty miles north of Cape Town. On July 29, the *Alabama* dropped anchor in the bay, and Semmes learned that no Union vessels had been seen in the area for several months. *Mr. Welles was asleep,* Semmes commented, *the coast was all clear, and I could renew my "depredations" upon the enemy's commerce whenever I pleased.*

Semmes described the savage beauty of the view from the *Alabama's* deck: *The country around was wild and picturesque in appearance; the sub-*

Captain Raphael Semmes (foreground) and his First Lieutenant John M. Kell on the deck of the *Alabama* at Cape Town. Semmes is posed, leaning nonchalantly on the aft 8-inch pivot.

*stratum being of solid rock, and nature having played some strange freaks, when chaos was being reduced to order. Rocky precipices and palisades meet the beholder at every turn, and immense boulders of granite lie scattered on the coast and over the hills, ... A few farm houses are in sight from the ship, surrounded by patches of cultivation, but all the rest of the landscape is a semi-barren waste of straggling rocks and course grass.*

Semmes put his crew to work caulking, painting and replacing some of the *Alabama's* torn sails. All was not work, however, and hunting and fishing parties were organized with the men alternating between chores on board and relaxation ashore. Semmes sent his paymaster ashore to purchase fresh provisions and to inform the governor at Cape Town of his arrival. The *Alabama's* commander was at last able to relax his vigilance: *As I turned into my cot that night, with a still ship, in a land-locked harbor, with no strange sails, or storms to disturb my repose, I felt like a weary traveler, who had laid down, for the time, a heavy burden.*[26]

As usual, the *Alabama* was inundated with curious visitors, and soon the shore was crowded with people, some coming from as far away as Cape Town to get a look at the famous Confederate cruiser. While some of the officers were busy conducting tours of the ship for the Dutch farmers of the area, an unfortunate accident occurred which marred the *Alabama's* visit to Saldanha Bay. Three officers were returning to the *Alabama* by small boat, and Lieutenant Sinclair sadly described what happened:

*A hunting party formed for duck-shooting, and composed of Engineer Cummings, Master Bulloch, and the writer, had passed the day, Aug. 3, 1863, at the head of the bay. Late in the evening, on the return to the ship, Cummings shot himself through the heart in an effort to pull the gun to himself by the muzzle. The hammer of the gun caught the thwart (seat of the boat). Without an outcry or groan, but with a look of despair and appeal never to be forgotten, he sank into the bottom of the boat, his body coming together limp as a rag. It was so sudden and unexpected as to stun and appall, and used as both of us had been to sudden death, tears only relieved and restored our straying senses.*[27]

When the boat bearing the engineer's body reached the side of the *Alabama*, the tragic news was conveyed to Semmes, and Sinclair was ordered to report to the commander's cabin. *Semmes was deeply affected, trembling with emotion,* wrote Sinclair, *and brushing away a tear creeping down his weather-beaten cheek, he said, "That will do, sir; good-night." Slowly and carefully the body is carried below, the wound examined by Llewellyn, and with a watch by it, left for the night, the officers and men with soft step and bated breath retiring to their quarters. ... Morning comes, the Confederate flag for the first time at half-mast on our ship, ... In single file the full complement of ship's boats, with muffled oars and flags at half-mast, form the funeral 'cortege,' and in a quiet spot, the gift of a sympathizing farmer, we laid our shipmate to rest.*[28]

One hundred and thirty-one years later, another funeral procession made its way slowly from Columbia, Tennessee, to "Elm Springs," the headquarters of the Sons of Confederate Veterans on the outskirts of town. Inside the wooden casket, carried on the horse-drawn wagon, were the remains of Second Assistant Engineer Simeon W. Cummings. With the help and assistance of friends in South Africa, including the South African Navy, Cummings' remains had been exhumed and flown to the United States. On Sunday, May 29, 1994, before the eyes of 1,000 attendees singing "What a Friend We Have in Jesus," reenactors of a Confederate Marine Honor Guard fired a twenty-one gun salute, and Engineer Cummings was laid to rest in the soil of his beloved Southland.[29]

As the *Alabama* lifted her anchor the following morning, and got under way for Cape Town, Sinclair's thoughts were of a distant land struggling for its very survival and wrote that our *thoughts will often stray to that far-away home, in the throes of a desperate and unequal struggle. We know that thoughts tending this way are futile, that to do, to act, is practical; yet we cannot dismiss the haunting fear that our brave fellows are but actors in a forlorn hope, a useless struggle; hence 'cui bono,' this knight-errantry of the Alabama? But steady; we must strangle these whisperings of the weaker side of our manhood, and resolve to strive against all discouragement.*[30]

As the *Alabama* steamed leisurely down the coast toward the Cape, she met the *Tuscaloosa* coming northward to join her. Lieutenant Low, having been delayed by light winds, was finally on his way to his rendezvous with the *Alabama* at Saldanha Bay. The *Tuscaloosa's* commander reported with disappointment that, while they had stopped about 40 ships, only one proved to be American, and she contained a neutral cargo. Semmes instructed Low to take the *Tuscaloosa* to Simon's Town, east of Cape Town, and there refit and secure fresh provisions.

The *Alabama* was within sight of the city when the familiar cry of "Sail ho!" came from the masthead. With little effort, the *Sea Bride* of Boston inbound to Cape Town was taken just short of the marine league. Semmes placed Fullam with a prize crew on board her and instructed him to take the vessel to Saldanha Bay and await his instructions.

With advanced notice of the coming of the Confederate cruiser, thousands of excited citizens watched the capture of the *Sea Bride* and were eager to welcome the *Alabama*. Within minutes of dropping anchor, the cruiser's deck was crowded with well-wishers all striving to welcome and congratulate Semmes and the men of his ship. Officers, wearing their now slightly faded gray uniforms, were kept busy showing the elite of the British Colony around the decks of the Confederate ship. Her Majesty's officers from the English squadron stationed at

Cape Town were eager to see the Confederate warship and meet her commander. Baskets of fruit were brought on board and Semmes' cabin and the *Alabama's* deck were soon garlanded with bouquets of fresh flowers. Semmes was overwhelmed by the press of ladies wishing to meet him: *I simply surrendered at discretion, and whilst Kell was explaining the virtues of his guns to his male visitors, and answering the many questions that were put to him about our cruises and captures, I found it as much as I could do, to write autographs, and answer the pretty little perfumed billets that came off to me.*[31]

A newspaper reporter for the South African *Advertiser and Mail* was among the throng of people visiting the deck of the *Alabama*, and later he printed his impression of her commander: *He has nothing of the pirate about him — little even of the ordinary sea captain. He is rather below middle statue with a spare body frame. His face is care-worn and sunburnt, the features striking — a broad brow with iron-gray locks straggling over it, gray eyes, now mild and dreamy, then flashing with fire as he warms in conversation. ... He was dressed in an old gray, stained uniform, the surtout, with battered shoulder straps and faded gold trimmings buttoned close up to the throat. In look, manners and dress he had more of the military than naval officer about him. He is 53 years old but looks somewhat older.*[32]

Not everyone, however, was enthralled with the *Alabama's* visit. At the urging of the American consul, South African Governor Philip E. Wodehouse reluctantly accused Semmes of capturing the *Sea Bride* within his country's territorial waters. Semmes had anticipated such a move and had been careful to record his bearings from all points of land and had requested and received affidavits from prominent citizens on shore stating that he was clearly beyond the three mile limit. With this evidence of the legality of his capture of the *Sea Bride*, Cape Town officials rejected the American consul's claims.[33]

Semmes still had the problem, however, of what to do with the *Sea Bride*, which was still at Saldanha Bay with Master's Mate Fullam. Fortunately, a British merchant approached Semmes with a proposition to buy the *Sea Bride*, if he could take possession at some secluded spot along the coast. Aware of the semi-legality of such a transaction, Semmes nevertheless agreed and sold the vessel, to be delivered later, for $16,940.

On August 9, the *Alabama* sailed out of Table Bay and headed for Simon's Town. Heavy gales had been pounding the bay at Cape Town, and Semmes needed a more sheltered spot to complete the caulking and painting of the cruiser. Before reaching Simon's Town, the American bark *Martha Wenzell* was intercepted, but Semmes astonished her master by announcing that he would not bond or burn his vessel, being they were both in the territorial waters of South Africa. At 2:00

p.m. that afternoon, the *Alabama* joined the *Tuscaloosa* at Simon's Bay, the British Naval Station for the crown colony.[34]

Semmes instructed Low to take the *Tuscaloosa* as soon as he was finished loading provisions, and to proceed to Saldanha Bay, pick up Fullam and the *Sea Bride*, and meet him at Luderitz Bay on the desolate coast of Angra Pequena (present day Namibia) where none of the great powers claimed jurisdiction.

For the next week, while work was progressing on the *Alabama*, Semmes and his officers were wined and dined by the officers of the British Fleet. Except for the work details, Kell gave the crew liberty, and it began to look like Jamaica all over again. *Most of them went over to Cape Town in the stagecoach that was running between the two places,* Semmes wrote, *and put that lively commercial town in "stays."... They all overstayed their time, and we only got them back by twos and threes. It was no use to muster, and inspect them now. Their tidy, new suits, in which they had gone on shore, were torn and draggled, and old-drunks were upon nearly all of them.*[35]

The *Tuscaloosa* sailed on August 14, and the *Alabama* followed the next day. While Low was gathering up the *Sea Bride*, Semmes planned on stationing the *Alabama* off the Cape of Good Hope in the steady stream of commerce coming from the East Indies. The Confederate cruiser sailed leisurely among this traffic for ten days, but while numerous sails were constantly in sight, not one American-owned ship was among them. Disappointed, but realizing that the lack of American ships was much the result of his own activities, Semmes headed for Luderitz Bay to rendezvous with the *Tuscaloosa* and the *Sea Bride*. Arriving on August 28, Semmes completed his sale and delivery of the *Sea Bride* to the English merchant.

While at secluded Angra Pequena, the *Alabama's* condenser broke down and water had to be rationed. Fortunately, Low discovered that the English merchant's schooner had an abundant supply of water and arrangements were made to transfer 1,500 gallons to the *Alabama*. On August 31, the *Alabama* returned to sea after Semmes, again ill with fever, left instructions with Low to depart and cruise off the coast of Brazil for a time, and then meet the *Alabama* back at Cape Town on her return from the East Indies.[36]

For two weeks the *Alabama* cruised the waters off the Cape of Good Hope but with no better luck than before. American ships were either avoiding the passage around the Cape or were being sold to foreign shippers. Within a few days, the condenser, which had been repaired, again broke down, and the men had to be put on half-rations of water. Disappointed anew, and now in need of coal, Semmes had steam raised and proceeded to Simon's Bay.

Master Arthur Sinclair, Jr., (left), and Lieutenant Richard F. Armstrong on the deck of the CSS *Alabama*. Photo taken at Cape Town, South Africa in August, 1863. The gun is a 32-pounder of Sinclair's division.

Upon arrival on September 16, Semmes learned that there was no coal available, for two steamers had recently stopped in the harbor and had exhausted the entire supply. One of them, Semmes gladly noted, was the CSS *Georgia*. The other, however, was the huge sidewheel steamer USS *Vanderbilt* which was now out looking for the *Alabama*. Coal was ordered from Cape Town and the crew was granted shore leave. Even with the help of the local police, it was difficult to recover the wayward sailors, and fourteen never could be found. Semmes was forced to purchase eleven hungry and destitute vagabonds off the docks of Simon's Town as replacements and ship them as "passengers" to avoid violating the Foreign Enlistment Act.[37]

Learning that the *Vanderbilt* had returned to Cape Town, Semmes hurried his preparation for departure. Finally, on the night of September 24, 1863, all was ready. Although the sky was clear, a strong gale was blowing from the southeast, but with the *Vanderbilt* so close, Semmes could delay no longer. Just past 11:00 p.m., the *Alabama* steamed away from the continent of Africa and turned her head toward the Indian Ocean. Semmes described their departure:

*The struggle of the little ship with the elements was a thing to be remembered. The moon, ... was near full, shedding a flood of light upon the scene. The Bay was whitened with foam, as the waters were lashed into fury by the storm. Around the curve of the "horse-shoe" arose broken, bald, rocky mountains, on the crests of which were piled fleecy, white clouds, blinking in the moonlight, like banks of snow. ... The scene was wild and weird beyond description. It was a picture for the eye of a poet or painter to dwell upon. ... At three A.M. we cleared the Cape, and keeping the ship off a few points, gave her the trysails, with the bonnets off. She bounded over the seas like a stag-hound unleashed. I had been up all night, and now went below to snatch some brief repose, before the toils of another day should begin.*[38]

# *Chapter Seven*

## Rendezvous at Cherbourg

The morning following her departure from Simon's Bay found the *Alabama* well launched upon the Indian Ocean. Semmes' plan was to sail south to the fortieth parallel, turn east, and sail the more than 4,000 miles across the Indian Ocean. Once across this boundless expanse of ocean, he would enter the South China Sea through the Strait of Sunda that separates Java and Sumatra. In the vastness of this part of the Indian Ocean, gale force winds and violent storms were of constant occurrence, and a sharp lookout had to be maintained for icebergs which floated north from the shores of Antarctica. In an attempt to predict their presence, Semmes ordered the water and air temperature to be taken and recorded every hour.[1]

On September 27, Semmes observed his fifty-fourth birthday. From the solitude of his cabin, he wrote in his journal an introspective account of himself at this moment: *My life has been one of great vicissitude, but not of calamity or great suffering, and I have reason to be thankful to a kind Providence for the many favors I have received. I have enjoyed life to a reasonable extent, and trust I shall have fortitude to meet with Christian calmness any fate that may be in store for me. ... My dear family I consign with confidence to His care, and our beloved country I feel certain He will protect and preserve, and in due time raise up to peace, independence and prosperity.*[2]

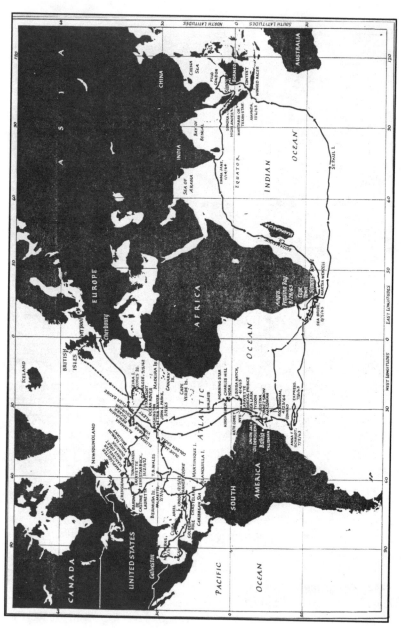

The cruises of the CSS *Alabama.*

Reaching the fortieth parallel on the September 30, Semmes marveled at what the sailors called the "Brave West Winds," which blew constantly at gale force, driving rain and snow before them. With icebergs a possibility, sailing through this area could be a frightening experience: *As we are driven on dark nights before these furious winds,* Semmes wrote, *we have only to imitate the Cape Horn navigator — "tie all fast, and let her rip," iceberg or no iceberg. When a ship is running at a speed of twelve or fourteen knots, in such thick weather that the lookout at the cat-head can scarcely see his own nose, neither sharp eyes, nor water thermometers are of much use.*[3]

As the *Alabama* raced eastward before the howling wind, Semmes described the magnitude of the storms and the vastness of the waters upon which they were venturing: *These winds continued to blow from day to day, hurrying us forward with great speed. There being a clear sweep of the sea for several thousand miles, unobstructed by continent or island, the waves rose into long, sweeping swells, much more huge and majestic than one meets with in any other ocean. As our little craft, scudding before a gale, would be overtaken by one of these monster billows, she would be caught up by its crest, like a cork-boat, and darted half-way down the declivity that lay before her, at a speed that would cause the sailor to hold his breath. Any swerve to the right or the left, that would cause the ship to "broach to," or come broadside to the wind and sea, would have been fatal.*[4]

On October 17, Semmes noted that he was exactly halfway around the world from his home in Alabama. Doubtless he must have reflected upon that desperate and unequal struggle in which his beloved country was engaged at the moment. Perhaps it was these thoughts that enabled him to endure the hardships and isolation of his command and to continue his relentless war against his country's enemy.

Four days later, the *Alabama* crossed the Tropic of Capricorn and almost immediately picked up the gentle southeast tradewinds. On October 26, Semmes learned from the captain of an English vessel, who had just come through the Strait of Sunda, that the USS *Wyoming*, along with a tender, was prowling the strait watching for the Confederate cruiser. As the *Alabama* approached the strait, sails were sighted in abundance, but they were all under foreign flags. Finally, on November 6, the bark *Amanda* of Boston, with a cargo of hemp and sugar, was captured. The *Amanda* was the first of the enemy's vessels destroyed in four months and it was with a certain amount of satisfaction that night that she was set ablaze. Semmes explained that *the conflagration lighted up the sea for many miles around, and threw its grim and ominous glare to the very mouth of the Strait.*

The next day, during a rainstorm, the *Alabama* passed through the Strait with no sign of the *Wyoming*. Where the Strait debauches into the China Sea off the north coast of Java, a beautiful American clipper ship was spotted. She was the *Winged Racer* out of Manila and bound for her home port of New York with an assorted cargo of sugar, hides, and jute. Allowing her crew and the prisoners from the *Amanda* to go ashore in the clipper's boats, she was anchored for the night while the *Alabama's* boarding officers directed the transfer of stores and provisions. The next day, to the astonishment and terror of the numerous Malay "bummers" gathered around her, the magnificent *Winged Racer* had the torch applied, causing her to burst into a raging inferno.[5]

On November 11, the Alabama under steam headed north toward the Gasper Strait. Not wanting to arrive at the busy commercial passage during darkness, Semmes ordered the propeller hoisted and was about to put the cruiser under leisure sail when the lookout at the masthead sighted another New York clipper. Keeping off her lee bow so as not to excite suspicion, the hoisting operation was suspended, and the engine room began working feverishly to rebuild steam pressure. When within about four miles of the quarry, Semmes ordered the U.S. flag hoisted and the clipper responded with the same colors. *Feeling now quite sure of her,* Semmes wrote, *we fired a gun, hauled down the enemy's flag, and hoisted our own to the breeze. (We were now wearing that splendid white flag, with its cross and stars, which was so great an improvement upon the old one.) So far from obeying the command of our gun, the gallant ship kept off a point or two — probably her best point of sailing — gave herself top-gallant and topmast studding-sails, and away she went!*

The graceful clipper was now in a race for her life, and at first it looked as though she would pull away from the Alabama. With a full head of steam now in the cruiser's boilers, the power of the propeller was added to her sails, yet still the *Alabama* was not gaining in the chase. Two forward 32-pounders were moved aft, and Semmes had the entire crew crowd aft on the quarterdeck in an effort to trim the *Alabama* to her best possible speed. The chase had begun around midmorning, and as the day progressed the sun's heat beat down on the ocean, and the breeze began to die, and with it the *Contest* out of Yokohama for New York was doomed.

The business of burning ships, even ships of an enemy, was distasteful at best to the sailor. Semmes never enjoyed his work, but felt it was necessary to inflict as much damage as possible on those that were invading his homeland. He especially hated destroying the graceful *Contest*, and for lack of armament, would have converted her into another Confederate cruiser. Semmes congratulated the clipper's captain on his skillful handling of his ship, and reluctantly, later that night, applied the torch.[6]

The difficulty of overtaking the *Contest* illustrated the deterioration in the sailing qualities of the *Alabama*. It had been almost sixteen months since that sunny day in July and the "trial trip" down the Mersey. Not once during this period had she been able to visit a shipyard where facilities existed for repairs and overhaul. The pounding she had taken on the passage across the Indian Ocean had opened her seams again, and her copper sheathing was beginning to peel off in rolls. The *Alabama* was badly in need of a dry-dock and was no longer the greyhound of the seas. Semmes knew he would have to adopt different tactics from now on, if he was to continue destroying the enemy's commerce.

During the balance of November and well into December, the *Alabama* sailed the treacherous waters of the South China Sea. Semmes, knowing that this part of the China Sea with its hidden currents and coral reefs was one of the most dangerous in the world, spent many sleepless nights pacing the quarterdeck and listening to the cry of the leadsmen. Cruising along the coast of Cochin China (Vietnam), the *Alabama* entered the desolate harbor at Pula Condore, a group of rugged islands 45 miles off the coast of Cochin and on the trade route between Saigon and Singapore. The islands had only recently become a French possession, and Semmes was welcomed by a dilapidated Chinese junk flying the French flag. The little gun-boat's commander, along with the "governor," were the sole French authority in the islands, and they quickly granted permission for the *Alabama* to make repairs and refit.

With no saloons, dance halls, or brothels in the area, the *Alabama's* gray clad tars had to make do with swimming, fishing, hunting, and teasing a family of apes that came down to the beach every morning to watch the activities around the ship. While enjoying this secluded harbor, William Robinson, the ship's carpenter, constructed an ingenious coffer, or caisson, which could fit snugly to the side of the hull, and when the water was pumped out, workers could make repairs to the copper sheathing well below the waterline. While work progressed on the vessel, a sharp lookout was kept at all times for the *Wyoming*. Semmes felt, however, that if she should appear, the *Alabama* would be more than a match for her. With the rudimentary repairs completed, the *Alabama* departed for Singapore on December 14, where Semmes hoped to replenish his coal supply before heading back to the Cape of Good Hope.[7]

Upon arrival on December 21, in the thriving Asian port of over 100,000 inhabitants, it was immediately evident why no American ships had been encountered. Lying at anchor and rotting by the wharves were no less than twenty-two U.S. merchant ships which were unable to

The CSS *Alabama* stops a merchant ship on the high seas.

The Illustrated London News

obtain cargoes. From the moment the *Amanda* was set afire at the entrance of the Strait of Sunda, word had spread that a Confederate cruiser was in the area, and all American vessels had fled to port where they now lay deserted or for sale. Semmes heard reports of others abandoned in Bangkok, Canton, Shanghai, Japan, and the Philippines. It was gratifying to know that, while the *Alabama* had not destroyed many enemy ships in these waters, the mere presence of the *Alabama* was having the same result.

While the ship was being coaled, and the *Alabama's* officers were overnight guests at the residence of Her Majesty's governor, some of the crew slipped ashore with the usual result. *When an old salt once gets a taste of the forbidden nectar,* Semmes wrote, *he is gone — he has no more power of resistance than a child. The consequence on the present occasion was, that a number of my fellows "left" on a frolic. We tracked most of them up during the night, and arrested them ... and brought them on board. ... When it came to call the roll, there were half a dozen still missing.* Semmes accepted six "passengers" from sailors that desired to enlist, and on Christmas Eve, bright and early, the *Alabama* sailed from Singapore.

Steaming through the Strait of Malacca off the coast of Sumatra, the familiar cry of "Sail ho," was heard from the masthead. About 1:00 p.m. the *Alabama* overtook an American-looking bark which hoisted the British ensign. Sending Master's Mate Fullam to board her and examine the vessel's papers, Semmes prepared to receive her captain in his cabin. The ship's papers, which were presented to Fullam, indicated she was the British ship, *Martaban*, belonging to parties in Maulmain, a port in India. She was American built, formerly the *Texan Star*, but had been sold to her English owners, supposedly, within the last ten days. When Fullam ordered the *Martaban's* commander, Captain Pike, to accompany him to the *Alabama*, Pike refused, claiming the protection of the British flag flying above his head. Fullam returned emptyhanded to the side of the *Alabama*, and reported, that while her papers appeared to be in order, he recommended that Captain Semmes take a look at her.

Not wanting to compel an "English" master to come on board the Confederate cruiser, Semmes ordered his gig lowered and was rowed to the side of the *Martaban* (the only ship he ever personally boarded). *I could not but admire the beautiful, "bran new" English flag, as I pulled on board,* Semmes recorded, *but, ... every line of the ship was American — her long, graceful hull, with flaring bow, and rounded stern, taunt masts with sky-sail poles, and square yards for spreading the largest possible quantity of canvas. Passing up the side, I stepped on deck. Here every thing was, if possible, still more American, even to the black, greasy cook, who, with his uncovered woolly head, naked breast, and up-rolled sleeves in the broiling sun, was peeling his Irish potatoes for his codfish. ... The master received me at the gangway, and after I had paused to take a look at things on deck, I proceeded with him into his cabin, where his papers were to be examined.*

Semmes began the examination of these documents: *When the papers were produced, I found among them no bill of sale or other evidence of the transfer of the property. His crew list, which had been very neatly prepared, was a mute but powerful witness against him. It was written, throughout, signatures and all, in the same hand — the signatures all being as like as two peas.*

*The master had sat with comparative composure during this examination,* Semmes continued, *evidently relying with great confidence upon his English flag and papers; but when I turned to him and told him that I should burn his ship, he sprang from his chair, and said with excited manner and voice, — "You dare not do it, sir; that flag — suiting the action to the word, and pointing with his long, bony finger up the companion-way to the flag flying from his peak — won't stand it!" "Keep cool, captain," I replied, "the weather is warm, and as for the flag, I shall not ask it whether it will stand it or not — the flag that 'ought' to be at your peak, will have to stand it though."*

Within thirty minutes, after transferring the crew to the *Alabama*, the *Texan Star*, alias the *Martaban*, was a mass of flames. Later that afternoon, Semmes had Captain Pike brought to his cabin, and during the taking of his formal deposition, Pike admitted that the papers were fraudulent. The *Alabama's* commander gently pointed out to him that if his English cargo of rice had been properly documented, instead of falsifying the ship's papers, Semmes would have been forced to bond the *Texan Star* and she would have been saved.[8]

Later that night, with the moon casting its bright light on the waters of the strait, the *Alabama* anchored off the tiny village of Malacca on the Malay peninsula, a former Portuguese settlement that was now claimed by Britain. Despite the pleas of the Malay-English officials for Semmes and his crew to spend Christmas day with them, the *Alabama* hoisted anchor, and by mid-morning was steaming up the strait. The crew spent Christmas day, 1863, "splicing the main-brace," while the cruiser steamed carefully through the Malacca Strait.

Early the next day the lookout spotted two large ships at anchor that looked "sort o' Yankee." They were waiting for the breeze to freshen in order to continue into the Indian Ocean, and the *Alabama* hoisted the Confederate ensign and pulled along side of them. They were the 708-ton *Sonora* and the 1,050-ton clipper *Highlander*, both of Boston. There was no question of the neutrality of their cargoes, for both ships were in ballast and headed for Akyab, Burma for a cargo of rice. The captain of the *Highlander* accepted his ship's fate with a certain amount of relief. Climbing aboard the *Alabama* with his ship's papers tucked under his arm, he extended his hand to Semmes and said, "*Well, Captain*

*Semmes, I have been expecting every day for the last three years to fall in with you, and here I am at last!"* I told him I was glad he had found me after so long a search, Semmes replied. *"Search!"* said he; *"It is some such search as the Devil may be supposed to make after holy water. The fact is,"* continued he, *"I have had constant visions of the Alabama, by night and by day; she has been chasing me in my sleep, and riding me like a night-mare, and now that it is all over, I feel quite relieved."* Within a short time, with their crews pulling toward shore in their own boats, the two vessels were a raging inferno.[9]

Cruising off the western end of Sumatra for a few days, the *Alabama* finally set sail on the first day of January, 1864, for the long crossing of the Bay of Bengal, and the island of Ceylon off the south coast of India. Nothing but neutral flags were seen; however, many of these were boarded by the *Alabama's* boarding officers to verify their nationality. On boarding one of these, the cruiser's officer was asked by the Moslem pilgrims on board, if the rumor was true that the *Alabama* kept several black giants chained in the hold and fed them live Yankees. The Confederate officer, without blinking an eye, responded that "they had made the experiment, but the Yankee skippers were so lean and tough, that the giants refused to eat them."

By January 14, the island of Ceylon had been passed, and the *Alabama* was sailing off the coast of Malabar, India, when the 1,097-ton *Emma Jane* of Bath, Maine was captured. Unable to obtain freight at Bombay because of the fear of shipping in American vessels, she had sailed in ballast for Burma, where she had hoped to find a cargo. After removing her chronometer and flag, she was set ablaze. Landing his prisoners at the small Portuguese village of Anjenga and taking on a few supplies, Semmes set the *Alabama's* course for the east coast of Africa.[10]

On January 20, the Equator was crossed and on the 30th, the *Alabama* dropped anchor at the Comoro Islands, remaining there for a week. With no night spots on the islands, Semmes' tars behaved themselves and dutifully reported to the beach every night to be returned to the ship. With fresh provisions filling the larder, the Alabama sailed on February 15, and headed south, bound for Cape Town.

Sailing through the Mozambique Channel off the south tip of Madagascar, the *Alabama* ran through a horrendous electrical storm and Lieutenant Sinclair described its awesome power: *It was the first watch of the night, about half-past eight. The sky had been promising for some time a rain squall, and it did not tarry long once the lightning lit up the horizon. ...The flashes approached very rapidly, accompanied by torrents of rain, such as must have visited old man Noah, but with little wind. The lightning ran down the three conductors to the masts in constant streams, entering the water with a hissing sound, and jumping from gun to gun, and even to the engine below.*

*The crash was like the explosion of a heavy mine blast, or battery of artillery; and between the flashes the night was as black as Erabus. ... Nearly blinded by the flashes, there was nothing to do but recline on the horseblock, and take the deluge of rain with our mouth shut to keep from being drowned. The captain, putting his head out the companion hatchway, and looking around for a few moments, remarked, "Well, sir, you do not seem to be getting any wind out of it, though, on the whole, I do not envy you your watch;" and retired to his law books again.*

During the pitch blackness, interrupted by blinding flashes of lightning, little could be seen on deck. Suddenly, Sinclair was aware that someone was beside him: *As a flash of lightning lit up the deck, Midshipman Maffitt of the watch was noted close beside the writer. His post was on the forecastle; and to the query, "What can I do for you, Mr. Maffitt?" "Nothing," is the reply; then for some time we gaze at each other inquiringly, as the flashes allow, "Well, sir," he said at last, "I came aft because it is so lonesome." The reason was appreciated fully; but his place was forward. So with an "I'm sorry, sir, I would like to have your company, but it won't do; you had better go forward," we parted. It must be confessed I would have preferred to pass the remainder of the watch near somebody to divide the scare with myself.*[11]

On March 11, the aging *Alabama* and her weary crew, arrived at the their old cruising ground off the Cape of Good Hope. Plying these waters for nine days, it was evident that the *Alabama* had done her work well, for while many vessels were stopped and boarded, none proved to be American. Semmes ordered the *Alabama's* head turned toward Cape Town, and early the next morning ran into Table Bay and anchored.

Old friends greeted the *Alabama,* but an unexpected problem had developed while the cruiser was away. After returning in January from her cruise off the coast of Brazil, the *Tuscaloosa* was seized by the British authorities when she entered Table Bay at Cape Town. The English government had treated the *Tuscaloosa,* while she was at Simon's Bay in August, as a commissioned Confederate warship. Now, however, Her Majesty's government had reversed its position and was threatening to return the ship to her former Northern owners. Despite strong protests from Low, pointing out that the legitimacy of his warship had already been established, Governor Wodehouse refused to release the cruiser, claiming that he was under orders from the home government. Not knowing when, or if, Semmes and the *Alabama* might return, Low paid off his crew, and he and Sinclair returned to England.

Learning of this seizure, Semmes was furious. Sitting in his cabin, and gleaning from his extensive knowledge of international law, he wrote a lengthy letter to British commander, Admiral Walker, explaining in detail why "one nation cannot inquire into the antecedents of the ships of war of another nation." Although the case would eventually be heard in the House of Commons, Semmes finally won his argument, and the *Tuscaloosa* was ordered returned to Low or any other representative of the Confederate government. Unfortunately, there was no such representative in South Africa by the time the order was reversed, and the vessel languished at dockside until the end of the war when she was handed over to U.S. authorities.[12]

By now the *Alabama* was desperately in need of a total overhaul. Her boilers were encrusted and almost eaten through from the corrosive effect of salt water, while the furnace, where the fires were rarely allowed to go out completely, needed scraping and cleaning. Her condenser was broken, her copper cladding was coming off in rolls, and no amount of caulking could seal the seams in her hull. Semmes knew that the only way to accomplish these repairs was to put the ship in dry-dock. With England tightening her neutrality policies, the feasibility of going to an English port and effecting repairs looked doubtful. Learning that France was building several ironclads for the Confederacy, Semmes decided that Cherbourg, a French port on the English Channel with good facilities yet difficult to blockade, would be his destination.

With this plan in mind, Semmes and his officers bid an emotional farewell to all their Cape Town friends. After taking on a full load of coal, the *Alabama* steamed out of Table Bay for the last time on March 25, 1864, and headed north.[13]

Before reaching the three mile limit, the *Alabama* met the *Quang Tung*, a fast U.S. steamer built for the China trade as she was entering the bay. With the United States flag at her peak and the Confederate ensign flying from the *Alabama's*, the two vessels passed one another with their yard-arms almost touching, while the crews lined the rails and glared at one another in silence.[14]

While in Cape Town, Semmes had been given a supply of newspapers, and now that they were at sea, he found time to read: *The news was not encouraging,* he wrote sorrowfully. *Our people were being harder and harder pressed by the enemy, and post after post within our territory was being occupied by him. The signs of weakness on our part, which I mentioned as becoming, for the first time painfully apparent after the battle of Gettysburg, and the surrender of Vicksburg, were multiplying. The blockade of the coast, by reason of the constantly increasing fleets of the enemy, was becoming more and more stringent. Our finances were rapidly deteriorating, and a general demoralization, in consequence, seemed to be spreading among our people. From the whole review of the situation, I was very apprehensive that the cruises of the Alabama were drawing to a close.*[15]

The *Alabama* steamed northwest into the south Atlantic and positioned herself in the broad sealane of vessels homeward bound from the Pacific. Semmes had not taken a prize since January 14, and it must have been gratifying to hear the cry of the lookout proclaiming a "Yankee" ship in sight on April 22. After a long chase, which lasted all night, the 976-ton *Rockingham* of Portsmouth, was brought to with a blank cartridge. She was loaded with fertilizer and attempted to cover her cargo with false papers; however, Semmes discovered the fraud and condemned her. After transferring to the *Alabama* what stores and provisions were needed, Semmes instructed Kell to exercise his gunners on the Northern ship. Although Semmes wrote that the firing was of "good effect," Kell found the results to be disappointing. Of twenty-four rounds fired, only seven had any material effect, and upon further investigation, many of the shell fuses were found to be faulty. Several barrels of dampened powder, which had been stored near the condenser, were thrown overboard, and even cartridges sealed in airtight containers were found to have lost much of their strength.[16]

Four days later, and a little south of the equator, the lookouts spotted a large ship off the bow which was headed directly toward them. Waiting until she was within hailing distance, the 717-ton bark *Tycoon* out of New York, was ordered to heave to, as Semmes raised the Confederate flag to the cruiser's masthead. She had an assorted cargo with no attempt to claim it as neutral, and she was soon ablaze. The *Tycoon* was the sixty-fifth prize captured by the *Alabama*, and she would prove to be her last.[17]

On May 2, the cruiser crossed the equator and paused in her old hunting grounds off the Azores. On the night of May 24, she chased a schooner that was out of Nova Scotia and bound for Rio. When a blank cartridge failed to stop her, a shell was fired — it failed to explode.

The *Alabama* now set her course toward the coast of Spain and Portugal, and while the crew was happy to be headed home at last, Semmes and his officers were gloomy and downcast as they sailed even farther away from their troubled and strife-torn Southern homeland. Several years after the war, the pain was still evident in Semmes' heart as he wrote in the third person concerning himself: *Her commander, like herself (the Alabama), was well-nigh worn down. Vigils by night and day, the storm and the drenching rain, the frequent and rapid change of climate, now freezing, now melting or broiling, and the constant excitement of the chase and capture, had laid in the three years of war he had been afloat, a load of a dozen years on his shoulders. The shadows of a sorrowful future, too, began to rest upon his spirit. The last batch of newspapers captured were full of disasters. Might it not be, that, after all our trials and sacrifices, the cause for which we were struggling would be lost? Might not our federal system of government be destroyed, and state independence become a phrase of the past; the glorious fabric of our American liberty sinking, as so many others had done before it, under the invasion of Brennuses and Attilas? The thought was hard to bear.*[18]

On June 10, after battling stiff headwinds and rough seas, the *Alabama* finally made landfall off the coast of France. Taking a pilot on board just as night was falling, and with a heavy storm brewing, she steamed slowly up the English Channel arriving off Cape La Hague by ten the next morning. A French pilot now came on board, and at thirty minutes past noon, the Confederate cruiser dropped anchor in the beautiful French port of Cherbourg.[19]

During the twenty-two months the *Alabama* had roamed the seas, she had overtaken and stopped a total of 294 vessels. Fifty-five of these were American merchant ships which were burned and sent to the bottom, and ten others bonded. The total estimated value of these vessels, including their cargoes, came to $5,062,000. No other Confederate cruiser during the entire war caused so much damage to Northern commerce.[20]

With Cherbourg being a National French Naval Base, Semmes went on shore the next day to formally request permission from the Port Admiral for the use of the government dry-dock. Because only Emperor Napoleon III could grant permission, and he was away from Paris for a few days, Semmes was told he would have to await the Emperor's return. He was, however, given permission to land his prisoners from the *Rockingham* and the *Tycoon*, and to take on a small supply of coal.

When the *Alabama's* anchor splashed into the waters of Cherbourg harbor, telegraph wires all over Europe were announcing her arrival. The news soon reached the commander of the USS *Kearsarge* lying in the Scheldt, off Flushing, the Netherlands, and three days later, on June 14, the Union warship steamed into the harbor at Cherbourg. Her commander was Captain John A. Winslow, and ironically, he and Semmes had served together on board the USS *Cumberland* during the Mexican War. Later, both men served on the USS *Raitan* and became close friends, even sharing a cabin together. Without dropping anchor, the *Kearsarge* lowered a boat which proceeded to shore to request from the French officials that the prisoners, recently dispatched from the *Alabama*, be brought on board. Semmes objected to this because, he argued, it would be augmenting her crew within a neutral port. French authorities agreed, and the request was denied, whereupon Winslow steamed out and anchored the *Kearsarge* just beyond the three mile limit.[21]

The Federal warship under Winslow's command was a 1,031-ton steam sloop-of-war, and mounted one rifled 30-pounder, four 32-pounders, and two 11-inch Dahlgrens. Her officers and crew numbered 162. While the *Alabama* had the advantage in that she carried one more gun than the *Kearsarge*, the Federal's arsenal was much heavier and could fire 430 pounds of projectiles in one broadside compared to the *Alabama's* 360 pounds. Semmes believed he would have an advantage in speed, however, but as events would prove, the *Kearsarge* was faster because of the deteriorating condition of the *Alabama's* hull.

Before the *Kearsarge* left port, Lieutenant Kell stood on the *Alabama's* quarterdeck and through his marine glasses studied the Federal ship while she was on the other side of the harbor. She had a low rakish hull that was smooth and painted black, but because most of her guns were pivot-mounted, little could be seen of her armament. Both Semmes and Kell had seen the *Kearsarge* up close at Gibraltar back in 1862, and both men failed to notice a slight alteration in her appearance since then. To protect her engines and boilers, large anchor chains had been stretched vertically over her midsection on each side and attached with heavy eyebolts. To make this "less unsightly," the chains were covered with three-quarter inch boards and painted black. From a distance, and looking broadside on, it was impossible to detect the slight protrusion made by the boxed-in chains.[22]

With the *Kearsarge* guarding the exit from the harbor, and no word yet on when, or if, the dry-dock would be made available, Semmes was faced with several options. First, he could continue to await the return of the Emperor and trust that Napoleon III would grant the needed permission to use the dry-dock. If the *Alabama* was finally put in for repairs, it would take at least a couple of months for them to be completed, and by then most of his crew would be gone, and a score of Federal warships, by that time, would be patrolling off Cherbourg. A second option was to attempt to steal out on a dark, rainy night, slip by the *Kearsarge*, and head for the open sea. But what then? Where could he go? With British and most French ports now looking with disfavor on visiting Confederate vessels, with the *Alabama* desperately in need of repairs, and with the war clouds looming darker and darker over his Southern homeland, it may have seemed to Semmes that it was time for drastic action. It may also have been, and it seems evident that this was Semmes' primary reason, that he was just so very tired of running. In any event, he chose a third option — he would fight the *Kearsarge* as soon as the *Alabama* could be made ready.

Semmes summoned Kell to his cabin, and revealed his decision by the statement that "I am tired of running from that flaunting rag!" Asked of what he thought of the decision to fight the *Kearsarge*, Kell gently reminded his captain that the Federal ship carried heavier ordnance than the Confederate, and when the *Alabama's* gunners had fired on the *Rockingham* for practice, only one in three shells exploded. "I'll take the chances of one in three!" Semmes snapped. "Yes sir! I'll fit the ship for action, sir!" was Kell's response. Semmes then wrote a note to be delivered to Winslow, that if he would wait until the *Alabama* finished coaling, he would come out and give him battle.[23]

The next four days were spent in intense preparation for the coming engagement, and while the coaling operation continued, Kell ran the crew through boarding practice. Semmes hoped to damage the *Kearsarge* badly enough with his long range guns, so that he could then close with her and throw his tough English tars on board. The guns were overhauled and the gun crews ran through the drill one last time. On Saturday, June 18, Semmes notified the port admiral that he would give battle the following day, a Sunday. The crew felt it was their captain's "Lucky Day."[24]

Semmes felt that his men were ready: *My crew seem to be in the right spirit, a quiet spirit of determination pervading both officers and men. The combat will no doubt be contested and obstinate, but the two ships are so equally matched that I do not feel at liberty to decline it. God defend the right, and have mercy upon the souls of those who fall, as many of us must.*[25]

Lieutenant Kell wrote of the *Alabama's* departure: *Accordingly, on Sunday morning, June 19th, between 9 and 10 o'clock, we weighed anchor and stood out of the entrance of the harbor, the French iron-clad frigate Couronne following us. The day was bright and beautiful, with a light breeze blowing. Our men were neatly dressed, and our officers in full uniform. The report of our going out to fight the Kearsarge had been circulated, and many persons from Paris and the surrounding country had come down to witness the engagement. With a large number of inhabitants of Cherbourg they collected on every prominent point on the shore that would afford a view seaward.*[26]

Some observers estimated that as many as 15,000 persons were gathered on the high ground and roof tops to watch the engagement. As the *Alabama* weaved her way through the crowded harbor, she passed near the French liner *Napoleon,* and Lieutenant Sinclair described a spirit lifting incident: *We were surprised and gratified as she manned the rigging and gave us three rousing cheers, her band at the same time playing a Confederate national air. It must have been an enthusiasm of local birth, a sort of private turn-out of their own. It was much appreciated by us, and no doubt stirred our brave lads to their center.*[27]

In addition to the French ironclad, which was intent on making sure that French territorial waters were not violated, various small craft followed in the wake of the *Alabama,* including the English yacht *Deerhound,* owned and operated by John Lancaster. Lancaster and his family happened to be vacationing in the area, and earlier that morning the family members had taken a vote on whether to go to church or see

The battle between the CSS *Alabama* and the USS *Kearsarge*, June 19, 1864, off Cherbourg, France.

the battle. Little nine-year-old Catherine had cast the deciding vote, and Semmes with forty-one of his officers and men would soon owe their lives to this small girl's decision.[28]

As the *Alabama* rounded the breakwater, the *Kearsarge* could be seen approximately seven miles to the northeast. Winslow was steaming slowly away in an effort to lead the *Alabama* farther from the sanctuary of French territorial waters. It took nearly 45 minutes to steam within range of the enemy and Sinclair gives us a vivid picture of the *Alabama* during this time: *Our ship as she steams offshore for her antagonist, hull down in the distance and waiting for us, presents a brave appearance. The decks and brass-work shine in the bright morning sunlight from recent holystoning and polishing. The crew are all in muster uniform, as though just awaiting Sunday inspection. They are ordered to lie down at their quarters for rest while we approach the enemy, A beautiful sight — the divisions stripped to the waist, and with bare arms and breasts looking the athletes they are. The decks have been sanded down, tubs of water placed along the spar-deck, and all is ready for the fray.*[29]

The shrill cry of the boatswain's pipe now pierced the morning air, and all hands were ordered aft to the quarterdeck. Mounting a gun carriage, Semmes delivered his only other speech to the crew since the commissioning ceremony almost two years ago:

*Officers and seamen of the Alabama! — You have at length another opportunity of meeting the enemy — the first that has been presented to you since you sank the Hatteras! In the meantime, you have been all over the world, and it is not too much to say, that you have destroyed, and driven for protection under neutral flags, one half of the enemy's commerce, which, at the beginning of the war covered every sea. This is an achievement of which you may well be proud; and a grateful country will not be unmindful of it. The name of your ship has become a household word wherever civilization extends. Shall that name be tarnished by defeat?* ("Never! Never!" shouted the crew.) *The thing is impossible! Remember that you are in the English Channel, the theater of so much of the naval glory of our race, and that the eyes of all Europe are at this moment upon you. The flag that floats over you is that of a young republic, who bids defiance to her enemies, whenever, and wherever found. Show the world that you know how to uphold it! Go to your quarters!*[30]

When the *Alabama* had approached to within a mile of the still slowly retreating Federal ship, the *Kearsarge* suddenly wheeled and steamed directly for her attacker. At a range of 900 yards, she sheared to port and with smoke and flame enveloping her side, her starboard battery opened fire. The shells from her smooth bores fell short and the crew of the *Alabama* cheered. Before the spray from the *Kearsarge's* shells had settled, the booming voice of Kell shouted, "Fire!" Sinclair had shifted one of his port 32-pounders to the starboard side, and with a thunderous roar, all six guns spat fire and smoke as their missiles streaked toward the *Kearsarge*. The *Alabama* trembled from the recoil, but the guns were aimed too high, and the rifled shots whistled through the Union ship's rigging doing her no harm.

With a full head of steam and her extra margin of speed, the *Kearsarge* now attempted to maneuver into a raking position off the *Alabama's* stern. To counter this, the Confederate cruiser also turned to starboard, and thus the entire engagement was fought with both ships steaming around a common center and fighting their starboard batteries. Before the battle ended, seven complete circles would be made, with both antagonists maintaining a distance from each other of three quarters to one-half mile, all the while drifting westward in a three-knot current.[31]

The engagement now became general, and the *Alabama's* gunners were firing rapidly, twice as fast as the *Kearsarge*, but in their enthusiasm and inexperience, most of their shots were wild. Semmes, standing on the horse-block shouted to the gun captains to aim low. A ricochet was as effective as a direct hit. Peering through his marine glass, he watched as a shell from the forward Blakely pivot rifle crashed into the *Kearsarge's* sternpost. Holding his breath, he waited for the explosion that never came. Semmes would later claim that this one shot, if it had exploded, would have won the battle.[32]

The *Alabama* was now feeling the effects of the slow but accurate firing of the *Kearsarge's* 11-inch guns. Soon the spanker-gaff was shot away and the colors floated to the deck. Another flag was quickly raised to the mizzen-mast head. *Our bulwarks are soon shot away in sections,* Sinclair reported, *and the after pivot-gun is disabled on its port side, losing, in killed and wounded, all but the compressor-man. The quarter-deck thirty-two pounder of this division is now secured, and the crew sent to man the pivot-gun.*[33]

Semmes, noting the splinters flying from the side of the *Kearsarge* every time a shell struck, but seeing no damage, shouted to his first lieutenant, "Mr. Kell, use solid shot; our shells strike the enemy's side and fall into the water." After firing solid shot for a time, the *Alabama's* gunners began to alternate between solid shot and explosive shells. Many of the latter, however, failed to explode due to defective primers.[34]

After firing franticly for almost twenty minutes, the *Alabama's* gun crews settled down and began to make some of their shots count. With the *Alabama's* starboard side enveloped in smoke from her flaming guns, the forward pivot gun sent an 8-inch shell which exploded on the *Kearsarge's* quarterdeck, wounding three men at the aft pivot gun, one of whom later died. Another shell exploded in the hammock nettings, which set the Union ship on fire, while two more shots crashed through open gun ports but caused only minor damage. One of Sinclair's 32-

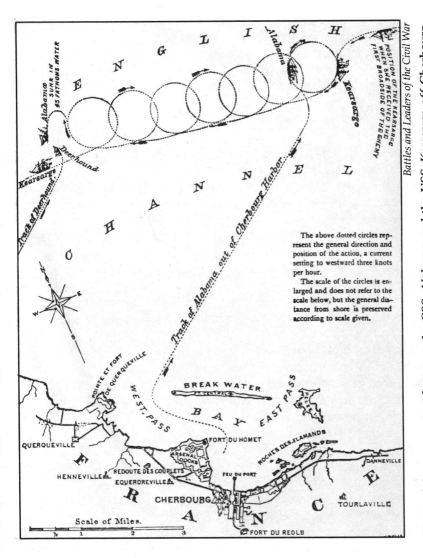

*Battles and Leaders of the Civil War*

Chart of the engagement between the CSS *Alabama* and the USS *Kearsarge* off Cherbourg, France, June 19, 1864.

pounders sent a shell crashing onto the *Kearsarge's* deck near the forward 11-inch pivot, but like the Blakely shell in the sternpost, it too,
failed to explode.[35]

The *Kearsarge's* guns were by now exacting a terrible toll upon the
*Alabama*. Kell wrote that, *The enemy's 11-inch shells were now doing severe
execution upon our quarter-deck section. Three of them successively entered
our 8-inch pivot-gun port; the first swept off the forward part of the gun's
crew; the second killed one man and wounded several others; and the third
struck the breast of the gun carriage, and spun around on deck till one of the
men picked it up and threw it overboard. Our decks were now covered with
the dead and the wounded, and the ship was careening heavily to starboard
from the effects of the shot holes on her water-line.*[36]

For a brief moment there was anticipation of a victory on the *Alabama* as one of her shells was seen to crash through the *Kearsarge's*
engine room skylight, but it also failed to explode. Down in the
*Alabama's* engine room, the engineers, working amidst suffocating
smoke and fumes, with water rising about their knees, struggled to
keep the engines running. *An eleven-inch shell enters us at the water-line,
in the wake of the writer's gun,* Sinclair wrote, *and passing on, explodes in
the engine-room, in its passage throwing a volume of water on board, hiding
for a moment the guns of the division. Our ship trembles from stem to stern
from the blow.*[37]

The battle had lasted almost an hour, and the *Alabama* was in trouble.
A spinning fragment of an 11-inch shell caught Semmes on the hand,
and blood began to drip on the horseblock. A quartermaster wrapped
a bandage around his hand and placed his arm in a sling. Lethal
wooden splinters and fragments of jagged iron spun through the air,
ripping into men and machinery before falling hissing into the water.
Still, the guns that were serviceable continued to thunder away at the
*Kearsarge*. Observers noted, however, the dull boom of the *Alabama's*
guns compared to the crisp report from the *Kearsarge*. With the Federal
ship continuing to pour her devastating fire into the *Alabama*, a gasping and choking engineer reported to Semmes that the rising water in
the hold was now exceeding the capacity of the pumps.

Semmes knew his ship was crippled and he decided to make a desperate attempt to reach shore. *Captain Semmes ordered me to be ready to
make all sail possible when the circuit of fight should put our head to the coast of
France;* Kell recounted, *then he would notify me at the same time to pivot to
port and continue the action with the port battery, hoping thus to right the ship
and enable us to reach the coast of France. The evolution was performed beauti-
fully, righting the helm, hoisting the head-sails, hauling aft the fore try-sail
sheet, and pivoting to port, the action continuing almost without cessation.*[38]

One of the seamen sent aloft by Kell to loose the jib, amid the hurricane of shot and shell, was an Englishman named John Roberts. Succeeding in his appointed task, he was beginning to return when a shell ripped open his abdomen. Sinclair remembered the horrifying scene: *Roberts in this desperate plight clung to the jib-boom, and working along the footrope, reached the top-gallant-forecastle, thence climbed down the ladder to the spar-deck, and with shrieks of agony, and his hands over his head, beating the air convulsively, reached the port gangway, where he fell and expired.*[39]

With the *Alabama* now turning for the coast, her stern was exposed to a raking attack from the *Kearsarge*, but for some reason, Winslow held his fire. Kell now attempted to resume the fight: *The port side of the quarter-deck was so encumbered with the mangled trunks of the dead that I had to have them thrown overboard, in order to fight the after pivot-gun. I abandoned the after 32-pounder, and transferred the men to fill up the vacancies at the pivot-gun under the charge of Midshipman Anderson. ... At this moment the chief engineer came on deck and reported the fires put out, and he could no longer work the engines. Captain Semmes said to me, "Go below, sir, and see how long the ship can float." As I entered the wardroom the sight was indeed appalling. There stood Assistant-Surgeon Llewellyn at his post, but the table and the patient upon it had been swept away from him by an 11-inch shell, which opened in the side of the ship an aperture that was fast filling the ship with water.*

Kell continued: *It took me but a moment to return to the deck and report to the captain that we could not float ten minutes. He replied to me, "Then, sir, cease firing, shorten sail, and haul down the colors; it will never do in this nineteenth century for us to go down, and the decks covered with our gallant wounded."*[40]

The colors were hauled down and after the *Alabama's* flag was lowered, the *Kearsarge* sent five more well-aimed shots crashing into the stricken ship. Winslow later admitted that he feared Semmes was trying some type of "ruse," and ordered his men to continue firing. With no white flag on board the *Alabama*, two crewmen held up the white portion of the Confederate national ensign at the stern and the firing finally ceased. The battle had lasted over an hour, but the struggle for life for the men of the *Alabama* was still not over.

With the ship settling by the stern, Semmes ordered Fullam to take the small dinghy, which was undamaged, and row to the *Kearsarge* and ask for their assistance, for there was no sign that she was lowering her boats. Kell, finding one quarterboat that was only slightly damaged, had all the wounded placed in it, and along with Surgeon Galt, they were sent off to the *Kearsarge*. Still no help appeared to be coming from the Union ship. Semmes now gave the order to abandon ship and it was every man for himself. Grasping anything available — a spar, a grate, an

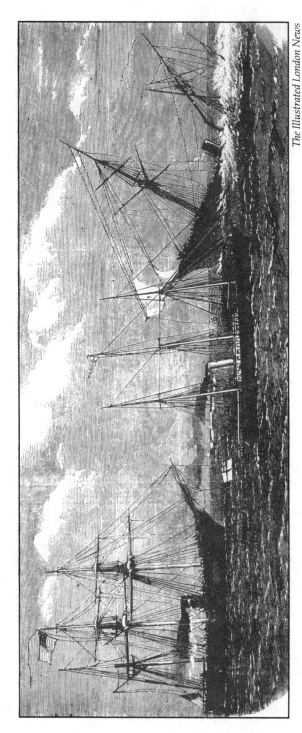

*The Illustrated London News*

The English yacht *Deerhound* (center) steams to the rescue of the *Alabama's* crew.

oar, — the men began jumping into the cold channel waters and struggling to get away from the sinking ship. Semmes and Kell, not wanting their swords to decorate some Union wardroom, unbuckled them and heaved them into the sea. *To enforce the order,* (to abandon ship) wrote Kell, *I walked forward and urged the men overboard. As soon as the decks were cleared, save of the bodies of the dead, I returned to the stern-port, where stood Captain Semmes with one or two of the men and his faithful steward,* (A. G. Bartelli) *who, poor fellow, was doomed to a watery grave, as he could not swim. The Alabama's stern port was now almost at the water's edge. Partly undressing, we plunged into the sea, and made an offing from the sinking ship, Captain Semmes with a life-preserver and I on a grating.*[41]

Kell tried to assist Semmes who was weak from loss of blood and could only use his uninjured arm. As he struggled to hold both their heads above water, he looked in vain for a rescue boat. Fortunately, John Lancaster of the *Deerhound,* recognizing the grave situation, steamed into the midst of the struggling men and lowered all his boats. Still no boats came from the *Kearsarge. Had victory struck the dumb, or helpless,* Kell wrote — *or had it frozen the milk of human kindness in their veins.* By now, in spite of his best efforts, Kell and Semmes had become separated. The *Deerhound's* steward, William Roberts, having met Semmes at Gibraltar two years earlier, recognized him as he struggled in the water and dragged him aboard one of the yacht's boats.[42]

Sinclair was one of the last to leave the sinking *Alabama,* and he paints a graphic picture of her demise: *The ship is settling to her spar-deck, and her wounded spars are staggering in the "steps," held only by the rigging. The decks present a woeful appearance, torn up in innumerable holes, and air bubbles rising and bursting, producing a sound as though the boat was in agony. ... From the wake of the Alabama, and far astern, a long, distant line of wreckage could be seen winding with the tide like a snake, with here and there a human head appearing amongst it. The boats were actively at work, saving first those who were without assistance.* At long last, some boats from the *Kearsarge* had been lowered and were now helping rescue the struggling men.

It had been an hour and twenty-seven minutes since the guns opened fire, and plunging into the water with Engineer O'Brien, Sinclair described the famous cruiser's last moments: *The Alabama's final plunge was a remarkable freak, and witnessed by O'Brien and self about one hundred yards off. She shot up out of the water bow first, and descended on the same line, carrying away with her plunge two of her masts, and making a whirlpool of considerable size and strength.*[43]

The *Alabama* was gone.

Kell described the struggle still taking place in the water: *The sea now presented a mass of living heads striving for their lives. Many poor fellows sank*

Battles and Leaders of the Civil War

The fatal plunge of the CSS *Alabama.*

*for want of timely aid. Near me I saw a float of empty shell-boxes, and called to one of the men, a good swimmer, to examine it; he did so and replied, "It is the doctor, sir, dead." Poor Llewellyn! He perished almost in sight of his home. The young midshipman, Maffitt, swam to me and offered his life-preserver. My grating was not proving a very buoyant float, and the white-caps breaking over my head were distressingly uncomfortable, to say the least. Maffitt said: "Mr. Kell, take my life-preserver, sir; you are almost exhausted." The gallant boy did not consider his own condition, but his pallid face told me that his heroism was superior to his bodily suffering, and I refused it. After twenty minutes or more I heard near me some one call out, "There is our first lieutenant," and the next moment I was pulled into a boat, in which was Captain Semmes stretched out in the stern-sheets, as pallid as death.*[44]

Shortly after Kell was pulled into one of the *Deerhound's* boats, a boat from the *Kearsarge* passed closely, and the Union sailors asked if anyone had seen Semmes. "Captain Semmes is drowned," Kell answered, and the Union boat continued its belated look for more survivors. The *Deerhound's* boats saved 42 men including 12 officers. The *Kearsarge* rescued 70 men, including the wounded brought in the *Alabama's* boat, but only five officers were among this group. Two French pilot boats rescued 15 more. Nine men had been killed on the *Alabama*, and 21 were listed as wounded. Twelve men were lost by drowning including David White, the mess steward-boy, who could not swim.[45]

The *Deerhound* steamed for Southampton, thus cheating the United States out of taking the hated "Pirate" Semmes alive. Until his dying day, Semmes would claim that he knew nothing of the chain armor on the *Kearsarge* and if he had, he would not have fought her. Others, including Sinclair, would say differently. The war continued for another year, and some of the men of the *Alabama* served in the cold and vastness of the Arctic Ocean on board the cruiser CSS *Shenandoah*. Semmes, after a tour of Europe to recover his health, returned to the beleaguered Confederacy in its dying days to command the James River Squadron.

The *Alabama* could not have found a more fitting grave, for she had lived her entire life on the oceans of the world. On that bright Sunday morning, Raphael Semmes, while struggling for life in the cold channel waters, turned to have one last look at his gallant ship as she slid rapidly, stern first, beneath the waves: *A noble Roman once stabbed his daughter, rather than she should be polluted by the foul embrace of a tyrant. It was with a similar feeling that Kell and I saw the Alabama go down. We had buried her as we had christened her, and she was safe from the polluting touch of the hated Yankee!*[46]

# Chapter Eight

## Gun Flashes on the Neuse

The brightly colored autumn leaves were gone by now. The majestic, old shade trees that lined the principal avenues of Richmond, Virginia were leafless and barren. The winter of 1863 was fast approaching and cold December winds whistled around the buildings and down the streets of the picturesque Confederate capital on the James River. Almost every day, just before sundown, passersby noticed a tall, stately man emerge from the unpretentious white mansion on Clay Street. Unmindful of the cold wind, he would mount his Arabian, and set off alone for a mind-clearing ride into the country. The cares and concerns of his office bore heavily upon the Confederate president. He desperately needed to get away from the constant duties of his position, if only for an hour, to commune with himself and his God.[1]

Occasionally, a handsome, young naval officer accompanied Davis on his lonely rides. John Taylor Wood, the president's nephew, was now assigned to his uncle as an aide. Wood, who had served on the *Virginia* during her battles in Hampton Roads, had been promoted to commander effective August 23, 1863, for "gallant and meritorious conduct" in his small boat operations on the Chesapeake Bay. As the two rode slowly out of Richmond and into the surrounding Virginia countryside, a weary Davis reviewed the probable future course of the war, and discussed with Wood his suggestions and ideas as to the

*140*

navy's role. During one of these cold rides, Wood revealed a daring plan to the president.[2]

Ever since the Federals had captured Roanoke Island in February of 1862, they had occupied Albemarle Sound, Pamlico Sound, and most of the eastern shore of North Caro-

lina. They had extended their fortifications to include the principal rivers and towns several miles inland. One North Carolina town whose occupation by the enemy was particularly objectionable, Wood explained, was New Bern. Located at the confluence of the Neuse and Trent Rivers, New Bern had been heavily fortified by the Federal occupying troops, and continued to provide a base for foraging expeditions against the citizens of the area. More importantly, Wood undoubtedly hastened to add, New Bern was only 45 miles from the all important Wilmington and Weldon Railroad over which most of the supplies for Lee's army in Virginia passed. If the Union forces from

**Commander John Taylor Wood, circa 1867. Leader of the small boat attack on the Federal gunboat USS *Underwriter*.**

New Bern should attack and cut this railroad line, the Army of Northern Virginia could be in deep trouble.

With Lee's army about to enter winter quarters, Wood believed that enough troops could be temporarily spared and sent to North Carolina. If this force attacked New Bern from the land side, coupled with a surprise naval attack from the river, Wood believed the town could be recaptured. The president must have listened intently, for he issued "verbal instructions" for Wood to journey to North Carolina, assess the feasibility of recovering New Bern, and to report his findings. Undoubtedly, he was also ordered to inspect the three ironclads under construction in eastern North Carolina. The vessels to which the president referred included the *Albemarle* being built at Edward's Ferry along the Roanoke River, the *Neuse*, under construction at Kinston on the Neuse River, and an unnamed ironclad just being laid down at Tarboro on the Tar River. If one or more of these vessels could be completed during the coming winter, they could possibly become the naval element in the anticipated attack on New Bern.[3]

During the first week of January, 1864, with the season's first mantle of snow covering the Confederate capitol, Wood left Richmond en route to eastern North Carolina to carry out the president's instructions. The young navy lieutenant riding the worn-out rails to Weldon, North Carolina, had spent nearly his entire adult life as a professional military officer. Born at the army outpost of Fort Snelling, then Iowa Territory (present day St. Paul, Minnesota), on August 13, 1830, Wood was the grandson of Zachary Taylor, twelfth president of the United States. On June 10, 1853, he was graduated second in his class at the Naval Academy at Annapolis. Making Maryland his home, John was commissioned a lieutenant in 1855, and was teaching gunnery and tactics at the academy when the war came. Although his father remained loyal to the Union, and even became Assistant Surgeon General of the United States, Wood resigned his commission on April 21, 1861, and traveled to Richmond to offer his services to the Confederacy. John's younger brother, Robert C. Wood, Jr., a graduate of West Point, also offered his allegiance to the Confederacy and rose to the rank of colonel in the cavalry command of John Hunt Morgan.[4]

Upon arriving in North Carolina, Wood probably inspected the ironclads under construction, and his findings would not have been encouraging. None of the vessels, it appeared, would be operational before spring. By then, any troops dispatched from Lee's army would be needed for the spring campaigns in Virginia and would have to be returned. If the ironclads could not be completed in time, the only other solution was to capture one or more of the enemy's gunboats, and use them to attack the fortifications around New Bern, while the army attacked from the land side. To accomplish this, Wood planned on staging a surprise night attack employing a force of sailors and marines in small boats. Hastening back to Richmond he reported his findings and plans to the president, who gave his approval, and sent him on to Lee to discuss the troops that would be needed.[5]

Lee recognized at once the potential for increased supplies that might be garnered from the eastern counties of North Carolina if the Federals could be driven out. In addition, the security of the railroad was reason enough to undertake the effort. On January 20, 1864, Lee wrote to Wood informing him that he was sending Brigadier General Robert F. Hoke's brigade to Kinston and that Major General George E. Pickett would be in command of the operation. Wishing him success, he commended Wood "to the care of a merciful Providence."[6]

Wood spent the final two weeks in January organizing the naval part of the operation. Surgeon Daniel B. Conrad, who would accompany the expedition, wrote afterwards: *In January, 1864, the Confederate officers on duty in Richmond, Wilmington and Charleston were aroused by a telegram from the Navy Department to detail four boats' crews of picked men and officers, who were to be fully armed, equipped and rationed for six days; they were to start at once by rail for Weldon, North Carolina, reporting on arrival to Commander J. T. Wood, who would give further instructions.*

*So perfectly secret and well guarded was our destination that not until we had all arrived at Kinston, North Carolina, by various railroads, did we have the slightest idea of where we were going or what the object was of the naval raid. We suspected, however, from the name of its commander, that it would be "nervous work," as he had a reputation for boarding, capturing and burning the enemy's gunboats on many previous occasions.*[7]

Tne James River Squadron supplied four cutters, each manned by ten seaman and two officers, under the command of Lieutenant Benjamin P. Loyall. Lieutenant Loyall, commandant of midshipmen at the Confederate Naval Academy on the *Patrick Henry*, would be Wood's second in command. The men were well armed with cutlasses, revolvers, and a few axes, and each wore heavy clothing including a pea jacket to ward off the January cold.[8] The sailors were from the various ships of the squadron, but also included were twenty-five Confederate Marines of Company C under the command of Captain Thomas S. Wilson. The Enfield rifles of these marines would soon prove their worth in the forthcoming attack.[9]

To avoid unnecessary attention, Wood instructed Loyall to launch his contingent in the James River and pull down stream to Petersburg where he would meet them. At 9:00 a.m., on the cold Thursday morning of January 28, Loyall and his command left the city of Richmond behind, and at a measured gait, headed their cutters south. Loyall wrote later that they, *reached Petersburg before daylight* (next day). *There was a railway train waiting for us, and we hauled our boats out of the water, and, by hard work, loaded them on the flat cars before the people were up and about.*

The boats were lashed onto the cars right-side-up, and once all equipment was loaded aboard, the sailors and marines took their places in the boats. Loyall was amused at the scene: *We started off at once, and it was a novel sight to see a train like that ... Jack sitting up on the seats of the boats and waving his hat to the astonished natives, who never saw such a circus before.*[10] "Jack" also exacted a promise from some of the girls along the route that the pretty Southern belles would bestow a kiss on them for every enemy flag they brought back.

Reaching Kinston before daylight on the 31st, Wood had the boats unloaded and dragged to the Neuse River. Putting Loyall in command, he sent them downstream a few miles where they landed on a small island in the middle of the river and set up camp. Meanwhile, an impatient Wood paced the depot platform waiting for the contingents to arrive from Wilmington and Charleston.[11]

In Wilmington, Lieutenant George W. Gift had experienced difficulty obtaining the four cutters specified in the orders from Richmond. Finally securing two boats and two heavy launches armed with a twelve-pound howitzer, Gift left for Goldsboro, North Carolina. Here he was to rendezvous with the Charleston contingent under the command of Lieutenant Philip Porcher. Leaving Goldsboro, their train finally pulled into Kinston at noon on the 31st, and Gift along with Porcher, found Wood still pacing the station platform. The Charleston and Wilmington boats were unloaded, all except the two heavy launches, and dragged to the river. Eager to join his men at the island, Wood instructed Gift to find a couple of mules, hitch them to the launches, move them to the river, and join him as soon as possible. Leaving eighty men with Gift, Wood and the remaining sailors pulled out into mid-stream, and with the sun sinking low on the western horizon, turned the cutters down river.[12]

It was almost sunset by the time Wood stepped onto the island where the rest of his men were waiting. Calling the group together, he explained the details of the mission to them. Dividing the 150 sailors and marines into two divisions, he placed Lieutenant Loyall in command of one and the other under himself. *Commander Wood, in distinct and terse terms,* Surgeon Conrad remembered, *gave orders to each boat's crew and its officers just what was expected of them, stating that the object of the expedition was to, that night, board some one of the enemy's gunboats, then supposed to be lying off the city of New Bern, now nearly sixty miles (actually less than 30 miles) distant from where we then were by water. He said that she was to be captured without fail. Five boats were to board her on either side simultaneously, and then when in our possession we were to get up steam and cruise after other gunboats. It was a grand scheme, and was received by the older men with looks of admiration and with rapture by the young midshipmen, all of whom would have broken out into loud cheers but for the fact that the strictest silence was essential to the success of the daring undertaking.*[13]

Wood passed out white strips of cotton cloth and instructed each man to tie it around his left arm. The password for the night would be *Sumter.* Everyone now realized that some severe hand-to-hand fighting was in store. Conrad remembered those final moments before casting off on this dangerous mission:

*In concluding his talk, Commander Wood solemnly said: "We will now pray;" and thereupon he offered up the most touching appeal to the Almighty that it has ever been my fortune to have heard. I can remember it now, after the long interval that has elapsed since then.*[14] Lieutenant Loyall also recalled this experience: *It was a solemn and impressive scene — just as the shades of evening were falling — this unusual assemblage of armed men. Then with muffled oars, a single line was formed, and we pulled with a measured stroke down the stream.*[15]

Midshipman J. Thomas Scharf, who would later write a history of the Confederate navy, was in charge of one of the boats. He described the journey down the Neuse: *Bending silently to the muffled oars, the expedition moved down the river. Now, the Neuse broadened until the boats seemed to be on a lake; again, the tortuous stream narrowed until the party could almost touch the trees on either side. Not a sign of life was visible, save occasionally when a flock of wild ducks, startled at the approach of the boats, rose from the banks, and then poising themselves for a moment overhead, flew on swift wing to the shelter of the woodland or the morass. No other sound was heard to break the stillness save the constant, steady splash of the oars and the ceaseless surge of the river. Sometimes a fallen log impeded the progress, again a boat would run aground, but as hour after hour passed by, the boats still sped on, the crews cold and weary, but yet cheerful and uncomplaining. Night fell, dark shadows began to creep over the marshes and crowd the river; owls screeched among the branches overhead, through which the expedition occasionally caught glimpses of the sky. There was nothing to guide the boats on their course, but the crews still kept hopefully on, and by eleven o'clock the river seemed to become wider, and Commander Wood discovered that we had reached the open country above New Bern.*[16]

Wood and his boats surged on, and in the early morning hours they drew near their objective. Even though they were dead tired from the long pull down the river, the men's spirits rose as they could smell the salt air from the water of Pamlico Sound. Surgeon Conrad wrote that, *at about half past three o'clock we found ourselves upon the broad estuary of New Bern Bay. Then closing up in double column we pulled for the lights of the city, even up to and close in and around the wharves themselves, looking (but in vain) for our prey. Not a gunboat could be seen; none were there.*[17]

Wood searched cautiously looking for a target, but there were no Federal ships in sight. Lieutenant Loyall explained that they *searched in vain to find something afloat, although we got close enough to the wharf to hear talking, probably the sentries on the dock. There was nothing to be done but find some refuge out of sight until next night, but it was hard letting down from the pitch of excitement and expectation we had been under — the unbending of the bow that had been strung for action.*[18]

With daylight approaching, Wood led his men two to three miles back up the Neuse and entered Bachelor's Creek. Finding a small desolate spot, the boats were pulled into the weeds and carefully hidden in the high grass and brush. With pickets posted to give the alarm, the men threw themselves on the soggy ground and attempted to get some sleep.[19]

As the morning sun began to burn the low-lying mist off the river, the men were startled to see in plain sight of their bivouac, a tall crow's nest occupied by a Union lookout on picket duty. Loyall wrote that *I assure you it gave us a creepy, uneasy feeling to think that our whole movement and intention might be discovered.* By staying well hidden, the presence of the gray clad sailors and marines went unnoticed by the lookout.

*Shortly after sunrise,* Conrad remembered, *we heard firing by infantry. It was quite sharp for an hour, and then it died away. It turned out to be, as we afterwards learned, a futile attack by our lines under General Pickett on the works around New Bern. We were obliged to eat cold food all that day, as no fires were permissible under any circumstances; so all we could do was keep a sharp lookout for the enemy, go to sleep again, and wish for the night to come.*[20]

The musket firing that Conrad heard was indeed the sound of the attack launched at daylight by Pickett on the fortifications surrounding New Bern. Leaving Kinston at 1:00 a.m. on February 1, Pickett had divided his 4,500 man force into three columns. Two brigades were to attack the Federal fortifications in front of New Bern at sunrise, while another force, under the command of Colonel James Dearing, was sent across the Neuse to attack Fort Anderson opposite the town. Meanwhile, General Seth M. Barton's command, consisting of twelve companies of cavalry accompanied by artillery, had left the day before and crossed the Trent River. Their assignment was to prevent reinforcements by swinging south of the town and cutting the Atlantic and North Carolina Railroad between New Bern and Morehead City. Once that was done, they were to cross the Trent using the railroad bridge and drive toward New Bern from the south in conjunction with Pickett's frontal assault.

The Federals offered stiff resistance along Bachelor's Creek, adjacent to where Wood's men were hiding, but General Hoke's brigade splashed across the creek, slammed into the Union troops, and drove them back toward their fortifications. Soon the heavy guns of the forts were lobbing shells into the Confederate ranks as Pickett listened anxiously for the sound of Barton's guns to the south. The day wore on, and still there was no sign of Barton. Late that afternoon, two trains loaded with Federal reinforcements from Morehead City arrived, and Pickett now knew that Barton had failed to reach his objective. Reluctantly, he issued orders to his commanders to pull their troops out after dark and return to Kinston. The land portion of the attack on New Bern was over.[21]

While the abortive Confederate land attack was taking place, Lieutenant Gift, in Kinston, had located a couple of mules, and with them, had dragged the two heavy launches to the river. With forty men manning the oars in each boat, they sped down the Neuse at over six knots.

Arriving at Swift Creek, about two miles up river from Bachelor's Creek, Gift sent a courier to Pickett to inquire about Wood's whereabouts. When the messenger returned with the information, Gift immediately cast off, rowed the remaining two miles, and turned into Bachelor's Creek, arriving at Wood's bivouac and hiding place at sunset. His two heavy launches, each armed with a 12-pounder howitzer, and the 85 plus men now brought Wood's strength to approximately 230 men and officers.[22]

Shortly after Gift and his men had arrived, with the welcome shadows of night stretching its protective veil over the river, Wood called for his swiftest boat and most experienced crew. Together with Loyall, they pulled noiselessly down the Neuse taking care to remain within the shadows of the river bank. *We had not gone two miles,* Loyall wrote, *when simultaneously we both cried, "There she is!" We discovered a black steamer anchored close up to the right flank of the outer fortifications of New Bern, where she had come that day.* Staying within the dark shadows of the shoreline, Wood studied the steamer closely with his night glasses. He noted with satisfaction that her low wooden rail would make her relatively easy to board. *...Having located her exactly,* Loyall continued, *we returned to our hiding place, with the understanding that we would attack her between 12 and 4 o'clock in the morning* (Tuesday, February 2).[23]

The Federal vessel that Wood and Loyall had spotted was the USS *Underwriter* commanded by Acting Master Jacob Westervelt. The gunboat was a sidewheel steamer of 325 tons, 186 feet long and 35 feet abeam, and her powerful engines developed 800 horsepower. She had fired the first shot at the battle for Roanoke Island in September 1861, and was considered by the Confederates as the most powerful and dangerous gunboat on the sounds of North Carolina. She carried two 8-inch guns, one 30-pound rifle, one 12-pound howitzer, and a crew of 12 officers and 72 men.

Assembling his men at 11:00 p.m., Wood went over the attack plan in detail. He explained that the enemy vessel was about one hundred yards from Battery Number Two and not far from Fort Stevenson. The boats would move in double columns with Loyall's division striking the *Underwriter* aft of the giant paddle wheels, while his own section would strike the ship forward. Gift's launches would follow with extra men and be prepared for towing if necessary. Wood reminded them to wear their white arm bands, and began assigning several marines with their Enfield rifles to each boat as sharpshooters. Pistols and cutlasses were strapped on, and ammunition was distributed. Light rain began to fall as the men filed silently to the boats. Looking up at the fast-fading stars, Midshipman Palmer Sanders was heard to mumble: *I wonder, boys, how many of us will be up among the stars by tomorrow morning.* [24]

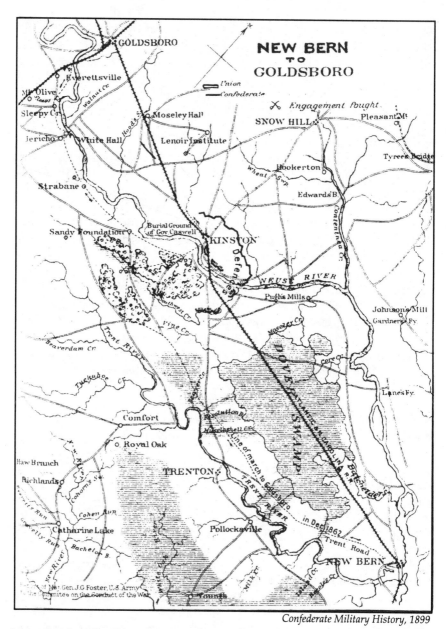

*Confederate Military History, 1899*

Map showing the Neuse River between Kinston and New Bern, down which Wood's men rowed to attack the USS *Underwriter*.

Midshipman Scharf, who refers to Wood by his army rank (Wood had been given the dual rank of colonel of cavalry by Davis on January 26, 1863), wrote a graphic and poignant description of the approach and attack on the Federal gunboat: *After forming parallel to each other, the two divisions pulled rapidly down the stream. When they had rowed a short distance, Col. Wood called all the boats together, final instructions were given, and this being through with, he offered a fervent prayer for the success of his mission. It was a strange and ghostly sight, the men resting on their oars with heads uncovered, the commander also bareheaded, standing erect in the stern of his boat; the black waters rippling beneath; the dense overhanging clouds pouring down sheets of rain, and in the blackness beyond an unseen bell tolling as if from some phantom cathedral. The party listened — four peals were sounded and then they knew it was the bell of the Underwriter, or some other of the gunboats, ringing out for two o'clock.*

*Guided by the sound, the boats pulled toward the steamer, pistols, muskets and cutlasses in readiness. The advance was necessarily slow and cautious. Suddenly when about three hundred yards from the Underwriter, her hull loomed up out of the inky darkness. Through the stillness came the sharp ring of five bells for half-past two o'clock, and just as the echo died away, a quick, nervous voice from the deck hailed, "Boat ahoy!" No answer was given, but Col. Wood kept steadily on. "Boat ahoy! Boat ahoy!!" again shouted the watch. No answer. Then the rattle on board the steamer sprung summoning the men to quarters, and the Confederates could see the dim and shadowy outline of hurrying figures on deck. Nearer Col. Wood came, shouting, "Give way!" "Give way, boys, give way!" repeated Lieut. Loyall and the respective boat commanders, and give way they did with a will.*[25]

With the boats only 100 yards out, the black silhouette of the *Underwriter* suddenly exploded in a wicked crimson line of flame as the Federals opened fire with muskets and pistols. Bending to their oars, their backs to the blazing Federal volleys, the Confederate sailors pulled with all their strength, and the cutters flew over the water. Stabbing tongues of orange and red suddenly erupted from twenty-five Enfields as Confederate marines, swaying to the motion of the oarsmen, stood in the bows and bravely returned the fire. *Our coxswain* (in Wood's boat), *a burly, gamy Englishman,* Conrad wrote, *who by gesture and loud word, was encouraging the crew, steering by the tiller between his knees, his hands occupied in holding his pistols, suddenly fell forward on us dead, a ball having struck him fairly in the forehead. The rudder now having no guide, the boat swerved aside, and instead of our bow striking at the gangway, we struck the wheelhouse, so that the next boat, commanded by Lieutenant Loyall, had the deadly honor of being first on board.*[26]

Wood's boats slammed against the side of the *Underwriter* forward of the wheelhouse and grappling hooks flew through the night air.

The second division arrived farther aft and Lieutenant Loyall wrote that, *our boats struck the vessel just abaft the wheelhouse, where the guards make a platform, an admirable place for getting on board. The ship's armory, where all the small arms were kept, was in a room just there under the hurricane deck, and they did not stop to reload, but loaded guns were handed to the men, as fast as they could fire. It seemed like a sheet of flame, and the very jaws of death. Our boat struck bow on, and our bow oarsman, James Wilson, of Norfolk, caught her with his grapnel, and she swung side on with the tide.*[27]

Loyall and Engineer Emmet F. Gill, revolvers and cutlasses in hand, were the first to scramble over the rail, falling in a heap on the slippery, rain-soaked surface. Engineer Gill, four bullets in his body, was dead before he hit the deck. Before Loyall could rise, four wounded sailors came tumbling down on top of him, while at the same moment, Confederate pistols were spitting flame from amidships as Wood and his men scrambled over the side. More boats came crashing against the *Underwriter*, and Lieutenant Gift, who had slowed his launches to avoid ramming the cutters, shouted for Scharf to fire the howitzer. With a loud bang, the little 12-pounder barked and sent a full load of canister whistling into the Union ship's pilot house. Before Scharf could reload, the launches, too, were against the *Underwriter*, and Gift's men were forcing their way aboard.

*Now the fighting was furious, and at close quarters*, Loyall reported. *Our men were eager, and as one would fall another came on. Not one faltered or fell back. The cracking of fire arms and the rattle of cutlasses made a deafening din. The enemy gave way slowly, and soon began to get away by taking to the ward room and engine room hatches.*[28]

Confederate Marines, who were among the first to scramble on board, were grasping their empty rifles by the barrel and wielding them as giant clubs with devastating effect. The deck was slippery from blood and rain, causing men to loose their footing, and as they fell, they wrestled with the enemy, tumbling and rolling in a frightful grapple of death. Wood kept urging his men on. Conrad remembered: *I could hear Wood's stentorian voice giving orders and encouraging the men.*[29]

Midshipman Scharf, his pistol blazing, was now in the middle of the desperate fighting and he later recalled the scene: *The enemy had by this time gathered in the ways just aft of the wheelhouse, and as the Confederates came up they poured into them volley after volley of musketry, each flash of which reddened the waters around. ... Cutlasses and pistols were the weapons of the Confederates, and each selected and made a rush for his man. The odds were against the attacking party, and some of them had to struggle with three opponents. But they never flinched in the life-and-death struggle, nor did the gallant enemy. The boarders forced the fighting. Blazing rifles had no terrors for them. They drove back the enemy inch by inch. Steadily, but surely,*

*The Confederate Soldier in the Civil War*

Confederate sailors and Marines led by John Taylor Wood, launch a night attack on the USS *Underwriter.*

*the boarders began to gain the deck, and crowded their opponents to the companion-ways or other places of concealment; while all the time fierce hand-to-hand fights were going on on other portions of the vessel. Now one of the Confederates would sink exhausted — again, one of the enemy would fall on the slippery deck. Rifles were snatched from the hands of the dead and the dying, and used in the hands as bludgeons did deadly work. Down the companion-ways the attacked party were driven pell-mell into the ward-room and steerage, and even to the coal bunkers, and after another sharp but decisive struggle the enemy surrendered.*[30]

Conrad recalled that *in less than five minutes, I could distinguish a strange synchronous roar, but did not understand what it meant at first; but it soon became plain: "She's ours!" everybody crying at the top of their voices, in order to stop the shooting, as only our men were on their feet.*[31] As the exhausted and bleeding Confederates gathered on deck, the night air was rent with a fierce "Rebel Yell."

There was little time to celebrate, however. After Wood gave the order to cease fire, he held a hurried conversation with Loyall. If they could raise steam and get the engines running, they could move the gunboat up the Neuse and put her in shape under Confederate colors. Because the *Underwriter* was the largest and most heavily armed vessel on the river, the Confederates would have temporary control of the waters around New Bern. Wood ordered his two engineers to hurry below to see if there was enough steam in the boilers to get the ship underway.

Meanwhile, Surgeon Conrad had begun tending to the wounded. *I examined a youth who was sitting in the lap of another, and in feeling his head I felt my hand slip down between his ears, and to my horror, discovered that his head had been cleft in two by a boarding sword in the hands of some giant of the forecastle. It was Passed Midshipman Palmer Sanders. Directing his body, and those of all the other killed, to be laid out aft on the quarter deck, I went down below, looking for the wounded in the ward-room, where the lights were burning, and found half a dozen with slight shots from revolvers.*[32]

While Conrad was attending the wounded below, the engineers reported disappointing news to Wood. The fires in the furnaces were banked, steam pressure was low, and it would take at least an hour to build enough to turn the big paddle wheels. Wood ordered Gift to tow the vessel with his launches, but the ship had been moored so securely that it was estimated it would take another hour to slip the chains which held her fast. At that moment, the *Underwriter* was rocked by the explosion of a shell which crashed into her upper works. The gunners at Fort Stevenson, alerted by the firing, in addition to escaped Federal crewmen, had opened fire on the gunboat. *All the shore batteries then opened fire on the doomed vessel,* Scharf recalled, *either careless of or not realizing the fact that their own wounded must be on board; and the captors soon found that a rapid movement would have to be made.*[33]

The *Underwriter* had become a trap. As more and more shore batteries opened fire, Wood made his decision to destroy the vessel. Conrad recalled that, *very calmly and clearly he directed me to remove all dead and wounded to the boats, which the several crews were now hauling to the lee side of the vessel, where they would be protected from the shots from the fort. The order was soon carried out by willing hands.* There was no time, however, to remove the Federal dead and they were left on board. While the wounded and the prisoners were being hurried into the boats, the guns of the *Underwriter* were quickly loaded and pointed toward the Federal fortifications.

*After an extended search through the ship's decks, above and below,* Conrad continued, *we found that we had removed all the dead and wounded, and then, when the search ended, reported to Captain Wood on the quarter-deck, where, giving his orders where the fire from the fort was deadly and searching, he called up four lieutenants to him, to whom he gave instructions as follows: Two of them were to go below in the forward part of the ship, and the other two below in the afterpart, where from their respective stations they were to fire the vessel, and not to leave her until her decks were all ablaze, and then at that juncture they were to return to their proper boats and report.*[34]

Loyall, who had instructed one of the four lieutenants, Francis L. Hoge, to take fire from the furnace, and set the ship ablaze, recounted the final act of the drama: *When we had gotten (a) half mile from the ship, Wood pulled up toward our boats and asked if I had ordered the ship set afire. I said: "Yes," but it looked as if it had not been done successfully. Just then Hoge came along in his boat and said that he had set fire to her.* Not seeing any flames, Wood ordered Hoge to return to the *Underwriter* and make sure, a dangerous undertaking with every Federal gun that could be brought to bear now firing on the vessel.

*In about ten minutes we saw flames leap out of a window forward of the wheelhouse, where the engineer's supplies were kept,* Loyall continued, *and Hoge pulling away. In a very few minutes the whole expanse of water was lighted up, and you may be sure we struck out with a vim to rendezvous at Swift Creek, about six miles up the river.* (In the haste to leave, one of the boats was found to contain twenty Union prisoners and only two Confederate guards. In the confusion of the darkness and exploding shells from the forts, the Federals easily overpowered their captors and escaped to shore.) ...*As we were pulling up we could hear now and then the boom of the guns of the Underwriter as they were discharged by heat from the burning ship, and just before reaching our landing place we heard the awful explosion of the sturdy vessel, when the fire reached her magazine.*[35]

The rain was falling in torrents as the exhausted Confederates pulled slowly up Swift Creek. From almost every boat could be heard the groans and cries of the wounded. With morning light just breaking over the eastern horizon, the cutters landed on the soggy creek bank and the injured were gently lifted ashore. Five Confederates had been killed: Engineer Gill, Midshipman Saunders, Seamen Hawkins and Sullivan, and Private William Bell of the Marine Corps. Eleven sailors and four Marines had been wounded. The Federals lost nine killed, including the *Underwriter's* commander, Westervelt, whose body washed ashore a month later. The bodies of the remaining Federal dead burned in the conflagration that consumed the *Underwriter*. Twenty Union sailors were wounded but carried away and cared for by Wood's men, and twenty-six more were taken up Swift Creek as prisoners. Twenty-three of the *Underwriter's* crew had escaped. The two division's cutters bore stark evidence to the ferocity of the Federal's fire with each one averaging fourteen white plugs to seal the jagged bullet holes.

Later that afternoon, a solemn funeral service was held on the banks of Swift Creek. With Lieutenant Loyall reading the church service, five comrades in navy gray were lowered into North Carolina soil. That night, and for the next two nights, the Confederates pulled against the strong current of the Neuse and arrived at Kinston on February 5. There they waited while Wood proceeded on to Richmond. Loyall sent the Wilmington and Charleston contingents on home, and finally, on February 9, Wood telegraphed orders for the remainder to return to Petersburg.[36]

The objective to capture New Bern had failed, owing in part to the lack of aggressiveness by Pickett and the failure of Barton to cut the rail line. The Confederate navy, however, and indeed the entire country, was elated over the destruction of the Federal's most powerful gunboat in the sounds of North Carolina, and done so under the very guns of the Union fortifications. While the Confederate Congress passed a resolution offering its thanks to Wood and his command, perhaps the highest compliment was given by Union Admiral Porter: *This was rather a mortifying affair for the (Union) navy, however fearless on the part of the Confederates. This gallant expedition was led by Commander John Taylor Wood. It was to be expected that with so many clever officers, who left the Federal navy, and cast their fortunes with the Confederates, such gallant action would often be attempted.*[37]

The boats were again loaded on the flatcars, and on a bleak and frigid day in February, with the men in their seats, the train clattered northward on its way to Petersburg. Bundled up in their pea jackets and blankets, the gray-clad sailors had not forgotten the charming young belles that they had met on their southbound journey: *On the return trip the young men, never for an instant forgetting the bargain they had made, manufactured several miniature (Union) flags,* Conrad remembered. *We old ones purposely stopped at all the stations we had made coming down in order to see the fun. The young ladies were called out at each place, and after the dead were lamented, the wounded in the cars cared for, then the midshipmen brought out their flags, recalled the promises made to them, and demanded their redemption. Immediately there commenced a lively outburst of laughter and denials, a skirmish, followed by a slight resistance, and the whole bevy were kissed 'seriatim' by the midshipmen, and but for the whistle of the train warning them away, they would have continued indefinitely.*[38]

# *Chapter Nine*

## Gray Warriors Beneath the Waves

Some of the citizens of Charleston, South Carolina had become accustomed to the sight; others had not. Visible from the waterfront and the "Battery" almost every evening during the approaching winter of 1863 was the long, low shape of a peculiar looking vessel. Usually around sundown, observers would see a lone sailor cast off the lines and then disappear into the boat's interior. Slowly, the strange craft would ease into the channel and begin to make its way out of the harbor. With no protruding sail or smokestack, its upper surface was barely visible above the water. Two open hatchways, one forward and one aft, were all that interrupted the black silhouette. Gently rising and falling with the swells of the outgoing tide, the mysterious vessel glided silently out toward the green waters of the Atlantic Ocean. Occasionally, as the boat would rise on an unusually large swell, a long spar could be discerned protruding from the bow with a sinister looking black cylinder attached to the end.

As the bizarre craft proceeded out in the direction of the Federal blockading fleet, perceptive viewers, perhaps with a high quality telescope, could see the hatch covers close, and suddenly, in a surge of bubbles, the boat would disappear beneath the surface. At that point, some may have turned sadly away or started for home thinking another boat had sunk in the harbor and more wives and mothers may

*156*

be crying by morning. But if they lingered long enough, perhaps twenty minutes or more, and there was still enough light, they might catch a distant glimpse farther down the channel. Silently, it would break the surface briefly, and then would sink again to be lost from view in the gathering darkness. Usually, it would return to its mooring by morning. Several times, however, it had not returned, at least not by its own power. On those occasions, it took several days for divers to locate the sunken craft. When finally raised by cranes from the bottom, and the hatches opened, there would then be weeping in Charleston.

Little did the residents of the city realize that they were historic witnesses to what would become the world's first successful submarine. Forerunner of all the great and fearsome undersea craft to come in a later century, this historic vessel they were watching was the Confederate submarine, CSS *H. L. Hunley*. No other vessel built by or for the Confederacy is as intriguing and innovative as the *Hunley*. Even the swift cruisers such as *Alabama* or *Shenandoah*, the mighty ironclads like *Virginia*, *Arkansas*, or *Tennessee* cannot rival the little *Hunley* for sheer genius in concept, construction, and operation. This vessel, as events have shown, introduced a whole new concept and dimension to naval warfare which still influences our lives today.[1]

The *Hunley* may have found its moment of glory at Charleston, but its life began in Mobile, Alabama. Designed and financed by James R. McClintock, Baxter Watson, and Horace L. Hunley, the builders were able to incorporate lessons learned in the building and testing of several earlier undersea boats, first at New Orleans and later at Mobile. To save time in construction, they used an existing ship's boiler that was twenty-five feet in length and four feet in diameter as the basis for the hull. This was cut in half lengthwise and reinforcing iron bars added to the inside of each half. The upper and lower halves were then rejoined by riveting two twelve-inch strips of iron between them on either side, and all seams were tightly caulked and sealed. Tapered sections were bolted to both ends to form the bow and stern, while on the exterior, a twelve-inch strip of iron was bolted to the top to form a deck. Inside the boat, bulkheads were fabricated fore and aft.[2] The space between these bulkheads and the ends of the boat served as water-ballast tanks which were, unfortunately, left open at the top causing at least one accident by allowing the interior to flood when they overflowed. Both ballast tanks were equipped with inlet valves or "sea cocks" which, when opened, would allow sea water to fill the tanks, causing the boat to sink. In addition, each tank was equipped with a hand pump to force the water out causing the boat to rise. In an emergency, these pumps could also operate as bilge pumps.

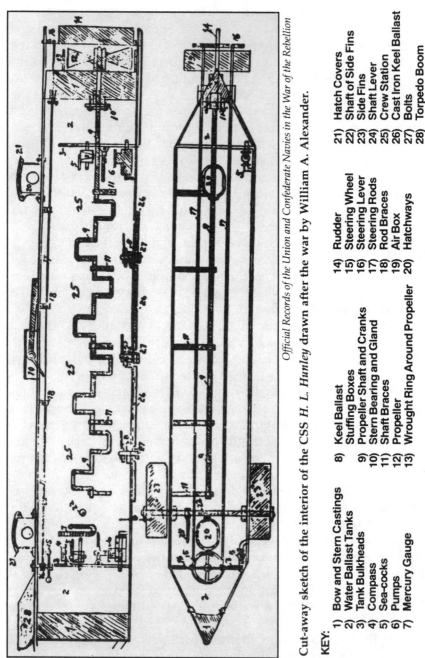

Cut-away sketch of the interior of the CSS *H. L. Hunley* drawn after the war by William A. Alexander.

Official Records of the Union and Confederate Navies in the War of the Rebellion

KEY:

1) Bow and Stern Castings
2) Water Ballast Tanks
3) Tank Bulkheads
4) Compass
5) Sea-cocks
6) Pumps
7) Mercury Gauge
8) Keel Ballast
9) Stuffing Boxes
10) Propeller Shaft and Cranks
11) Stern Bearing and Gland
12) Shaft Braces
13) Propeller
14) Wrought Ring Around Propeller
15) Rudder
16) Steering Wheel
17) Steering Lever
18) Steering Rods
19) Rod Braces
20) Air Box
21) Hatchways
22) Hatch Covers
23) Shaft of Side Fins
24) Side Fins
25) Shaft Lever
26) Crew Station
27) Cast Iron Keel Ballast
28) Bolts
Torpedo Boom

The CSS *H. L. Hunley* on a dock at Charleston, South Carolina. Photo is from a painting completed on December 6, 1863, by Confederate artist Conrad Wise Chapman.

To give the boat a weighted keel, which would serve to keep it upright, additional iron ballast was placed under the hull. These were attached with special T-bolts that could be turned from the inside, which would drop the ballast in case of an emergency. Diving vanes, five feet long and eight inches wide, were positioned on either side of the forward part of the boat. A one and one-quarter inch rod passed through stuffing boxes at the rear of the commander's station and connected these vanes to the diving lever. This lever was positioned by the commander's side, and when raised or lowered would change the depth of the boat without having to disturb the water level in the ballast tanks.

Running fore to aft through the center of the boat, and supported by brackets attached to the starboard side, was a long crankshaft which was connected to the propeller. Power was supplied by eight crewmen sitting along the port side of the hull (the aft-most position being occupied by the officer controlling the aft ballast tank), each turning his respective part of the crank. Around the three-bladed propeller was a shroud to prevent fouling, and attached to this was the rudder. Approximately 14 feet apart on the top of the hull were two small entrance hatchways measuring 16 by 12 inches, each with 8-inch coamings containing three glass portholes. Both hatches were equipped with heavy hinged lids incorporating rubber gaskets, and special bolts that could be tightened from inside or out.[3]

For cruising just below the surface or when surfaced and rough seas required the hatches to be kept closed, an iron "air box" was positioned on the top side of the hull just to the rear of the forward hatch. This box was equipped with two 4-foot tubes lying parallel with the hull. These could be rotated by a lever inside the boat to a vertical position when air was needed and the vessel was near the surface. A single tube led from this air box through stuffing boxes to the interior. The end of this tube was equipped with a key control which, when turned, could close off the upper end to prevent water from entering when the boat dove any depth below the surface. Available records seem to indicate that, because of the fear of flooding the interior, this air supply system was seldom used.[4]

All seams and crevices were tightly sealed on the interior, and wrought iron ladders led up to each hatch. The captain stood so that when the boat was partially submerged, he could sight through the glass of the coamings of the forward hatch. At his hands were the diving lever which controlled the vanes on the exterior, a sea cock used to flood the forward ballast tank, a hand pump to pump out the water, a mercury depth gauge (manometer), a magnetic compass, and a small ship's wheel connected to the rudder. A petty officer occupied the rear hatch position with a sea cock and hand pump to control the aft ballast tank. Interior light was provided by a single candle, and when the flame went out in 20 to 25 minutes, it was an indication that it was time to surface for air. When launched in the spring of 1863, the *Hunley* measured forty feet long and was the best underwater boat that had been completed to date. Considering all the handicaps and shortages under which the Confederacy was struggling, it is simply amazing that such a unique and sophisticated craft was designed and built at all.[5]

To begin an attack, the forward crew members, followed by the captain, would enter through the forward hatch. The remaining crew boarded via the aft hatch, followed by the second officer after he had cast off the lines. While remaining on the surface, the boat would then proceed under its own power, or at times, be towed by a steam tug or a "David" torpedo-boat to a point where the approach toward the enemy fleet could begin. Because of the *Hunley's* spar torpedo, this operation could be very dangerous to the towing vessel. For this reason, most sorties began by utilizing the boat's "internal" power. When all was ready, the hatch covers were closed, the candle lit, and the sea cocks opened, which allowed the boat to settle until the outside water level could be seen through the portholes. This would put the hull approximately three inches beneath the surface. The sea cocks were then closed, and the crew was instructed to turn the crank, putting the boat under way. The captain, after sighting on a distant object and checking the compass heading, would then lower the diving lever very slightly, noting on the mercury gauge the depth below the surface. When the desired depth was reached, he would bring the lever back to neutral, and the boat would proceed at that depth. Raising the diving lever would bring the boat back to just beneath the surface.[6]

The torpedo was a copper cylinder which held ninety pounds of explosive. Percussion primers on the front and sides would detonate the charge when contact was made against the hull of a ship. It appears from existing records, however, that the *Hunley* used a different type of torpedo when it made its final attack on the *Housatonic*.[7] The original mode of assault was to tow a torpedo at the end of a two hundred foot line. When near the target, the boat would dive underneath and then surface on the other side, meanwhile pulling the torpedo into the side of the enemy. Trials in Mobile Bay proved that this method worked well at times, but if the water was rough with a strong current or wind, the torpedo could not be controlled. Hunley, who had taken over the project by now, decided upon the forward torpedo suspended on a twenty-two foot wooden spar. After extensive testing in Mobile Bay, it was determined to be impractical to attack the Union fleet because of the rough water. Consequently, in August, the submarine was loaded aboard two flat cars and shipped by rail to Charleston, South Carolina.[8]

A contemporary sketch depicting the *Hunley's* torpedo exploding beneath the USS *Housatonic*.

On Saturday, August 29, 1863, the Hunley was being towed across Charleston harbor when disaster struck. The boat became entangled in some ropes and was drawn over on its side. The hatches being open, the craft quickly filled with water and five crewmen drowned. As a consequence, General Beauregard, commander of the city's defenses, asked Hunley to come to Charleston to take charge of the project. Hunley brought with him, Lieutenants George E. Dixon and W. A. Alexander, of the 21st Alabama Infantry Regiment. Both of these men had been with the project since its inception in Mobile. The boat's designer was convinced that the reason for the previous mishap was the lack of experience with the submarine's crew. Hunley established a rigid training program and demanded that all those serving on board have an ample amount of practice. With Dixon in command and Alexander as second officer, the *Hunley* and her crew trained constantly as summer lapsed into fall.

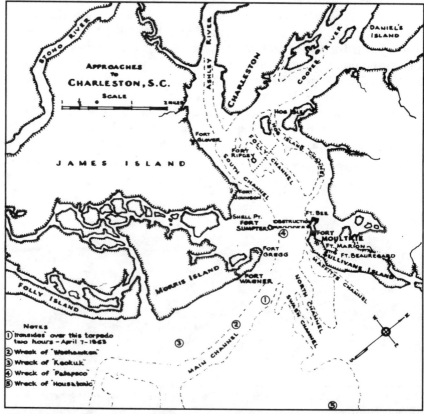

Chart of the approaches to Charleston, South Carolina, showing the location of wrecked U.S. ships, including the USS *Housatonic*. (5)

On October 15, 1863, with Dixon absent on business in Charleston, Hunley determined to continue the crew's training with himself at the controls. Tragically, on this day, the submarine claimed another crew, including its designer. Some reports indicate that the boat had made several passes underneath the tender *Indian Chief* after which it failed to surface. Within a few days it was located, and cranes were brought in which raised the hull and placed it on a dock. After completing a thorough investigation, Alexander explained what happened:

*The boat when found, was lying on the bottom at an angle of about 35 degrees, the bow deep in the mud. The holding-down bolts of each cover had been removed. When the hatch covers were lifted considerable air and gas escaped. Captain Hunley's body was forward, with his head in the forward hatchway, his right hand on top of his head (he had been trying, it would seem, to raise the hatch cover). In his left hand was a candle that had never been lighted, the sea cock on the forward end, or Hunley's ballast tank, was wide open, the cock-wrench not on the plug, but lying on the bottom of the boat. Mr. Park's body was found with his head in the after hatchway, his right hand above his head. He also had been trying to raise his hatch cover, but the pressure was too great. The sea cock to his tank was nearly empty. The other bodies were floating in the water. Hunley and Parks were undoubtedly asphyxiated, the others drowned. The bolts that held the iron keel ballast had been partially turned, but not sufficient to release it.*

Alexander then summarized what he felt must have taken place during those tragic final moments:

*At this time the boat was under way, lighted through the dead-lights in the hatch-ways. He partly turned the fins to go down, but thought, no doubt, that he needed more ballast and opened his sea cock. Immediately the boat was in total darkness. He then undertook to light the candle. While trying to do this the tank quickly flooded, and under great pressure the boat sank very fast and soon (the tank) overflowed, and the first intimation they would have of anything being wrong was the water rising fast, but noiselessly, about their feet in the bottom of the boat. They tried to release the iron keel ballast, but did not turn the keys quite far enough, therefore failed. The water soon forced the air to the top of the boat and into the hatchways, where Captains Hunley and Parks were found. Parks had pumped his ballast tank dry, and no*

Horace L. Hunley in an undated photograph. Hunley was the designer of the submarine that bore his name, and lost his life in the boat on October 15, 1863.

*doubt Captain Hunley had exhausted himself on his pump, but he had forgotten that he had not closed his sea-cock.*[9]

Undaunted, Dixon and Alexander were now more determined than ever to turn this novel and dangerous craft into an offensive weapon, and to strike a blow at the Federal blockading fleet. After refurbishing the boat, now officially named CSS *H. L. Hunley* in honor of her designer, Dixon sought another crew from the sailors on board the tender *Indian Chief*. With more volunteers than he could use, the young lieutenant embarked on a very rigid training program. He and Alexander established America's first submarine training school at Mount Pleasant, on the north side of the harbor.[10] The submarine was moored off Battery Marshall on Sullivan's Island, and as the long nights of winter approached, the crew became more and more proficient. With Dixon at the helm, and Alexander controlling the aft ballast tank, they began to undertake nightly sorties of up to five miles each way.

*In comparatively smooth water and light current, the Hunley could make four miles an hour,* Alexander explained, *but in rough water the speed was much slower. It was winter, therefore necessary that we go out with the ebb and come in with the flood tide, a fair wind, and dark moon. This latter was essential to our success, as our experience had fully demonstrated the necessity of occasionally coming to the surface, slightly lifting the hatch-cover, and letting in a little air. On several occasions, we came to the surface for air, opened the cover, and heard the men in the Federal picket boats talking and singing.*[11]

As their skill increased, an endurance dive became inevitable. On a calm, clear December day, Dixon signaled observers ashore who noted the time on their watches. The hatches and air valve were closed, the sea cocks opened, and the *Hunley* gently bumped against the bottom of the harbor. The candle was lit and the "engineers" were instructed to turn the propeller just enough to enable Dixon to hold her steady against the tide. By common consent among the crew, it was agreed that at the very moment anyone gave the "Up!" signal, the boat would surface. Within twenty-five minutes the candle flame, which had grown smaller and smaller, finally flickered and went out. As the inside atmosphere became warm and humid, the interior walls of the hull began to sweat. Crew members gasped and coughed as their breathing air turned foul. Occasionally, Dixon would call out, *How is it?* Each time the reply came from Alexander at the rear hatch, *All Right.* On shore the soldiers who had been watching studied their timepieces and shook their heads. An hour passed, an hour and-a-half; two hours. Slowly the observers began drifting away thinking that the worst must have happened. It was getting dark and a message was dispatched to Beauregard to inform him that the submarine had claimed another crew.

Beneath the dark surface of the water, however, Dixon and his men were still very much alive though gasping desperately for oxygen. Gagging and smothering, some crew members realized they were dying and were close to losing control of themselves, yet no one wanted to be the first to give in. Suddenly, almost in unison, the cry "Up!" was given and Dixon and Alexander began pumping furiously on their hand pumps. Slowly the bow began to rise higher and higher, but in spite of Alexander's pumping, the stern refused to budge. Wenches, lines, and other equipment began sliding toward the rear and the men in desperation hung on to keep from doing the same. Alexander was certain he had closed the line leading from the bilge and the pump should be throwing water from the ballast tank. Perhaps the valve was stuck open. Working quickly, he pulled the cap from the pump and yanked out the valve. In the pitch blackness he could feel something wet and slippery. Seaweed! He cleaned the fitting, rammed the valve back in place, and began pumping with all his remaining strength. Slowly, very slowly, the stern began to rise. Soon, though it must have seemed like an eternity, the boat broke the surface and the hatches were torn open. Fresh Air! A match was struck and Dixon looked at his watch; they had been submerged for two hours and thirty-five minutes.[12]

Almost every evening now, as the nights became longer in the deepening winter, Dixon and his crew would run the *Hunley* out into the cold Atlantic waters looking for an opportunity to attack the Federal blockading ships. *During this time we went out on an average of four nights a week,* Alexander wrote, *but on account of the weather, and considering the physical condition of the men to propel the boat back again, after going out six or seven miles, we would have to return. This we always found a task, and many times it taxed our utmost exertions to keep from drifting out to sea, daylight often breaking while we were yet in range.*

In February, Alexander, much to his disappointment, was ordered to another project, and a replacement volunteer quickly took his place. As dusk settled over Charleston on Wednesday evening, February 17, 1864, the *Hunley*, with no fanfare and few observers, cast off her lines for the last time and sailed into history.[13]

It was a bitterly cold, clear night as the *Hunley* drove toward the open sea. A full moon cast its eerie glow on the green Atlantic waters. On this fateful night, the Union warship USS *Housatonic* was anchored some distance off the battery on Breech's Inlet. Her position placed her approximately five and one-half miles east, southeast of Fort Sumter. The Union ship was a wooden-hulled cruiser of 1,240 tons and mounting thirteen heavy guns. Being part of the inner ring of blockading vessels, she was under strict orders to maintain a constant lookout, keep steam up, and be ready to move at a moment's notice.[14]

Suddenly, a few minutes before 9:00 p.m. she was rocked by a tremendous explosion on her starboard quarter. The *Hunley* had rammed her torpedo into the side of the *Housatonic*, and in only a few minutes the Union vessel lay shattered on the ocean floor. Unfortunately, the *Hunley* and her crew of nine including her commander Lieutenant Dixon, never returned. While comrades and loved ones watched anxiously the next morning, her mooring continued to remain empty. Finally it was presumed that she, too, was lost in the explosion of her own torpedo.[15]

After exhaustive research it is now possible to prove that the *Hunley* did not go down with the Union ship. In fact, the men of the *Hunley* had successfully accomplished their mission and were on their way back when some unknown tragedy struck. Using every scrap of evidence that is available, it is now feasible to piece together an amazing picture of the events of that night. When fully understood, one is simply astounded at the courage and ingenuity of the *Hunley's* crew.

At approximately 8:45 p.m., a lookout on the *Housatonic* spotted what appeared to be a "wooden plank" off the starboard side about 75 to 100 yards out and heading straight for them. The alarm was sounded and several sailors and officers commenced firing rifles and pistols at the intruder. Evidence taken at a court of inquiry held by the United States Navy a few days after the sinking revealed that the *Hunley* came on at right angles to the starboard quarter at about four knots. Additional Confederate documentation provides what is perhaps the most fascinating aspect, and until now the most misunderstood aspect of the attack. Indications are that instead of the standard contact torpedo, the *Hunley* used an experimental type that was intended for wooden vessels. This torpedo had been designed by Captain Francis D. Lee, an engineer officer from Charleston serving on General Beauregard's staff, and included a steel point equipped with saw-tooth edges. It was mounted on the boom in such a way that, after being rammed into the side of an enemy, it would slip off as the submarine backed away. A lanyard mounted in a reel on the boom would play out as the boat backed off, and when it reached its full length and became taut, it pulled a trigger on the torpedo which caused the explosion. This is evidently exactly what the *Hunley* did, for the explosion did not occur on impact.[16]

In addition, the *Housatonic* did not back down on the *Hunley* as many have thought. According to Third Assistant Engineer James W. Holihan of the *Housatonic*, who testified at the inquiry, the ship's engine was in motion only about ten seconds prior to the explosion. In those ten seconds the propeller had gone from a dead stop to only about 30 revolutions per minute. The *Housatonic* certainly could not have gathered much headway in such a short period of time. In addition, all Federal reports indicated that the *Hunley* approached at right angles to the starboard quarter. Even if the *Housatonic* had begun to move, that movement would have been at 90 degrees to the path of the *Hunley*. This would not have resulted in the Union ship's "backing down" on the *Hunley*.[17]

The most convincing proof that the *Hunley* affixed its torpedo and then backed away comes from Ensign Charles Craven of the *Housatonic's* crew. Ensign Craven testified: *I was in my room about 9:00 p.m. ... when I heard the officer of the deck give the order "Call all hands to quarters." I went on deck and saw something in the water on the starboard side of the ship, making towards the ship, about 30 feet off, and the captain and executive officer were firing at it. It looked to me like a water logged plank.*

*I fired two shots at her with my revolver as she was standing towards the ship as soon as I saw her, and a third shot when she was almost under the counter, having to lean over the port to fire it. I then went to my division, which is the second, and consists of four 32-pounder guns in the waist, and tried with the captain of number six gun to train it on this object, as she was backing from the ship, and about 40 or 50 feet off then. I had nearly succeeded, and was about to pull the lock string when the explosion took place.*[18]

Because the blast was under water, there was no fire and much of the sound was muffled. In fact, the rest of the Federal fleet was unaware of the attack until approached by one of the *Housatonic's* boats carrying survivors. The *Housatonic* settled by the stern and sank in 27 feet of water, the crew scrambling into the rigging. Five crew members were never found.

By prior agreement, the *Hunley* had arranged for a signal to be displayed from shore after they had completed their attack to help guide them on their return. Dixon and Lt. Colonel O. M. Dantzer, commander of Battery Marshall, had settled on two blue lights to be shown from the *Hunley* and a single white light to be displayed from shore. A full one-half hour after the attack, a Federal sailor, Robert Flemming, who was in the rigging awaiting rescue, testified that he saw a blue calcium light off the starboard quarter. Colonel Dantzer, in his official report, confirms that the blue lights were observed and answered from his station on shore.[19]

The little *Hunley* and her crew, therefore, were on their way in. What elation they must have felt! With their new weapon, they had attacked and sunk one of the largest warships in the U. S. Navy. All their training and perseverance had finally paid off. The sacrifice of Horace L. Hunley, killed in that tragic accident back in October, had not been in vain. Then, at some point, tragedy struck. Perhaps one of the glass portholes had been hit by rifle fire and finally gave way. Possibly, while showing the blue lights, a swell swept over them and with the hatches open the interior was flooded. Like other great undersea craft of a later century, the *Hunley* just simply disappeared.

Much has been written since the war about what might have happened to the *Hunley*. Until now, most have supported the theory that since the *Housatonic* reportedly backed her engines just prior to the impact, the *Hunley* was carried into the hole in the side of the Union vessel, caused by the explosion, and was unable to back out. Being trapped, the submarine was thus carried to the bottom with her. The fact that the torpedo boat, as it was called, was never found near the wreck of the Union vessel, lent credence to this theory. A few researchers, including this author however, have held a different view.[20]

A detailed examination of the wreck of the *Housatonic* was made in November of 1864, by Lieutenant W. L. Churchill of the Federal navy. He had the ocean bottom dragged for a distance of 500 hundred yards around the *Housatonic* and no trace of the *Hunley* was found. A salvage crew working several years after the war to clear the channel, however, claimed they found the *Hunley*, and in their enthusiasm for notoriety, swore they saw bodies of the crew and turned the propeller. Several published histories concerning operations in and around Charleston have repeated this account. Most historians, however, have discounted this report because it would have been impossible to see anything inside the submarine at a depth of twenty-seven feet, and corrosion over the years would have prevented any movement of the propeller.[21]

In 1909, army engineers blasted the wreck of the *Housatonic*, because it was proving a menace to navigation into and out of Charleston harbor. Some have speculated that the *Hunley* was mistaken as one of the ship's boilers and was blasted into oblivion. Recent research has uncovered a survey that was taken of the site before demolition, and divers reported finding several heavy guns and two boilers. The *Housatonic* had been built with two boilers, and they were still in the wreck in 1909. Had the *Hunley* been present, the divers would have reported three boilers.

All of this speculation and previous reports have now become meaningless. By plotting a course between the wreck site and the point where the *Hunley* departed that cold February night, researchers in 1994, using high tech electronic gear, uncovered two large metal anomalies buried deep beneath the mud and sand. It was believed that one of these anomalies represented the hull of the *Hunley*.[22] Finally, on May 3, 1995, these same researchers, led by the well-known author Clive Cussler, who has devoted fifteen years to the search, successfully uncovered one of the *Hunley's* hatches. With this positive identification, it was determined that the encrusted iron hull is intact and lies buried on her side in twenty feet of water, and only a couple of miles off shore.[23]

A set of coordinates now marks the spot where, beneath the mud and silt of the cold Atlantic floor, the *Hunley's* rusting hull still holds the remains of her brave crew. These nine gallant men, with no thought of turning back, continued on their course and successfully struck a blow for their country's cause. And like so many others in the Confederacy's struggle, they paid the price with their lives. For over 130 years their tragic fate and the whereabouts of their stalwart craft has been a mystery. Now, however, the CSS *Hunley* and her courageous men are missing no more.

# *Chapter Ten*

## Dash to the Gulf

Spring is usually a bright and cheerful time of year. In 1865, however, it was a very gloomy season for the dying Confederate States of America. By this time the Army of Northern Virginia had been stretched to the breaking point around Richmond and Petersburg attempting to hold Grant's masses at bay. The Army of Tennessee had bled its life away the previous December around Franklin and Nashville, and now, after checking Sherman's "Bummers" briefly in March at Bentonville, North Carolina, General Joseph E. Johnston was trying desperately to pull the remnants of it together to stop him. Sheridan had laid waste to the Shenandoah

First Lieutenant Charles W. Read, CSN. Shown in the uniform of a cadet at the United States Naval Academy at Annapolis, Maryland, where he was graduated last in his class in 1860.

*170*

Valley and the South's last port east of the Mississippi River, Wilmington, North Carolina had fallen.[1]

The Confederate navy, however, was not yet ready to admit final defeat. As long as there was any hope of striking a successful and damaging blow at the enemy, the men of the navy and Marine Corps were willing to keep trying. Charles W. Read had just returned from his abortive overland torpedo mission along the James River, and the young navy lieutenant from Mississippi had another idea. After service as a gunnery officer on the *Arkansas*, Read had joined Maffitt on the cruiser *Florida* and had been taken captive in the abortive *Caleb Cushing* affair in Portland, Maine. Exchanged in October of the previous year, he had spent time as a prisoner of war at Fort Warren in Boston Harbor where he had escaped once only to be re-captured. Now, with the consent of his superiors in the James River Squadron, he took his latest plan directly to Secretary Mallory at the Navy Department.

Lying at Shreveport, Louisiana on the Red River three hundred fifty miles above New Orleans, Read explained, was the Confederate ram CSS *Webb*. Read proposed to take the ram down the Red River, run the blockade at the mouth of the river, and steam south down the Mississippi. The Mississippi, of course, would be awash in patrolling Federal gunboats, but if he could pass them by using stealth and deception, and reach the mouth of the river below New Orleans, he could proceed to sea in the *Webb*. During this breakout into the Gulf, if the opportunity presented itself, he would board and capture the Federal gunboat USS *Pampero* which was known to be south of New Orleans. The *Pampero* was a 1,375-ton warship mounting four guns, which was engaged in guarding one of the channels leading to the Gulf of Mexico. Once the *Pampero* was in his hands, Read explained, he would then turn her into a commerce raider, proceed to Havana, Cuba to replenish her supplies, and then run the blockade back into Galveston, Texas. Along the way, he would capture and burn whatever enemy ships he might encounter. If the *Pampero* could not be taken, he would continue on with the *Webb*, using her as a commerce raider. Either way, it was a reckless and dangerous undertaking.[2]

Aware of all the brave exploits in which this young navy lieutenant had been involved during the war, Mallory probably felt that if anyone could accomplish such a desperate mission it would be Read. Taking a few select officers from the James River Squadron, Read left Richmond in mid-March en route to Shreveport. Traveling from Virginia to Louisiana in March of 1865 was a difficult undertaking in the war-torn Confederacy. Not only was the country swarming with Union troops, but the grandfather of rivers, the mighty Mississippi, which they would have to cross, had effectively been closed by patrolling

Lieutenant Charles W. Read is the man sitting in the center with the derby hat and facing the camera in this group of Confederate naval prisoners at Fort Warren, Boston Harbor.

Federal gunboats. Showing that "travel" in the Confederacy was still possible, Read and his naval party, traveling via Mobile, arrived in Shreveport in late March. Reporting with his sealed orders from Mallory to Lieutenant Jonathan H. Carter, commander of the Red River Defenses, Lieutenant Read was given command of the *Webb* on the March 31, 1865.[3]

The CSS *Webb* was still in excellent condition with well-maintained engines; however, her guns had been removed and she had no crew.

Known as the *William H. Webb,* she had been built in New York several years prior to the war and was used there as a tow boat and as an ice breaker during the cold northern winters. Just prior to the outbreak of war, she was purchased by a group of New Orleans merchants. Because of her powerful engines, the Webb was put to work at the Crescent City towing heavily laden merchant ships into and out of the harbor. She was slightly over 200 feet long and weighed approximately 655 tons. Her powerful steam engines were of the low pressure type, and her huge sidewheels measured thirty-five feet high. With a draft of only nine feet, six inches and able to steam in excess of 25 knots, she was one of the fastest boats afloat. When war broke out she was seized at New Orleans by Confederate authorities, and due to her great strength, was converted into a ram and gunboat. Heavy, solid timbers were placed inside her bow running aft about thirty feet where they were bolted securely together. A 32-inch pivot rifle was placed on her foredeck and two 12-pounder howitzers placed on the stern. In addition, two "Quaker" guns (fake guns made of wood and painted black) were fabricated and one placed on either side.[4] In May, 1861, the *Webb* seized three Northern vessels off the mouth of the Mississippi and made prizes of them, sending them along with their cargoes into New Orleans. Once the Federal blockade was in place, however, it became impossible to bring captured prizes into New Orleans for adjudication, and the *Webb*'s privateering days were over.

Upon the passage of Fort Jackson by Farragut's fleet and the evacuation of New Orleans in 1862, the *Webb* was taken up the Red River in Louisiana to avoid capture by the advancing Union forces. In February of 1863, she descended the river to its juncture with the Mississippi, and in cooperation with the captured *Queen of the West* and two other Confederate vessels, attacked the Union ironclad *Indianola*. Ramming the *Indianola* several times, the Federal commander was forced to run his ship aground to keep from sinking and surrendered the ironclad along with its crew of one hundred men. After this action the *Webb* was taken back up the river and stationed at Shreveport, where she became part of the Red River Defense Fleet which guarded against Federal excursions into northern Louisiana. Now the *Webb* was about to embark on her most daring and, as fate would have it, her final journey.[5]

Read set out feverishly preparing the *Webb* for his reckless mission. The day before he left on the expedition, he wrote a letter to Secretary Mallory. He had no way of knowing that at the moment of his writing, the secretary was accompanying President Davis and the government on its flight through the Carolinas. Lee had surrendered 13 days before, and Johnston was negotiating with General Sherman.

*In pursuance of the instructions given me by you,* Read wrote, *I have reported, together with the officers ordered with me, to Lieutenant Commanding Jonathan H. Carter for duty on this vessel. Accordingly I took command of this ship, relieving Lieutenant Commanding J. L. Phillips on the 31st. ultimo. On assuming command I found the vessel totally unprepared for the service upon which I was ordered to take her, without a single gun on board, little or no crew, no fuel, and no small arms, save a few cutlasses, and as the vessel was some eighty miles below Shreveport on her way here, I was obliged to return to the first-named place, where I expected to obtain all my wants from General Kirby Smith, commanding this department.*

General Smith, commanding the Trans-Mississippi Department, came to his aid and provided, in addition to small arms, a 30-pounder Parrott rifle for the bow pivot and two small 12-pounders for the stern. A rough bulwark was hurriedly built around the forecastle to protect the vessel as much as possible from the pounding of heavy seas. On April 7, she was moved from Shreveport down the river to Alexandria, where 190 bales of cotton were manhandled on board. These were stacked two and three layers deep around her pilot house and machinery for the purpose of providing some protection against enemy fire.[6]

After an extensive search for coal, only one day's supply could be found and this was loaded on board. To supplement this meager supply of fuel, 250 tons of pine knots and a large amount of resin were hauled aboard. These highly flammable items, when added to the fires in the furnace, generated intense heat causing higher steam pressure, which in turn increased her speed appreciably. Water and a month's rations were loaded on board, and she was given a "dirty" white-washing which made her more difficult to see at night. William Biggio and James Kelly were both shipped as quartermasters, and the rest of the enlisted crew was composed of volunteers from the Red River Defense Fleet and army troops from General E. Kirby Smith's command.[7]

Read complained in his letter to the Secretary, of his lack of qualified engineers: *I have but two engineers understanding the machinery of the vessel, and two young third assistants whom I can not trust alone in the engine room for some time as yet; the two former will therefore be obliged to remain on watch whilst going out and whilst the double engines are unconnected, it not being advisable to work them connected when there exists a probability for rapid maneuvering.*

Read concluded his letter with a brief review for Mallory on how he planned to accomplish his goal: *The distance from the mouth of the Red to the mouth of the Mississippi is about 300 miles, and at regular distances in most of this length there are one or two of the enemy's gunboats. To be the first to notify these of my approach is my chief aim; toward effecting this I have arranged with General Thomas to cut the wires as far down as Plaquemine* by 8:00pm tomorrow. I shall myself cut the wires below that place, and shall take every precaution to prevent the forts (Jackson and St. Philip) from being informed of my movements, as these formidable fortifications will have to be passed in daylight. As I will have to stake everything upon speed and time, I will not attack any vessel in the passage unless I perceive a possibility of her arresting my purpose. In this event I am prepared with five torpedoes (100 Pounds), one of which I hold shipped on its pole on the bows.[8]

Meanwhile, the Federal navy had learned of the proposed expedition by the *Webb*, and to prevent her escape, they had dispatched the monitor *Manhattan* and the ironclads *Lafayette* and *Choctaw* to reinforce the gunboats already guarding the mouth of the Red River.[9]

Engineer William Smith had the engine room crew up and working early on Sunday morning. Fires which had been banked overnight were stirred and firemen began to shovel some of the precious coal in upon the glowing embers. Steam began to hiss through the valves and pressure climbed steadily in the boilers. Soon additional crew members and officers were scurrying about performing last minute tasks. Gunner T. B. Travers made one last check of the newly installed 30-pound Parrott on its bow pivot, and a poor substitute for coffee was served from the galley below. At 4:00 a.m. on April 23, 1865, light was just beginning to show faintly on the eastern Louisiana horizon when Read ordered the lines cast off, and the *Webb's* giant paddle wheels began to turn. Pulling into the middle of the river, the helmsman turned her head downstream, and the *Webb* was on her way into history.

Approximately forty miles below Alexandria, Read ordered a brief stop at Coot's Landing to take on board 250 cords of wood and to attach the thirty-five foot spar torpedo to the *Webb's* bow. As he had written to Mallory, this was to be used against one of the blockading ships, if it became necessary. Continuing on slowly, Read timed the *Webb's* speed so as to reach the Union blockade at the mouth of the Red River after dark on the 23rd.[10]

William Biggio, who was at the wheel, wrote afterwards about their passage from the Red into the Mississippi:

In front of the Webb, only a few hundred yards distant, lay the Federal fleet of about six vessels. It was a little after eight o'clock in the evening on a starlit night in April when we first descried the enemy's vessels. All of our lights were concealed and we were running very slowly in order not to make much noise. We approached close enough to distinguish every vessel and were within five hundred yards of them before they discovered us. I was at the wheel and we had slowed up the vessel as much as possible preparatory to making the final run of the gantlet. The steam in the engines was very high, and the engineer called to the captain that he could not stand it much longer without blowing the vessel up. At this moment a rocket went up from the

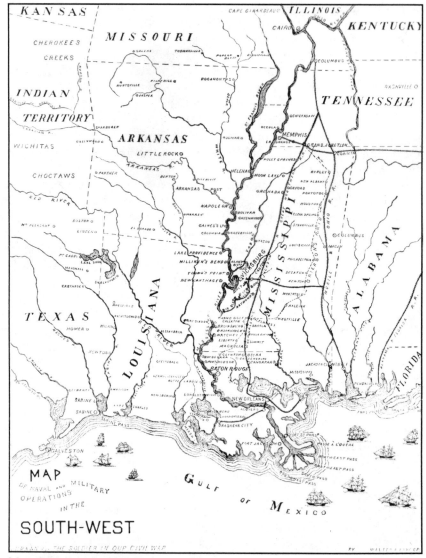

Map depicting the Red River and lower Mississippi River, the route taken by Read in his "Dash to the Gulf."

*Federal fleet, and we knew that we had been discovered. Captain Read then yelled, "Let her go!" and I rang the fast bell. The engineer threw the throttle wide open, and the Webb fairly leaped and trembled. "Keep her for the biggest opening between them!" shouted the captain, and I did as commanded. By this time every whistle of the fleet was screaming, drums were beating, rock-*

*ets were going up, and it seemed as if the very devil was to pay. I kept the Webb straight on her course, however, headed for the biggest opening, and before a gun was fired we had passed the blockade and had turned the bend and were making down the Mississippi River. We had run the gantlet and were now 'between the devil and the deep blue sea'. After we had gone down the river some distance the Manhattan fired a few shots, but did us no harm. Passing out of (the) Red River, and through the very jaws of death, it was only to encounter new and greater dangers before the Gulf could be reached.*[11] Greater and more serious dangers did indeed still lie ahead.

Leaving behind the Federal monitor *Lafayette*, which had started in pursuit, the *Webb's* speed was slackened, and she steamed along easily with the current. At approximately every five miles, the Federals had stationed gunboats in the Mississippi, and these all had to be passed without the Union lookouts discovering the *Webb's* identity. During the remainder of the night, the challenge from these gunboats was met with signal lamps. As they signaled the *Webb* inquiring as to "What ship goes there?" Kelly signaled back something they couldn't understand, and by the time the Federals translated the code, the *Webb* was gone. When daylight came, the same ruse was practiced using signal flags. Read's plan, which had now changed since his letter to Mallory, was to attempt to pass the forts below New Orleans at night, which would mean passing the city while it was still daylight. Several times Read sent ashore an officer along with a boat's crew and had the telegraph wires cut. Unfortunately, and unknown to Read, a message had been flashed to New Orleans just minutes before the wires went down that the *Webb* had passed the blockade at the mouth of the Red River. Thus the Union forces gathered at the city had about a three hours notice that the *Webb* was coming. A perplexing problem for them, however, was that because she passed the blockade so quickly and at night, they really did not know what she looked like.[12]

Ten miles above New Orleans, Read hoisted the United States ensign at half-mast as a ploy. (President Lincoln had been assassinated only a few days earlier.) He then had his crew don blue Federal overcoats over their Confederate uniforms and instructed them to sit casually on deck and smoke their pipes or play cards. While the Federal fleet was alerted that the *Webb* was coming, they were looking for something that resembled the *Virginia* or *Arkansas* rather than the innocent looking "army" transport loaded with troops and cotton that was steaming through their midst. By 1:00 p.m. on April 24, the *Webb* had passed most of the fleet lying north of the city. It was beginning to look as though their deception would take them all the way to the Gulf.[13]

As they entered the harbor of New Orleans, they passed within several hundred yards of the Federal twenty-four gun sloop, *Lackawanna*, the same warship that had rammed and battered the CSS *Tennessee* at the Battle of Mobile Bay the previous August. Suddenly, the pilot of the Federal ship, an old steamboat man from New Orleans, recognized the *Webb* and informed his captain. Orders were passed and in an instant one of the *Lackawanna's* guns roared. The howling shot crashed into the *Webb* abreast of the forehatch, tore bulkheads into splinters, and passed completely through the hull about four feet from the water line without exploding. Read shouted for Kelly to haul down the false colors and hoist the Confederate flag. The "fast bell" rang again in the engine room, and this time, with pine knots and resin burning fiercely in the furnace, the giant paddle wheels pounded the *Webb* forward at over twenty-five knots. The *Lackawanna* fired again. The shot was aimed at the pilot house but struck a bale of cotton, glanced upward, and passed over the top. A third shot streaked across the water, tearing through the funnel guy-wires, cutting one of them, but doing no additional damage. Because the *Webb* was now running abreast of the docks in downtown New Orleans, the remaining Federal vessels could not fire for fear of hitting their own ships or innocent people who were lining the streets and the levee and were watching in stunned disbelief.[14]

The excitement among the citizens thronging the waterfront was intense, and many were waving their hats and cheering the *Webb* on. After all these long years of occupation, right there before their very eyes, a Confederate warship with their nation's sacred banner snapping in the breeze was brazenly steaming right through the midst of the hated "Yankees." The frenzy spread like a wind-blown inferno. Rumor spread through the streets that the vessel contained the gold and silver of the Confederate treasury; that President Davis and General E. Kirby Smith were on board; and that John Wilkes Booth was at the wheel.[15]

Thousands watched in astonished pride as the *Webb* raced by New Orleans on that bright Monday afternoon. Her torpedo boom was hauled up at right angles to the bow. Every man was at his station, and the engines, under a full head of steam, were pounding away flawlessly. Giant rooster tails of spray trailed behind her massive revolving wheels, while the *Webb's* pointed bow parted the muddy Mississippi hurling white plumes of spray far out to either side. High above her from the tallest peak, streaming out for friend and foe to see, was her beautiful red and white "Stainless Banner," the national flag of the Confederacy, which was the Southern people's beloved symbol during their struggle for independence.

Anchored in the harbor was a French man-of-war. Speeding past, Read dipped his flag; the Frenchman returned the salute.[16] As the *Webb* neared a Federal ship, anchored close to the main channel, Read, thinking it was the Federal gunboat *Hartford*, ordered the torpedo lowered. When it came down, the spar snapped and the torpedo swung dangerously around threatening to strike the *Webb*. Orders were shouted, and axes flashed in the afternoon sun, cutting the lines and allowing the torpedo to sink harmlessly to the bottom. It was just as well, for the "gunboat" was the *Fearnaught*, a Federal ordnance ship loaded with over 300 barrels of gun powder. If she had been struck by the *Webb's* torpedo, both vessels would have been blown completely out of the water.[17]

With black smoke, hissing steam, and pounding engines, the speeding *Webb* raced on. New Orleans quickly receded into the background, but Read now knew that all the Federal forces were alerted. Telegraph wires were probably already humming, and the warships and the guns of the forts would all be waiting. "If only we had cut the telegraph wires a little earlier," he must have thought. Looking back he could see the Federal steamer *Hollyhock* trying to catch him. The *Hollyhock* was a low-bar tow boat much like the *Webb* and almost as fast. Read knew he had to stay ahead of her. Twenty-five miles south of the city, with only a few more miles before the forts and then the blue waters of the Gulf, they rounded a bend in the river, only to find the Federal sloop *Richmond* with twenty-four guns blocking the channel. The *Webb* was slowed, and Read called his officers together in front of the pilot house. The narrow channel meant they would have to pass immediately under the guns of the *Richmond*. The forts below her were now alerted, and the *Hollyhock* was fast approaching from the north. With saddened hearts, the officers all agreed that their luck had indeed finally run out. Read ordered Biggio, who was still at the wheel, to run the *Webb* ashore. Turning to port, Biggio headed for the east bank of the river and struck bottom about fifty yards out. Life lines were thrown over the bow and a boat was lowered. The crew was ordered to make their way to shore as best they could.[18]

Meanwhile, Read had ordered Travers to start a fire near the magazine. Once assured that the vessel was burning, Read joined his crew on the river bank. Dividing his men into three groups, they moved inland through the swamps far enough to be out of sight yet lingered close enough to keep the *Webb* in view.[19]

Soon the *Hollyhock* hove to beside the burning *Webb* and attempted to put out the flames with her fire hoses. With the fire burning so fiercely, however, this was soon deemed impossible, and she backed away. After a few more minutes, with a blinding flash, the *Webb* exploded.

Not wanting to fall into the hands of the Federal cavalry patrolling the area, but preferring to surrender to the Federal navy, Read and his

*Harper's Weekly*, May 20, 1865.

An artist's concept of the destruction of the CSS *Webb* below New Orleans, on April 24, 1865.

officers, along with some crew members, returned to the river bank and hailed the *Hollyhock*. Sending a boat, they were received on board the *Hollyhock* as prisoners of war. The rest of the *Webb's* crew were captured the following day by Union cavalry.

Conveyed to New Orleans, Read and his crew were marched through the streets of the city like captured animals. Much to the chagrin of the escorting Federal troops, however, the citizens lined the streets and cheered, ladies waved their handkerchiefs and threw flowers in their path. Lieutenant Read, along with some of his officers, was put on board the Federal steamer *Florida* which soon set sail for New York. Arriving there on May 6, he was later taken to Fort Warren in Boston Harbor where he was imprisoned.[20] Finally, on July 24, 1865, Lieutenant Read was granted his parole and allowed to return home.[21]

After the war, Charles Read captained a fruit schooner in the Caribbean and delivered warships to South American republics. Later he became a steamboat pilot at New Orleans guiding merchant ships to and from the Gulf.[22] Many times he must have passed that spot along the river bank where the remains of the *Webb* lay. As he glided past in his nameless merchant vessel, his thoughts must have drifted back to that sunny Monday afternoon in April of 1865, when he almost made it. — "Yes, if only those telegraph wires had been cut a bit earlier."

# Conclusion

The Confederate navy and Marine Corps have, for the most part, been largely neglected in the accounts of the War Between the States. While there are thousands of volumes dealing with the campaigns of the Southern armies, the publications devoted to the Confederate navy could probably be stored in one small bookcase. This is understandable, for the role of the navy during the war was overshadowed in a conflict that saw massive armies fighting bloody and protracted land campaigns. In addition, many of the navy records were destroyed during the evacuation of Richmond at the end of the war, which obviously makes any research that much more difficult. Then too, with a total strength that probably never exceeded 6,000 men and officers, there was a scarcity of post-war writings and memoirs generated by Confederate navy participants. For an agriculture-oriented nation, struggling to survive the loss of a war and the horrors of "reconstruction," the contribution of its navy at sea and on the nation's rivers and bays was uninteresting and unappreciated. Even today, to most students of the war, leaders such as Robert E. Lee, "Stonewall" Jackson, J. E. B. Stuart, and Bedford Forrest have no counterparts from their compatriots in the navy.

If for a moment, however, we turn our attention from these valiant gray armies and their superb general officers, and diligently research writings and records that are available, we will find that the same qualities existed in the men and officers who wore the navy gray. Men such as Raphael Semmes, Franklin Buchanan, James Bulloch, John Taylor Wood, Charles Read, Stephen Mallory, Catesby Jones, and John Maffitt, to name but a few, exhibited much the same character as the leaders of those gray legions on land. For the most part they were as competent, intelligent, and resourceful as their army counterparts, and their crews proved by their actions that most naval officers earned similar respect and devotion from their men. The majority of naval officers were professional career officers prior to the outbreak of war. The typical naval commander had spent many years in the "old navy," and had been thoroughly trained to respect his God, love his country, and fight savagely for her cause. By the end of 1861, 373 of these officers, painful for them that it was, determined that their first allegiance as a citizen was to their state. Discarding everything they had earned in the old service, they resigned their commissions and swore allegiance to the Confederate States of America. Duty, honor, and country were not just mere words to these men, they were the principles by which their very lives were governed.

The crewman of such ships as the *Virginia, Hunley, Webb,* and *Manassas,* for example, also exhibited the same courage and devotion to their cause and country as the valorous soldiers in the ranks of the Confederate armies. Because of the lack of seafaring men in the South, many crews of Confederate ships were composed of army units or former soldiers who had been transferred to naval service. It was their country, too, that was being invaded, and their peaceful homes and families that were being desecrated. Even on the ocean-roving cruisers, whose crews were composed of mostly foreigners or volunteers from their captured prizes, men seemed to catch the spirit of this new nation struggling for its freedom. When the time came, as it did for the crew of the *Alabama* off Cherbourg, they would fight for that nation in a way that is difficult for us to understand today. We who study the war are familiar with the image of long lines of blue and gray infantry firing volleys of musketry at one another from close range. The image of these men firing eleven and fifteen-inch guns at one another from a distance of forty feet is incomprehensible.

When the limited resources of the Confederacy, both in manpower and raw materials is considered, it is simply astounding that the Confederate Navy accomplished as much as it did. The old adage that, "Necessity is the mother of invention," was never more applicable than it was for this navy during the war. Faced with an aggressive enemy within the very first weeks of its existence, the Confederate Navy had to organize, begin operations, and fight an invader simultaneously. Because of this, many of the vessels initially thrown into the fray, which were nothing more than converted river steamers, had an "improvised" character about them. This is understandable, for with the loss of Norfolk, New Orleans, and Pensacola early in the conflict, new facilities had to be found to build warships. It took time to construct new shipyards, and with a scarcity of skilled workers, even more time to build new ships at these locations. One must be reminded that at the opening of hostilities, the timber for the vessels the South was ultimately able to construct was still growing in her forests, and the iron for their armor, engines, and machinery was still buried in the ground.

Yet, with all the difficulties and shortages that the country faced, approximately 150 warships were finally constructed within the boarders of the Confederacy. The keels for approximately fifty ironclads were laid, and twenty-two of these were commissioned and put into operation. The Confederate navy lead the way in the deployment of ironclads against obsolete wooden vessels, as the men in blue of the *Congress* and *Cumberland* discovered at Hampton Roads. The Confederacy was also a pioneer in the development and use of the underwater torpedo or mine, and she was the first to sortie forth with an operational submarine that actually destroyed an enemy warship. The predecessors of the fast torpedo boats of World War II also made their debut with the Confederate navy.

Overseas, ship design leapfrogged into the twentieth century with the building and launching of the fast and sleek blockade runners. Often referred to as the "Lifeline of the Confederacy," these swift British-built steamers, particularly when commanded by regular naval officers, managed to consistently slip through the Federal blockade with near impunity.

The determination and brilliance of Confederate naval officers in Europe brought about the birth of what proved to be the ultimate combination of sail and steam. The English built *Alabama* and *Florida* were acknowledged at the time, and still today, to be the finest cruisers the world has ever seen. Designed for a specific purpose, they accomplished that purpose devastatingly well.

In a letter written two years after the war, Secretary Mallory offered a brief and accurate appraisal of the Confederate navy: *I am satisfied that, with the means at our control and in view of the overwhelming force of the enemy at the outset of the struggle, our little navy accomplished more than could have been looked or hoped for; and if I have ever felt any surprise connected with its operations, it was that we accomplished so much.*

# *Appendix A*

## Officers assigned to the
## CSS *Virginia* - February, 1862

| NAME | RANK | PLACE OF BIRTH |
|------|------|----------------|
| | *(On Virginia)* | |
| Buchanan, Franklin | Captain (Commanding) | Maryland |
| Jones, Catesby ap R.. | Lieutenant (Executive Officer) | Virginia |
| Simms, Charles C. | First Lieutenant | Virginia |
| Minor, Robert D. | First Lieutenant | Virginia |
| Davidson, Hunter | First Lieutenant | District of Columbia |
| Wood, John Taylor | First Lieutenant | Minnesota |
| Eggleston, John R. | First Lieutenant | Virginia |
| Butt, Walter R. | First Lieutenant | Virginia |
| Foute, Robert C. | Acting Midshipman | Tennessee |
| Marmaduke, Henry H. | Midshipman | Missouri |
| Littlepage, Hardin B. | Acting Midshipman | Virginia |
| Craig, William J. | Acting Midshipman | Kentucky |
| Long, James C. | Acting Midshipman | Tennessee |
| Rootes, Lawrence M. | Acting Midshipman | Virginia |
| Semple, James A. | Paymaster | Virginia |
| Phillips, Dinwiddie B. | Surgeon | Virginia |

| Garnett, Algernon S. | Assistant Surgeon | Virginia |
| Thom, Reuben | Captain, CSMC | Virginia |
| Ramsey, Henery A. | Acting Chief Engineer | District of Columbia |
| Tynan, John W. | Acting First Asst. Engineer | Virginia |
| Campbell, Loudon | Second Assistant Engineer | Virginia |
| Herring, Benjamin S. | Acting Second Asst. Engineer | North Carolina |
| Jack, E. Alexander | Acting Third Asst. Engineer | Virginia |
| Wright, Robert | Third Assistant Engineer | Virginia |
| Hasker, Charles H. | Boatswain | England |
| Oliver, Charles B. | Gunner | Massachusetts |
| Lindsey, Hugh | Carpenter | Ireland |
| Sinclair, Arthur, Jr. | Captain's Clerk | Virginia |
| Forrest, Douglas | Lieutenant, CSA (Vol. Aide) | |
| Kevil, —— | Captain, CSA (Norfolk Artillery) | |
| Tabb, —— | Sergeant, CSA (Signal Corps) | |

# *Appendix B*

## Officers assigned to the
## CSS *Alabama* - August 24, 1862

| NAME | RANK *(On Alabama)* | PLACE OF BIRTH |
|------|------|------|
| Semmes, Raphael | Captain (Commanding) | Maryland |
| Kell, John M. | First Lieutenant (Executive Officer) | Georgia |
| Armstrong, Richard F. | Lieutenant | Georgia |
| Wilson, Joseph D. | Lieutenant | Florida |
| Sinclair, Arthur, Jr. | Acting Master | Virginia |
| Low, John | Master | Georgia |
| Galt, Francis L. | Surgeon | Virginia |
| Llewellyn, David H. | Assistant Surgeon | England |
| Younge, Clarence R. | Acting Assistant Paymaster | |
| Smith, William B. | Captain's Clerk | Louisiana |
| Howell, Becket K. | Lieutenant, CSMC | Mississippi |
| Freeman, Miles J. | First Asst. Engineer (Chief) | Louisiana |
| Brooks, William P. | Second Assistant Engineer | Louisiana |
| Cummings, Simeon W. | Acting Third Asst. Engineer | New York |
| O'Brien, Matthew | Third Assistant Engineer | Ireland |

| | | |
|---|---|---|
| Pundt, John W. | Third Assistant Engineer | South Carolina |
| Sinclair, William H. | Acting Midshipman | Virginia |
| Bulloch, Irvine S. | Acting Midshipman | Georgia |
| Maffitt, Eugene A. | Acting Midshipman | Georgia |
| Anderson, Edwin M. | Midshipman | Georgia |
| Fullam, George T. | Acting Master's Mate | England |
| Evans, James | Acting Master's Mate | South Carolina |
| McClaskey, Benjamin P. | Boatswain | Louisiana |
| Cuddy, Thomas C. | Gunner | South Carolina |
| Robinson, William | Carpenter | Louisiana |
| Alcott, Henry | Sailmaker | England |

# Appendix C

## Crew members lost
## on board the CSS *H. L. Hunley*

| August 29, 1863 | Frank Doyle, | CSN |
| | John Kelly, | CSN |
| | Michael Cane, | CSN |
| | Nicholas Davis, | CSN |
| | (Unknown), | CSN |

Lieut. John Payne, CSN (Commanding), and Lieut. Charles H. Hasker, CSN along with two other seaman escaped.

| October 15, 1863 | Horace L. Hunley, Civilian, (Commanding) |
| | Thomas Parks, | CSN |
| | Robert Brockbank, | CSN |
| | Joseph Patterson, | CSN |
| | Charles McHugh, | CSN |
| | John Marshall, | CSN |
| | Henry Beard, | CSN |
| | Charles Sprague, | CSN |

| February 17, 1864 | Lt. George E. Dixon, | CSA (Commanding) |
|---|---|---|
| | Cpl. C. F. Carlson, | CSA |
| | James A. Wicks, | CSN |
| | Arnold Becker, | CSN |
| | Fred Collins, | CSN |
| | C. F. Simpkins, | CSN |
| | —— Ridgeway, | CSN |
| | —— White | |
| | —— Miller | |

## Appendix D

### Officers Assigned to the CSS *Webb* - April, 1865

| NAME | RANK | PLACE OF BIRTH |
|---|---|---|
| Addison, W. J. | Assistant Surgeon | Maryland |
| Billups, James W. | Acting Master's Mate | |
| Blanc, Samuel P. | Master | Louisiana |
| Dubrock, A. | Signal Operator | |
| Duer(?), L. M. | Signal Operator | |
| Hale, George | Acting Boatswain | Texas |
| Lewis, John H. | Pilot | Louisiana |
| Lewis, Benjamin S. | Acting Master's Mate | |
| Lewis, Harry S. | Third Assistant Engineer | |
| Marsh, George R. | Third Assistant Engineer | |
| Read, Charles W. | First Lieutenant (Commanding) | Mississippi |
| Scott, Henry H. | Passed Midshipman | North Carolina |
| Smith, William | Second Assistant Engineer | |
| Travers, Thomas B. | Gunner | Virginia |
| Wall, William H. | First Lieutenant (Executive Officer) | Mississippi |
| Walters, Joseph F. | Third Assistant Engineer | Georgia |
| West, James W. | Pilot | Louisiana |

# Enlisted Men of the
# CSS *Webb* - April, 1865

| NAME | RANK |
|------|------|
| Anderson, J. P. | Landsman |
| Berthard, J. | Fireman |
| Biggio, William | Quartermaster (Pilot) |
| Brigham, J. | Ordinary Seaman |
| Burnes, E. | Coal Heaver |
| Chambers, J. H. | Landsman |
| Cornelius, J. N. | Coal Heaver |
| Cox, John | Second Steward |
| Davis, G. H. | Landsman |
| Davis, M. | Landsman |
| Davis, W. R. | Landsman |
| Durham, H. O. | Landsman |
| Fletcher, J. W. | Landsman |
| Haitly, G. B. | Landsman |
| Hall, J. W. | Landsman |
| Hancock, W. A. | Coal Heaver |
| Harper, N. B. | Landsman |
| Haynes, A. P. | Second Steward |
| Hines, H. | 1st. Chief Boatswain |
| Hunter, J. C. | Fireman |
| Hyde, M. | Master |
| Jernigan, J. H. | Landsman |
| Keith, J. | Ordinary Seaman |
| Kelly, James | Quartermaster |
| McDaniel, B. F. | Landsman |
| McDaniel, J. S. | Landsman |
| McDonald, J. S. | Coal Heaver |
| McLaughlin, P. | Fireman |
| McQueen, L. | Landsman |
| Moffitt, R. W. | Landsman |
| Moore, Thomas | Landsman |
| Morgan, D. A. | Master of Arms |
| Murphy, B. | Fireman |
| Oliver, H. | Quartermaster |
| Osborne, John C. | Second Steward |
| Preston, Charles | Landsman |

| | |
|---|---|
| Rice, T. C. | Landsman |
| Richards, E. | Captain Master |
| Riggins, N. B. | Landsman |
| Rook, Charles | W.R.C. |
| Rouse, G. W. | Coal Heaver |
| Sheffield, S. | Ordinary Seaman |
| Stewart, J. S. | Landsman |
| Taffe, W. | W.R.S. |
| Taylor, J. M. | Landsman |
| Thompson, T. J. | Landsman |
| Thurston, A. H. | Landsman |
| Turner, W. J. | Fireman |
| Walker, G. A. | Landsman |
| Williams, L. | Landsman |
| Wise, A. | Landsman |

Total Officers - 17
Total Enlisted - 51

Total Crew -   68

# Endnotes

## CHAPTER 1
## THE IRON TURTLE OF NEW ORLEANS

1. Maurice Melton, *The Confederate Ironclads*, New York: A. S. Barnes & Co., Inc., 1968, p. 65.
2. William Morrison Robinson, *The Confederate Privateers*, New Haven: Yale University Press, 1928, p. 156.
3. William N. Still, Jr., *Iron Afloat*, Nashville: Vanderbilt University Press, 1971, p. 47.
4. J. Thomas Scharf, *History of the Confederate States Navy*, New York: Rogers & Sherwood, 1887, p. 264.
5. Melton, p. 60.
6. Robinson, pp. 156–157.
7. Still, p. 48.
8. James Morris Morgan, "The Pioneer Ironclad," *United States Naval Institute Proceedings*, Annapolis: p. 2277.
9. Thomas Truxtun Moebs, *Confederate States Navy Research Guide*, Williamsburg: Moebs Publishing Co., 1991.
10. Morgan, pp. 2278–2279.
11. Still, p. 48.
12. Charles L. Dufour, *The Night the War was Lost*, Garden City: Doubleday & Company, Inc., p. 76.
13. Melton, pp. 66–67; Defour, pp. 77–78.
14. Dufour, pp. 77–80.
15. Ibid., pp. 81–83.
16. Ibid.
17. Ibid., p. 85.
18. Scharf, p. 243.
19. Dufour, p. 204.
20. A. F. Warley, "The Ram *Manassas* at the Passage of the New Orleans Forts," *Battles and Leaders of the Civil War*, 4 vols. New York: The Century Company, 1884–1888, p. 89.

21. William B. Robertson, "The Water-Battery at Fort Jackson," *Battles and Leaders of the Civil War*, 4 vols. New York: The Century Company, 1884–1888, p. 100.
22. B & L, vol. I, p. 89.
23. ———, *Official Record of the Union and Confederate Navies in the War of the Rebellion*, series I, vol. 18, p. 206.
24. B & L, vol. II, p. 90.
25. B & L, vol. II, p. 91.
26. B & L, vol. II, p. 66.
27. B & L, vol. II, p. 69.
28. Ibid., p. 90.
29. Ibid.
30. Charles W. Read, "Reminiscences of the Confederate States Navy," *Southern Historical Society Papers*, vol. I, No. 5, p. 343.
31. B & L, p. 91.
32. ORN, series I, vol. 18, p. 304.
33. Melton, p. 102.

## CHAPTER 2
## "A MATTER OF FIRST NECESSITY"

1. ———, *Official Records of the Union and Confederate Navies in the War of the Rebellion*, series I, vol. 5, p. 801.
2. Ibid., series II, vol. I, pp. 67–69.
3. Ibid., p. 783.
4. John M. Brooke, "The Plan and Construction of the *Merrimac*," *Battles and Leaders of the Civil War*, vol. I, New York: The Century Company, 1884–1888, pp. 715–716.
5. William N. Still, Jr., *Iron Afloat*, Nashville: Vanderbilt University Press, 1971, p. 15.
6. J. Thomas Scharf, *History of the Confederate States Navy*, New York: Rogers & Sherwood, p. 147.
7. Still, p. 18.
8. Scharf, p. 132; Still, pp. 24–25.
9. Maurice Melton, *The Confederate Ironclads*, New York: A. S. Barnes and Co., Inc., 1968, p. 30; Still, pp. 20–21.
10. Catesby ap R. Jones, "The Services of the *Virginia*," *The Confederate Soldier in the Civil War*, New York: The Fairfax Press, p. 396.
11. Still, p. 21.
12. Melton, p. 31.
13. William R. Cline, "The Ironclad Ram *Virginia* - Confederate States Navy," *Southern Historical Society Papers*, vol. XXXII, pp. 243–244.
14. ORN, Series II, vol. I.
15. Still, p. 23.
16. William C. Davis, *Duel Between the First Ironclads*, New York: Doubleday & Company, Inc., 1975, p. 38.
17. Royce Gordon Shingleton, *John Taylor Wood, Sea Ghost of the Confederacy*, Athens: University of Georgia Press, 1979, p. 39.
18. Ibid., pp. 39–40.
19. Melton, pp. 36.
20. Still, p. 26
21. Melton, p. 37.
22. Davis, pp. 80–81.
23. William H. Parker, *Recollections of a Naval Officer*, New York: Charles Scribners' Sons, 1883, p. 272.
24. Melton, p. 38.
25. Still, p. 29.
26. Melton, pp. 37–38

27. Virgil C. Jones, *The Civil War at Sea*, New York: Holt, Rinehart, and Winston, 1960–1962, vol. I, p. 415.
28. Ibid., pp. 415–417.
29. Melton, p. 41; Davis, p. 87.
30. Davis, p. 87.
31. Ibid., p. 88.
32. Ibid., p. 89.
33. Ibid., p. 90.
34. John Taylor Wood, "The First Fight of Iron-clads," *Battles and Leaders of the Civil War*, vol. I, New York: The Century Company, 1884–1888, p. 698.
35. Ashton Ramsey, "Most Famous of Sea Duels: The *Merrimac* and *Monitor*," *Harpers Weekly*, vol. LVI, pp. 11–12.
36. B & L, vol. I, p. 698.
37. Franklin Buchanan, "Battle between the *Virginia* and *Monitor*," *The Confederate Soldier in the Civil War*, New York: The Fairfax Press, p. 393.
38. Still, p. 30.
39. Davis, p. 100.
40. Parker, pp. 276–277.
41. Still, p. 31.
42. Davis, p. 101.
43. Ibid., pp. 105, 109.
44. Buchanan, p. 398.

## CHAPTER 3
## "IT IS QUITE A WASTE OF AMMUNITION"

1. Catesby ap R. Jones, "Services of the *Virginia* (Merrimac)," *Southern Historical Society Papers*, vol. XI, 1883, pp. 90–91.
2. Ibid.
3. William C. Davis, *Duel Between the First Ironclads*, New York: Doubleday & Company, Inc., 1975, p. 47.
4. Jones, p. 396.
5. Ashton Ramsey, "Most Famous of Sea Duels: The *Merrimac* and *Monitor*," *Harpers Weekly*, vol. LVI, p. 12.
6. Ibid.
7. John Taylor Wood, "The First Fight of the Iron-Clads," *Battles and Leaders of the Civil War*, vol. I, New York: The Century Company, 1884–1888, p. 702.
8. Ibid.
9. J. Thomas Scharf, *History of the Confederate States Navy*, New York: Rogers & Sherwood, 1887, p. 207.
10. Wood, p. 703.
11. Davis, p. 132.
12. Jones, p. 398.
13. ———, *Official Record of the Union and Confederate Navies in the War of the Rebellion*, series I, vol. VII.
14. Ibid.
15. J. H. D. Wingfield, "A Thanksgiving Service on the *Virginia*, March 10, 1862," *Southern Historical Society Papers*, vol. XIX, pp. 249–250.
16. Wood, pp. 705–706.
17. ORN, series II, vol. II.
18. Davis, p. 148.
19. Ibid., p. 148.
20. Wood, p. 40.
21. Wood, p. 707.

22. Davis, p. 150.
23. Wood, p. 709.
24. Maurice Melton, *The Confederate Ironclads*, New York: A. S. Barnes and Co., Inc., 1968, p. 57.
25. Wood, p. 710.
26. Ibid.
27. Davis, p. 155.

## CHAPTER 4
## PHANTOMS OF THE NIGHT

1. Stephen R. Wise, *Lifeline of the Confederacy*, Columbia: University of South Carolina Press, 1988, p. 226.
2. Wise, p. 221.
3. Royce Shingleton, *High Seas Confederate, The Life and Times of John Newland Maffitt*, Columbia: University of South Carolina Press, 1994, p. 41.
4. Ibid., p. 2.
5. Hamilton Cochran, *Blockade Runners of the Confederacy*, New York: The Bobbs-Merrill Company, Inc., 1958, p. 252.
6. Hamilton Cochran, reprinted from, *United States Service Magazine*, June–July, 1882.
7. Shingleton, p. 41.
8. Thomas Truxtun Moebs, *Confederate States Navy Research Guide*, Williamsburg: Moebs Publishing Co., 1991, p. 363.
9. Shingleton, pp. 97–98.
10. Wise, p. 99.
11. J. Thomas Scharf, *History of the Confederate States Navy*, New York: Rogers & Sherwood, 1887, pp. 462–463.
12. John Wilkinson, *Narrative of a Blockade Runner*, New York: Sheldon & Company, 1877, pp. 82–119.
13. Wilkinson, pp. 122–123.
14. Ibid., pp. 125–129.
15. Ibid., pp. 149–150.
16. Scharf, p. 481.
17. Wilkinson, pp. 149–152.
18. Ibid., pp. 154–156.
19. Ibid., p. 165.
20. Ibid., pp. 166–168.
21. Ibid., p. 169.
22. Ibid., pp. 169–171.
23. Wise p. 139.
24. Wilkinson, p. 175.

## CHAPTER 5
## GREYHOUND OF THE SEAS

1. Chester G. Hearn, *Gray Raiders of the Sea*, Camden: International Marine Publishing, 1992, p. 15.
2. J. Thomas Scharf, *History of the Confederate States Navy*, New York: Rogers & Sherwood, 1887, p. 783.
3. John McIntosh Kell, "Cruise and Combats of the *Alabama*," *Battles and Leaders of the Civil War*, vol. 4, New York: The Century Company, 1884–1888, p. 600; Hearn, pp. 153–154.
4. Kell, p. 600.
5. Hearn, p. 155.

6.  Warren F. Spencer, "Raphael Semmes," *Encyclopedia of the Confederacy*, vol. 3, New York: Simon & Schuster, Inc., 1992, p. 1392.
7.  Hearn, pp. 13–14.
8.  Ibid., p. 157.
9.  James D. Bulloch, *The Secret Service of the Confederate States in Europe; How the Confederate Cruisers were Equipped*, New York: Putnam Publishers, 1883, vol. I, pp. 241–242.
10. Bulloch, p. 243.
11. Raphael Semmes, *Memoirs of Service Afloat*, Baltimore: Kelly, Piet, 1869, pp. 402–404.
12. Ibid., p. 405.
13. Ibid., p. 409.
14. Ibid., p. 410.
15. Arthur Sinclair, *Two Years on the Alabama*, Boston: Lee and Shepard Publishers, 1895, p. 14.
16. Hearn, p. 160.
17. Semmes, p. 419.
18. Sinclair, pp. 16–17.
19. Hearn, pp. 162–163; Sinclair, pp. 260–288.
20. Semmes, p. 419.
21. Ibid., pp. 423–424.
22. Hearn, p. 166.
23. Semmes, pp. 429–430.
24. Ibid., pp. 431–434.
25. Norman C. DeLaney, *Ghost Ship, The Confederate Raider Alabama*, Middletown: Southfarm Press, 1989, p. 27.
26. Semmes, p. 437.
27. Ibid., p. 444.
28. Ibid., pp. 454–455.
29. Ibid., pp. 466–456.
30. Ibid., p. 458.
31. Hearn, p. 175.
32. Sinclair, p. 32.
33. Semmes, p. 469.
34. Ibid., pp. 474–475.
35. Sinclair, p. 38.
36. Semmes, p. 475–476.
37. Ibid., p. 476.
38. Ibid., p. 478.
39. Ibid., p. 482.
40. Hearn, p. 180.
41. Semmes, p. 509.
42. DeLaney, pp. 30–32.
43. Semmes, p. 513.
44. Ibid., pp. 515–516.
45. Semmes, p. 517.
46. DeLaney, p. 32.
47. Hearn, p. 183.
48. Semmes, p. 539.

## CHAPTER 6
## FROM GALVESTON TO CAPE TOWN

1.  Norman C. Delaney, *Ghost Ship, The Confederate Raider Alabama*, Middletown: Southfarm Press, 1989, p. 34.
2.  Raphael Semmes, *Memoirs of Service Afloat*, Baltimore: Kelly, Piet, 1869, p. 540.

3. Semmes, p. 549.
4. Ibid., p. 543.
5. Ibid., p. 544.
6. Delaney, p. 37.
7. ———, *Official Records of the Union and Confederate Navies in the War of the Rebellion*, Washington, D.C.: Government Printing Office, 1894–1927, series I, vol. 19, pp. 506–510.
8. Chester G. Hearn, *Gray Raiders of the Sea*, Camden: International Marine Publishing, 1992, pp. 188–189.
9. Arthur Sinclair, *Two Years on the Alabama*, Boston: Lee and Shepard, Publishers, 1895, pp. 64–65.
10. Hearn, p. 189.
11. Sinclair, p. 68.
12. Ibid., pp. 69–70.
13. Semmes, pp. 563–583.
14. Ibid., p. 586.
15. Ibid., pp. 586–587.
16. Hearn, p. 192.
17. Semmes, p. 594.
18. Hearn, p. 193.
19. Semmes, pp. 603–604.
20. Hearn, p. 195.
21. Ibid., p. 197.
22. Sinclair, p. 108.
23. Semmes, pp. 624–625.
24. Hearn, pp. 197–200.
25. Semmes, pp. 632–633.
26. Ibid., pp. 636–637.
27. Sinclair, p. 130.
28. Ibid., pp. 130–131.
29. ———, "Home is the Sailor," *Confederate Veteran*, July–August, 1994, pp. 12–13.
30. Sinclair, pp. 131–132.
31. Semmes, pp. 648–649.
32. Hearn, p. 205.
33. Ibid., p. 205.
34. Charles Grayson Summersell, CSS *Alabama, Builder, Captain, and Plans*, Tuscaloosa: University of Alabama Press, 1985, pp. 57–58.
35. Semmes, p. 664.
36. Hearn, p. 207.
37. Semmes, pp. 670–671.
38. Ibid., pp. 672–673.

## CHAPTER 7
## RENDEZVOUS AT CHERBOURG

1. Raphael Semmes, *Memoirs of Service Afloat During the War Between the States*, Baltimore: Kelly, Piet, 1869, p. 679.
2. ———, *Official Record of the Union and Confederate Navies in the War of the Rebellion*, Washington, D.C: Government Printing Office, 1894–1927, series I, vol. II, p. 768.
3. Semmes, p. 679.
4. Ibid.
5. Ibid., pp. 687–689.
6. Ibid., pp. 693–695.
7. Chester G. Hearn, *Gray Raiders of the Sea*, Camden: International Marine Publishing, 1992, pp. 213–214.

8. Semmes, pp. 716–718.
9. Ibid., pp. 720–721.
10. Ibid., pp. 721–722.
11. Arthur Sinclair, *Two Years on the Alabama*, Boston: Lee and Shepard Publishers, 1895, pp. 210–211.
12. Hearn, pp. 218–219.
13. Ibid., pp. 219–220.
14. Semmes, p. 745.
15. Ibid., p. 746.
16. Norman C. Delaney, *Ghost Ship: The Confederate Raider Alabama*, Middletown: Southfarm Press, 1989, pp. 50–51.
17. Semmes, p. 749.
18. Ibid., pp. 749–750.
19. Ibid., p. 750.
20. Delaney, p. 51.
21. Hearn, pp. 223–224.
22. Norman C. Delaney, "Fight or Flee," *Journal of Confederate History*, vol. IV, pp. 16–17.
23. Ibid., p. 22.
24. Hearn, p. 225.
25. Ibid.
26. John McIntosh Kell, "Cruise and Combats of the *Alabama*," *Battles and Leaders of the Civil War*, New York: The Century Company, 1884–1888, vol. IV, p. 607.
27. Sinclair, pp. 226–227.
28. Hearn, pp. 226–227.
29. Sinclair, p. 227.
30. Semmes, p. 756.
31. Hearn, p. 228.
32. Ibid., p. 228.
33. Sinclair, p. 230.
34. Kell, p. 608.
35. Hearn, p. 229.
36. Kell, p. 609.
37. Sinclair, p. 231.
38. Kell, p. 609.
39. Sinclair, p. 241.
40. Kell, pp. 609–610.
41. Ibid., p. 611.
42. Hearn, p. 232.
43. Sinclair, p. 233.
44. Kell, p. 611.
45. Hearn, p. 233.
46. Semmes, p. 765.

## CHAPTER 8
## GUN FLASHES ON THE NEUSE

1. Hudson Strode, *Jefferson Davis, Confederate President*, New York: Harcourt, Brace & World, Inc., 1959, p. 507.
2. Royce Gordon Shingleton, *John Taylor Wood, Sea Ghost of the Confederacy*, Athens: University of Georgia Press, 1979, p. 90.
3. Shingleton, p. 91.
4. Richard N. Current, *Encyclopedia of the Confederacy*, New York: Simon & Schuster, Inc., 1992, vol. IV, p. 1743.
5. Shingleton, pp. 91–92.

6. Clifford Dowdey, *The Wartime Papers of Robert E. Lee,* New York: Bramhall House, 1961, p. 657.
7. Daniel B. Conrad, "Capture and Burning of the Federal Gunboat *Underwriter," Southern Historical Society Papers,* 1892, vol. XIX, p. 93.
8. Shingleton, p. 92.
9. Ralph W. Donnelly, *The Confederate States Marine Corps,* Shippensburg: White Mane Publishing Company, Inc., 1989, p. 104.
10. B. P. Loyall, "Capture of the Underwriter," Southern Historical Society Papers, vol. XXVII, 1896, p. 137.
11. Shingleton, pp. 92–94.
12. Ibid., p. 94.
13. Conrad, pp. 93–94.
14. Ibid., p. 94
15. Loyall, p. 138.
16. J. Thomas Scharf, *History of the Confederate States Navy,* New York: Rogers & Sherwood, 1886, p. 396.
17. Conrad, p. 94.
18. Loyall, p. 138.
19. Conrad, p. 94.
20. Ibid.
21. _____, *The War of the Rebellion. A Compilation of the Official Records of the Union and Confederate Armies,* Washington, D.C.: Government Printing Office, 1880–1901, vol. XXXIII, series I, pp. 93–96.
22. Conrad, p. 95.
23. Loyall, p. 139.
24. Shingleton, p. 100.
25. Scharf, pp. 397–398.
26. Conrad, pp. 95–96.
27. Loyall, p. 140.
28. Ibid.
29. Conrad, p. 96.
30. Scharf, p. 399.
31. Conrad, p. 96.
32. Ibid.
33. Scharf, p. 400.
34. Conrad, p. 97.
35. Loyall, p. 142.
36. Shingleton, pp. 105–109.
37. Ibid., pp. 111–112.
38. Conrad, p. 100.

## CHAPTER 9
## GRAY WARRIORS BENEATH THE WAVES

1. W. A. Alexander, "Thrilling Chapter in the History of the Confederate States Navy. Work of Submarine Boats." *Southern Historical Society Papers,* vol. XXX, 1902, pp. 164–174.
2. James E. Kloeppel, *Danger Beneath the Waves,* Orangeburg: Sandlapper Publishing, Inc., 1987, p. 24.
3. Alexander, p. 166.
4. Ibid.
5. Ibid.
6. Ibid.
7. Kloeppel, p. 88.

8. Ibid., pp. 91–92.
9. Alexander, pp. 168–169.
10. Milton F. Perry, *Infernal Machines*, Baton Rouge: Louisiana State University Press, 1965, p. 102.
11. Ibid., p. 103.
12. Ibid.
13. Perry, p. 106.
14. ———, *Official Records of the Union and Confederate Navies in the War of the Rebellion*, Washington, D.C: Government Printing Office, 1894–1927, series I.
15. Perry, p. 107.
16. Kloeppel, p. 90.
17. Kloeppel, p. 89.
18. *Official Records*.
19. *ORN*, series I.
20. R. Thomas Campell, "Gray Warriors Beneath the Waves, Update," *Confederate Veteran*, May–June, 1993, pp. 10–13.
21. Kloeppel.
22. Mark K. Ragan, "Hunting for a Lost Confederate Submarine," *The Washington Times*, September 4, 1993.
23. Bruce Smith, "Hull of a Confederate Submarine is Found off Charleston," *The Philadelphia Inquirer*, Associated Press, May 12, 1995.

## CHAPTER 10
## DASH TO THE GULF

1. Thomas Truxtun Moebs, *Confederate States Navy Research Guide*, Williamsburg: Moebs Publishing Co., 1991.
2. Charles L. Dufour, *Nine Men in Gray*, Garden City: Doubleday & Company, Inc., 1963, p. 154.
3. Ibid., pp. 154–155.
4. ———, *Confederate Forces Afloat*, Naval History Division, vol. II, p. 581.
5. J. Thomas Scharf, *History of the Confederate States Navy*, New York: Rogers & Sherwood, 1887, p. 364.
6. ———, *Official Records of the Union and Confederate Navies in the War of the Rebellion*, Washington, D.C.: Government Printing Office, 1894–1927, vol. XXII, pp. 168–169.
7. Clarence Jeffries, "Running the Blockade on the Mississippi," *Confederate Veteran*, January, 1914.
8. ORN, p. 168.
9. Scharf, p. 365.
10. Jeffries.
11. Ibid.
12. Ibid.
13. Scharf, pp. 365–366.
14. Jeffries.
15. Scharf, p. 366.
16. Ibid.
17. Jeffries.
18. Ibid.
19. Ibid.
20. Scharf, p. 367.
21. Dufour, p. 158.
22. Ibid.

# Bibliography

——.*Official Records of the Union and Confederate Navies in the War of the Rebellion*, 31 volumes, Washington, D.C.: Government Printing Office, 1894–1927.

——.*The War of the Rebellion: A Compilation of the Official Records of the Union and Confederate Armies*. 130 volumes. Washington, D.C.: Government Printing Office, 1880–1901.

Alexander, W. A. "Thrilling Chapter in the History of the Confederate States Navy. Work of Submarine Boats." *Southern Historical Society Papers*. Volume XXX, 1902.

Barrett, John G. *The Civil War in North Carolina*. Chapel Hill: The University of North Carolina Press, 1963.

Besse, Sumner B. *C. S. Ironclad Virginia and U.S. Ironclad Monitor*. Newport News: The Mariners Museum, 1937.

Brooke, John M. "The Plan and Construction of the *Merrimac*." *Battles and Leaders of the Civil War*. 4 volumes. New York: The Century Company, 1884–1888.

Buchanan, Franklin. "Battle Between the *Virginia* and *Monitor*." *The Confederate Soldier in the Civil War*. Crown Publishers, Inc., circa 1880.

Bulloch, James D. *The Secret Service of the Confederate States in Europe, or How the Confederate Cruisers Were Equipped*. 2 volumes. New York: Putnam Publishers, 1883.

Burton, E. Milby. *The Siege of Charleston 1861–1865*. Columbia: The University of South Carolina Press, 1970.

Campbell, R. Thomas. "Gray Warriors Beneath the Waves, Update, " *Confederate Veteran*, May–June, 1993.

*203*

Cline, William R. "The Ironclad Ram *Virginia.*" *Southern Historical Society Papers.* Volume XXXII, December 1904.

Cochran, Hamilton. *Blockade Runners of the Confederacy.* New York: The Bobbs-Merrill Company, Inc., 1958.

Conrad, Daniel B. "Capture and Burning of the Federal Gunboat *Underwriter.*" *Southern Historical Society Papers.* Volume XIX, 1892.

Davis, William C. *Duel Between the First Ironclads.* New York: Doubleday & Company, Inc., 1975.

Davis, William C. *Jefferson Davis, The Man and His Hour.* New York: Harper Collins Publishers, 1991.

Delaney, Norman C. *Ghost Ship, The Confederate Raider Alabama.* Middletown: Southfarm Press, 1989.

Delaney, Norman C. "Fight or Flee." *Journal of Confederate History.* Brentwood: Southern Heritage Press, 1989.

Donnelly, Ralph W. *The Confederate States Marine Corps.* Shippensburg: White Mane Publishing Company, Inc., 1989.

Dowdey, Clifford, ed. *The Wartime Papers of R. E. Lee.* New York: Bramhall House, 1961

Dufour, Charles L. *Nine Men In Gray.* Garden City: Doubleday & Company, Inc., 1963.

Dufour, Charles L. *The Night the War was Lost.* Garden City: Doubleday & Company, Inc., 1960.

Duncan, Ruth H. *The Captain and the Submarine.* Memphis: S. C. Tool & Company, 1965.

Durkin, Joseph T. *Confederate Navy Chief: Stephen R. Mallory.* Chapel Hill: The University of North Carolina Press, 1954.

Gosnell, H. Allen. *Guns on the Western Waters.* Baton Rouge: Louisiana State University Press, 1949.

Guerout, Max. "The Wreck of the C.S.S. Alabama." National Geographic, Washington, D.C., December 1994.

Hearn, Chester G. *Gray Raiders of the Sea.* Camden: International Marine Publishing, 1992.

Horner, Dave. *The Blockade Runners.* Port Salerno: Florida Classics Library, 1992.

Jeffries, Clarence. "Running the Blockade on the Mississippi." *Confederate Veteran,* January 1914.

Jones, Catesby ap R. "The Services of the *Virginia.*" *The Southern Historical Society Papers.* Volume XI, January 1883.

Jones, Virgil C. *The Civil War at Sea.* 3 volumes. New York: Holt, Rinehart, and Winston, 1960–1962.

Kell, John McIntosh. "Cruise and Combats of the *Alabama.*" *Battles and Leaders of the Civil War.* 4 volumes. New York: The Century Company, 1884–1888.

Kell, John McIntosh. *Recollections of a Naval Life, Including the Cruises of the Confederate Steamers "Sumter" and "Alabama".* Washington: Neale, 1900.

Kloeppel, James E. *Danger Beneath the Waves.* Orangeburg: Sandlapper Publishing, Inc., 1987.

Loyall, Benjamin P. "Capture of the Underwriter." *Southern Historical Society Papers.* Volume XXVII, 1896.

Melton, Maurice. *The Confederate Ironclads.* New York: A. S. Barnes and Co., Inc., 1968.

Merli, Frank J. *Great Britain and the Confederate Navy.* Bloomington: Indiana University Press, 1970.

Moebs, Thomas Truxtun, comp. *Confederate States Navy Research Guide.* Williamsburg: Moebs Publishing Co., 1991.

Morgan, James Morris. "The Pioneer Ironclad." *United States Naval Institute Proceedings*, p. 2277.

Outlaw, P. J., and R. W. Betterton. "Home Is the Sailor." *Confederate Veteran*, July–August, 1994.

Parker, William H. *Recollections of a Naval Officer.* New York: Charles Scribners' Sons, 1883.

Perry, Milton F. *Infernal Machines.* Baton Rouge: Louisiana State University Press, 1965.

Ragan, Mark K. "Hunting For a Lost Confederate Submarine." *The Washington Times*, September 4, 1993.

Ramsey, Ashton. "Most Famous of Sea Duels: The *Merrimac* and *Monitor*." *Harper's Weekly.* Volume LVI.

Read, Charles W. "Reminiscences of the Confederate States Navy." *Southern Historical Society Papers.* Volume I, May 1876.

Robertson, William B. "The Water Battery at Fort Jackson." *Battles and Leaders of the Civil War.* 4 volumes. New York: The Century Company, 1884–1888.

Robinson, Charles M., III. *Shark of the Confederacy.* Annapolis: Naval Institute Press, 1995.

Robinson, William Morrison, Jr. *The Confederate Privateers.* New Haven: Yale University Press, 1928.

Scharf, J. Thomas. *History of the Confederate States Navy.* New York: Rogers & Sherwood, 1887.

Semmes, Raphael. *Memoirs of Service Afloat During the War Between the States.* Baltimore: Kelly, Piet, 1869.

Shingleton, Royce. *High Seas Confederate, The Life and Times of John Newland Maffitt.* Columbia: University of South Carolina Press, 1994.

Shingleton, Royce Gorden. *John Taylor Wood, Sea Ghost of the Confederacy.* Athens: University of Georgia Press, 1979.

Sinclair, Arthur. *Two Years on the Alabama.* Boston: Lee and Shepard Publishers, 1895.

Spencer, Warren F. "Raphael Semmes." *Encyclopedia of the Confederacy.* New York: Simon & Schuster, Inc., 1992.

Stern, Philip Van Doren. *The Confederate Navy, A Pictorial History.* New York: Bonanza Books, 1962.

Still, William N., Jr. *Iron Afloat.* Nashville: Vanderbilt University Press, 1971.

Still, William N., Jr. *Confederate Shipbuilding.* Columbia: University of South Carolina Press, 1987.

Strode, Hudson. *Jefferson Davis, Confederate President.* New York: Harcourt, Brace & World, Inc., 1959.

Summersell, Charles G., ed. *The Journal of George Townley Fullam.* Tuscaloosa: University of Alabama Press, 1973.

Summersell, Charles Grayson. CSS *Alabama: Builder, Captain, and Plans.* Tuscaloosa: University of Alabama Press, 1985.

Taylor, John M. *Confederate Raider.* Washington: Brassey's Inc., 1994.

Teaster, Gerald F. *The Confederate Submarine H. L. Hunley.* Summerville: Junior History Press, 1989.

Trotter, William R. *Ironclads and Columbiads.* Winston-Salem: John F. Blair, Publisher, 1989.

Warley, Alexander F. "The Ram *Manassas* at the Passage of the New Orleans Forts." *Battles and Leaders of the Civil War.* 4 volumes. New York: The Century Company, 1884–1888.

Wells, Tom Henderson. *The Confederate Navy, A Study in Organization.* Tuscaloosa: The University of Alabama Press, 1971.

Wilkinson, John. *Narrative of a Blockade Runner.* New York: Sheldon & Company, 1877.

Wingfield, J. H. D. "A Thanksgiving Service on the *Virginia,* March 10, 1862." *Southern Historical Society Papers.* Volume XIX.

Wise, Stephen R. *Lifeline of the Confederacy.* Columbia: University of South Carolina Press, 1988.

Wood, John Taylor. "The First Fight of the Ironclads." *Battles and Leaders of the Civil War.* 4 volumes. New York: The Century Company, 1884–1888.

# Index

*207*

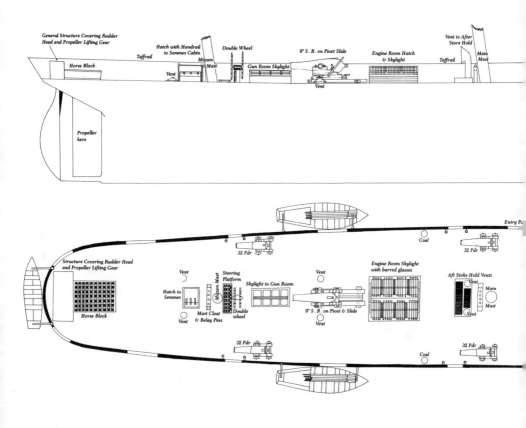

*Profile*

General Structure Covering Rudder
Head and Propeller Lifting Gear

Hatch with Handrail
to Semmes Cabin

Double Wheel

9" S. B. on Pivot Slide

Engine Room Hatch
& Skylight

Vent to After
Store Hold

Taffrail

Mizzen Mast

Main
Mast

Horse Block

Vent

Gun Room Skylight

Taffrail

Vent

Propeller
here

Structure Covering Rudder Head
and Propeller Lifting Gear

Entry Po

Coal

32 Pdr

32 Pdr

Vent

Steering
Platform

Engine Room Skylight
with barred glasses

Hatch to
Semmes

Mizzen Mast

Skylight to Gun Room

Vent

Aft Stoke Hold Vents

Vent

Mast Cleat
& Belay Pins

Double
wheel

Vent

9" S. B. on Pivot & Slide

Vent

Main
Mast

Vent

Horse Block

32 Pdr

Coal

32 Pdr

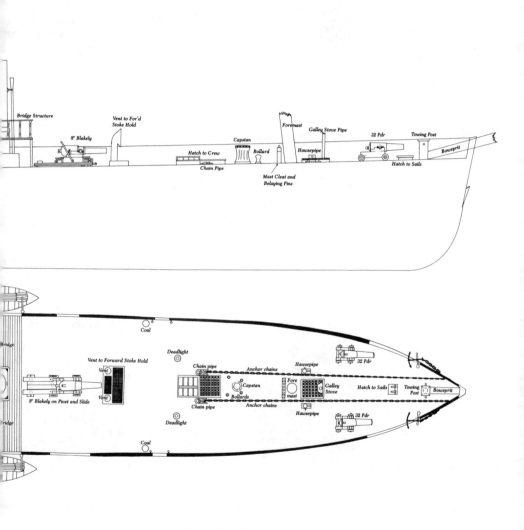

Bridge Structure

8" Blakely

Vent to For'd
Stoke Hold

Hatch to Crew

Chain Pipe

Capstan

Bollard

Mast Cleat and
Belaying Pins

Foremast

Hawsepipe

Galley Stove Pipe

32 Pdr

Hatch to Sails

Towing Post

Bowsprit

Vent to Forward Stoke Hold

Vent

Vent

8" Blakely on Pivot and Slide

Bridge

Bridge

Coal

Deadlight

Chain pipe

Chain pipe

Anchor chains

Anchor chains

Capstan

Bollards

Hawsepipe

Hawsepipe

Fore
mast

Galley
Stove

32 Pdr

Hatch to Sails

Towing
Post

Bowsprit

32 Pdr

Deadlight

Coal

# —ADDITIONAL WORKS BY R. THOMAS CAMPBELL—

## MIDSHIPMAN IN GRAY

*Midshipman in Gray* makes available the the first twenty-eight chapters of James Morris Morgan's book, *Recollections of a Rebel Reefer*. It is an intriguing and some-times humorous look at a young midshipman's exciting adventures in the Confederate States Navy.

ISBN 1-57249-061-6 • HC

## SEA HAWK OF THE CONFEDERACY
### *Lt. Charles W. Read and the Confederate Navy*

An intense and dramatic biography of Charles W. Read, including his early years, his desperate struggle for the Confederacy, and his eventful family life until his untimely death in 1890.

ISBN 1-57249-178-7 • HC

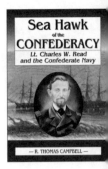

## ACADEMY ON THE JAMES
### *The Confederate Naval School*

This book contains the full story of the Confederate Naval Academy and reveals a different aspect of Confederate military history.

ISBN 1-57249-130-2 • HC

## CONFEDERATE NAVY QUIZZES AND FACTS

*Confederate Navy Quizzes and Facts* offers readers a complete guide to this most intriguing portion of military history.

ISBN 1-57249-236-8 • PB

## HUNTERS OF THE NIGHT
### *Confederate Torpedo Boats in the War Between the States*

The fascinating story of the design and development of Confederate torpedo boats and the courageous officers and men who took them into battle.

ISBN 1-57249-202-3 • PB

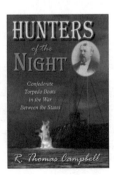

## BENEATH THE STAINLESS BANNER
### *John McIntosh Kell, CSN*

First Lieutenant John McIntosh Kell oversaw the day-to-day operation of the CSS Alabama. His recollections offer a fascinating glimpse into the activities of the Confederate navy.

ISBN 1-57249-147-7 • HC

---

## WINNER OF THE 1997
## NATHAN BEDFORD FORREST HISTORY AWARD
### *Exploits of the Confederate States Navy*

| | | |
|---|---|---|
| Southern Thunder | HC | ISBN 1-57249-029-2 |
| Southern Fire | HC | ISBN 1-57249-046-2 |
| Gray Thunder | HC | ISBN 0-942597-99-0 |
| Fire and Thunder | HC | ISBN 1-57249-067-5 |